Handbook for Educational Leadership Interns

A RITE OF PASSAGE

William G. Cunningham
Old Dominion University

PEARSON

Boston | New York | San Francisco
Mexico City | Montreal | Toronto | London | Madrid | Munich | Paris
Hong Kong | Singapore | Tokyo | Cape Town | Sydney

Senior Series Editor: Arnis E. Burvikovs
Series Editorial Assistant: Erin Reilly
Marketing Manager: Tara Kelly
Editorial Production Service: Omegatype Typography, Inc.
Composition Buyer: Linda Cox
Manufacturing Buyer: Linda Morris
Electronic Composition: Omegatype Typography, Inc.
Cover Administrator: Elena Sidorova

For related titles and support materials, visit our online catalog at www.ablongman.com.

Between the time Website information is gathered and then published, it is not unusual for some sites to have closed. Also, the transcription of URLs can result in typographical errors. The publisher would appreciate notification where these errors occur so that they may be corrected in subsequent editions.

ISBN: 0-205-46423-8

Printed in the United States of America

19

CONTENTS

PREFACE

This text/handbook lays out the critical elements that need to be considered in completing an effective internship experience. It provides the guidance and materials that clearly define and support the expectations, structure, procedures, knowledge, skills, ethics, and behavior necessary for an effective internship learning experience. It provides key insights regarding the application of knowledge, skills, and ways of thinking that are required to perform the responsibilities of educational leadership. The text/handbook facilitates your internship experience and allows for a higher level of performance and outcome.

Research findings suggest that clinical activities led by practicing administrators that are carefully and sensitively planned and arranged prove to be excellent learning opportunities and experiences that interns highly value (Browne-Ferrigno & Muth, 2004; Geisman, Morris, & Lieberman, 2000; Milstein, Bobroff, & Restine, 1991; SREB, 2004). Well-planned intern experiences greatly improve the preparation of future educational leaders and lead to "a stronger pipeline of effective school administrators" (Pounder & Crow, 2005, p. 57). A well-designed and supported internship expands the knowledge and skills of interns as it expands their knowledge of how to improve schools and student achievement.

Interns need assistance to negotiate the nature of their experiences, the types of efforts required, the activities through which they can gain the greatest benefit, and the needed documentation and structured reflections that allow for growth and continuous development, ultimately resulting in improved leadership capacity.

There is only one way to really comprehend the rigors of the job of an educational leader, unless you are a school administrator. That is to take on the job's responsibilities as an intern. This will be different from any other role that you have served in education and is not the same as classroom learning, even problem-based learning. Thus, it is an essential learning experience to actually go to the internship site and experience the responsibilities of an administrator.

You, as an intern, are expected to come to the table with some knowledge of what you will enter into during your internship experience. There are several steps you must take to ensure that level of preparedness. The internship portion of any school administration preparation program is where you will have an opportunity to apply what you have learned. You will learn what it takes for you to become an effective leader in the organizational setting. It cannot be stressed enough how important your internship experience is to your development as an administrator. This book is written to help you to have a high-quality experience that will allow you to get the most out of your time spent in an internship.

A four-year study (Zellner et al., 2002) found that those in line for the principalship needed contextual experiences in developing leadership skills. These experiences engage administrative interns in planning, developing, directing, and implementing school programs while receiving the needed mentoring for development and support. The Southern Regional Education Board (SREB) Leadership Initiative, which served as part of the impetus for writing this text/handbook, stresses the importance of

> Giving more time and attention to mentoring and internships that allow aspiring leaders to practice leadership skills by addressing school problems dealing with

student achievement under the coaching of master educational leaders in well-planned quality experiences.

Colleges across the country have been placing greater emphasis on internships in schools as powerful learning tools for future educational administrators.

The internship provides an opportunity for students to connect their knowledge and previous experiences and to implement and practice what they have learned in practical settings with the safety net of the internship process, university instructor, and practicing mentor in place for support. The internship also provides a unique setting to learn skills that can only be taught (or are at least *best* taught) in the real world setting. As a result, internships are being taken far more seriously than in the past (ELCC standard 7, NCATE, 2002).

TEXT/HANDBOOK DESIGN

Each intern brings unique knowledge to the internship experience and the job of administration. Therefore, this text/handbook engages readers in different ways. The internship handbook is a hands-on aid for all individuals completing internships in education. It focuses on making learning experiences enlightening, developmental, and enjoyable. It includes worksheets, competency guides, surveys, forms, self-reflection tools, internship aids, guided reflections, and—most important—planning techniques to ensure that students get the most from their internship experiences. Many of these types of documents can be found at the ends of select chapters. The text/handbook will integrate interns' practical experiences with learning aids, research and theory, and practioners' suggestions related to best practices.

It is intended to help students understand the possibilities that this experience provides—the lay of the land and the potential mine fields. It is designed to cover very practical skills by stimulating questions and providing guidance on how to plan and conduct a quality internship experience. This handbook suggests various windows through which students can view educational leaders' responsibilities, opening up vistas that they might have missed without such guidance. This opens up new areas of practice in which to become engaged, as well as some guidance on how to achieve success and avoid pitfalls.

The text/handbook is divided into three major sections, each of which has a very brief introduction. The first section, Introduction to the Internship, covers all of the elements of planning, successfully completing, documenting, and reflecting on and assessing the internship. This section provides guidance to ensure that the intern has a successful and rewarding experience. The second section, The Important Internship Tools, samples the technical aspects of leadership, providing some tools and techniques that the intern will need as he or she completes the internship experience. The third and final section, Assessment, Licensure, and Obtaining an Administrative Position, helps the intern make the transition into a career of educational leadership. The book provides powerful insights for a successful internship and outstanding practice.

ACKNOWLEDGMENTS

So many people at this point in my professional career have had significant impact on my work and my life, it is impossible to mention them all here. Many of them are cited throughout this text/handbook. Two that I particularly wish to thank are

Dr. Donald Walker and Dr. William Katzenmyer, who had such a profound influence on me when I was a student myself. Other people who have had an important impact on my professional life and my work, and for whom I have a deep sense of gratitude, include Bill Owings, Gene R. Carter, Paula A. Cordeiro, Paul A. Houston, Don W. Gresso, Michael Milstein, Lars G. Bjork, Paula M. Short, Joe Murphy, Terrance E. Deal, Rick Reitzug, Michael Fullon, and Diana Pounder.

I want to thank the students who have added so much to my professional life, who continuously provide new insights and enlightenments, and who have added considerable reality to the contents found within this book. Thank you to the educational leadership students who breathe such exciting life into the internship and then into our schools. I wish them Godspeed on their noble journey. I especially want to thank Gail VonMosch for examples used in Chapter 3, Kelly McCoig-Smith who helped develop Chapter 8, and Doug Parks who helped develop Chapter 15. They epitomize the types of students that inspire university faculty to teach and collaborate with students.

As always, I appreciate the wise counsel of my editor, Arnis E. Burvikovs. Particular thanks go to Dawn Hall and Sheila Jones, whose friendship, proofreading, and typing helped to make this book and others a reality. Many friends and colleagues who teach and practice educational administration provided wise counsel, inspiration, and direction as they gave of their time and interest. I would also like to thank the reviewers for their helpful comments on the mansucript: Felicia Blacher-Wilson, ITT Technical Institute; Alicia Cotabish, University of Arkansas at Little Rock; Lance Fusarelli, North Carolina State University; Patricia Guillory, Fulton County Schools; Reginald High, University of Tennessee, Martin; Paula Lester, Long Island University; Roger Shouse, Penn State; James Veitch, University of North Carolina, Chapel Hill; and Leigh Zeitz, University of Northern Iowa.

I would like to thank my father, Gerard J., my mother, Margaret M., and my sister, Gail Penn, for their continuing interest and support of my work and my life. Last, and most of all, I would like to thank my wife, Sandra L. Cunningham; daughter Kerri and her husband Chuck Joyner, and son Dr. Michael Cunningham and his wife Dottie; and grandchildren Cierra, Merrick, Keenan, Shealyn, Braidyn, and Alayna for their continuing encouragement and support and the happiness and love we share.

Many, many thanks go to all of you.

—W.G.C.

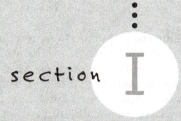

section I

INTRODUCTION TO THE INTERNSHIP

You are about to make a transition from one role to another. Your expectations, even the person you are, will change. That means you will want to be firmly placed on solid ground regarding who you are and how you will bring yourself into a new role with new responsibilities. You will need to be aware of your behavior and how you may need to let go of some aspects of yourself and develop others. This is why this process might be called a "rite of passage." This rite is much like that of the ancients before us, who went out on quests to discover and find who they were and how they might serve their people.

Even in traditional cultures today, changes in one's life station are marked by formal ceremonies of passage. Your internship experience is one of those rites of passage—from student to student and practitioner. If you do not participate in this passage, you forfeit entrance into the next stage of leadership development. Such passages or life transitions are challenges and opportunities of the highest order. The myths of humanity are replete with stories of the necessity to climb, cross over, and/or pass through if we are to fulfill our destiny and the promise of our lives. You are being asked to make such a journey as an educational leadership intern.

Interns are provided mentors to help them to understand the challenges and opportunities they face and to help them to discover their own spirit and style. Over time, leadership is mysteriously conferred upon the intern as the knowledge and best practices are handed down and experienced. These are the common origins that are essential in the smooth transition from student to effective educational leader.

One of the most difficult challenges for the intern is trying to apply textbook/classroom understanding to the real world of practice (Lashway, 2003). Educational administration is an applied field that is partially learned by experiencing the myriad of responsibilities, tasks, and activities that come with the administrative territory. As a result, field experiences or internships are vital to the preparation of future educational administrators. Interns need an opportunity to apply what they have learned through lectures, reading, discussion, problem-based activities, and study. Through field-based experiences, future educational administrators can make the essential connections that must be forged between discipline-based knowledge and professional practice.

This section of the text/handbook provides guidance on how to apply newly acquired knowledge to real-world problems in a relatively safe environment. Chapter 1 defines the internship and talks about the benefits for both the intern and the mentor, building a foundation for the development of the internship. Chapters 2 and 3 explain how this text/handbook complements internship course materials and discusses the goals and various components that might be a part of your internship experiences. Chapters 4, 5, and 6 help you develop the proper mindset for taking on the responsibility for internship activities and having a successful experience. Chapter 7 helps you consider the qualities needed in a mentor, to effectively engage the assistance of a mentor, and to maximize the benefits from this rewarding relationship.

Chapter 8 presents the activities or opportunities prerequisite to the development of skills you need to perform the work of an educational leader. Internship activities provide the opportunity for you to act on what you know, which is the fundamental purpose for the knowledge and skills you have developed. To achieve desirable goals, you must bridge your knowledge and research about administration to the accomplishment of practical activities that you have planned as an intern. This is the bridge that connects seeing the need to doing something about it. You, after all, are learning by doing—it is part conception and part application. Chapter 9 provides some final suggestions regarding the internship process and discusses the final transition from the intellectual pursuits to the pragmatic practice of leadership.

chapter 1

The Internship and Mentoring

It has long been known that the workplace provides a fertile opportunity for individuals to improve their craft. Smith (2003), Billet (1996), Beck (1994), Raelin and Schermerhorn (1994), and others have pointed out the importance of integrating knowledge and experience in real-world settings. The belief is that learning needs to be embedded or situated within the context of practice. What better way to do this than through the internship?

The mood across the United States could be described as a demand for changes in the way we prepare educators and the way we do business within our public schools. This has resulted in a call for reform in education that has continued into the new century. Part of this call is for changes in the ways that we prepare school leaders (Griffiths, Stout, & Forsyth, 1988; National Commission for the Principalship, 1990; National Policy Board for Educational Administration, 1989; SREB, 2002; Williamson & Hudson, 2001). A key part of this call for reform is a greater emphasis on making the knowledge-to-practice connections and providing students opportunities to work on real-world problems in the most authentic settings possible under the guidance of university faculty and experienced practitioners. As a result, an effort was begun in the 1990s to find ways to strengthen internships in principal preparation programs (Bass, 1990; Chance, 1990; Daresh, 1988; DeSpain & Livingston, 1997; Foster & Ward, 1998; Milstein, Bobroff, & Restine, 1991; SREB, 2002).

Internships have traditionally been an important part of professional preparation in a number of different fields, including medicine, law, social work, and education. The positive influence of purposeful engagement in school leadership on the ability of students to later perform administrative roles is widely researched and accepted (Henderson, 1989; Milstein, 1990; Milstein & Krueger, 1997; Mueller, Shea, & Andrews, 1989; Restine, Milstein, & Broboff, 1989). The National Council for the Accreditation of Teacher Education (NCATE) believed internship experiences to be of such importance that they made the internship one of their seven standards for preparing future administrators. Standard 7.0 for Advanced Programs in Educational Leadership states, "The internship provides significant opportunities for candidates to synthesize and apply the knowledge and practice and develop the skills identified in Standards 1–6 through substantial, sustained, standards-based work in real settings, planned and guided cooperatively by the institution and school district personnel for graduate credit" (NCATE, 2002).

The Southern Regional Education Board also stresses the importance of internships in their network of universities involved in improving educational administration preparation programs. This is a developmental grant program involving twenty-seven universities in twelve southeastern states. One of the major focuses of this program is: "Giving more time and attention to mentoring and internships that allow aspiring leaders to practice leadership skills by addressing school problems dealing with student achievement under the coaching of master educational leaders in well-planned quality experiences" (SREB, 2002). The Carnegie Foundation for the Advancement of Teaching and the Holmes Group recommended improved connections among university instructors and educational practitioners with a greater emphasis being placed on clinical experiences. The National Commission on Excellence in Educational Administration advocated that internships were essential for education administration preparation. The University Council for Educational Administration member preparation programs must include "concentrated periods of full-time and supervised clinical practice" (UCEA, 2001).

Through their research, Bowne-Ferrigno and Muth (2004) gained three major insights regarding the preparation of school leaders. First, principal acculturation occurs through socially constructed activities that require working closely with leadership mentors in authentic field-based experiences. Secondly, internship experiences and working with mentors "serve as effective professional development not only for aspiring and novice principals but also for veteran principals" (p. 471). Finally, they learned that this incredible internship opportunity "for leadership capacity building through reciprocal sharing between practicing and aspiring principals" results in the development of a community of practice that improves performance and can result in "successful school improvement." Successful internships have the ability to improve, expand, and deepen leadership capacity in schools and districts.

The result has been a more thoughtful and purposeful inclusion of school-based internship programs in principal preparation programs (Leithwood, Jantzi, & Coffin, 1995; Milstein & Krueger, 1997). These and other studies or reports that stress the importance of internships in educational administrative preparation programs have resulted in an increased emphasis on internships in state councils of higher education and in educational administration preparation programs throughout the United States.

DEFINITIONS

The NCATE standards for accreditation define the internship as a process that results from the application, in a workplace environment, of the strategic, instructional, organizational, and contextual leadership program standards. When coupled with integrating experiences through reflective thinking and cohort seminars, the outcome is a powerful synthesis of knowledge and skills.

Most definitions of internships incorporate the acquisition of skills and the application of knowledge by participating in authentic tasks with the support and guidance of persons more seasoned or experienced with the work. This typically requires that interns have opportunities to explore and discuss questions, to reflect on practices and related theory and research, to log activity and record behavior and thinking, to participate in seminars and diad and triad meetings, to review mentor assessments, to develop culminating reports, and to modify or refine leadership platforms and portfolios. Internships will never replace the development of knowledge within the classroom; however, internships complement classroom teaching.

Interns are immersed in situations and intensive clinical opportunities that prepare them to take on important responsibilities of administrative roles. Mentors and university supervisors help interns to recognize patterns, organize expertise, access and apply knowledge, and look for and reflect on solutions to unfamiliar challenges.

Collins (1997) suggests characteristics that are needed to build the scaffolding that interns need to be able to learn as they are actively involved in activities.

- *Authenticity.* Material to be learned is embedded in tasks and settings that reflect the uses of those competencies in the real world.
- *Interweaving.* Learning alternates between a focus on accomplishing tasks and a focus on gaining particular competencies.
- *Articulation.* Learners articulate their thinking and what they have learned.
- *Reflection.* Learners reflect and compare their own performance with that of others.
- *Learning cycles.* Learning occurs through repeated cycles of planning, doing and reflecting.
- *Multimedia.* Each medium is used to do what it does best.

Central to all of this is the need for human interaction and guidance from experienced experts (Smith, 2003). This works best when the intern, university supervisor, and practicing administrator work hand-in-hand to create the best possible internship experience under the guidance of a clear, comprehensive, and complementary text/handbook that supports the intern in designing, implementing, and assessing and reflecting on his or her internship.

MENTORING

It is now fairly widely accepted that wise, mature mentoring has always been around to help new professionals and others to learn their craft in ways that are not covered in classroom courses (Daresh, 2004). Success stories in all fields are full of statements of appreciation for a mentor who showed the individual the road to success in his or her work and provided support throughout the socialization and induction process. Roche (1979) found that 75 percent of the top executives in the United States gave some credit to the mentoring process for their success. These relationships typically began in an intern/mentor setting, and the people often became lifetime mentors and friends. A 2003 Public Agenda report showed that 52 percent of principals felt that advice and practical experiences that they received under the guidance of experienced mentors were their most valuable preparation (Farkas, Johnson, & Duffett, 2003).

Most definitions of the internship/mentorship process focus on the development and advancement of a protégé by someone in a position of authority within the professional context (Chao, Walz, & Garder, 1992; Mertz, 2004). An individual with good to outstanding experience and knowledge provides time to mentor someone who is advancing in his or her profession. The underlying belief that supports this process is that this relationship will ultimately be beneficial to all parties concerned. As mentioned above, research does suggest that mentoring across all disciplines is an overwhelmingly positive learning experience for mentors and mentees alike (Hansford, Tennent, & Ehrich, 2002). Studies of educational administration preparation students (Brause, 2002; Browne-Ferrigno, 2003; Browne-Ferrigno & Muth, 2001; Cordeiro, & Smith-Sloan, 1993) have shown that respondents do recognize the importance of mentoring, and contain references that describe students' need for "more experience" or "on-the-job training."

"Experience" was the most common need that new administrators expressed, when asked what else they needed to learn in order to feel competent, confident, and comfortable to lead a school. They needed opportunities to take on administrative responsibilities and lead in authentic settings. This is what they planned to get out of their internship experiences. They wanted to test their knowledge and ability in real-world settings, to have an opportunity to demonstrate their abilities to themselves and others as they experienced the day-to-day running of a school.

BENEFITS OF THE INTERNSHIP

There are a number of benefits that are typically derived from involvement in internships and mentoring programs. Daresh (2004) suggests "that protégés report that they feel more confident about their professional competence" (p. 503). He further reports that interns and mentees "begin to see daily translations of educational theory into daily practice. . . . Thus, having a guide and mentor who already speaks the language of school administration as an ally ready to interpret real-word problems allows the novice to begin to understand subtle relationships between what was learned in books with what now must be learned through daily interactions with parents, teachers, staff, and students" (p. 503).

Daresh also found that communication skills were often increased through mentoring. Regular interactions between mentees and mentors bring about a sharing of views often not seen in settings where mentees work (Forrest, Turban, & Dougherty, 1996). Daresh (2004, p. 504) states:

> Mentoring programs bring about discussions not limited to concerns of beginners alone. Instead, discussions take place concerning a wide array of issues of concern to mentors and protégés. Collegiality begins to develop.
>
> Mentoring provides beginning administrators with opportunities to learn some of the tricks of the trade from colleagues. Often, this benefit is described as the only benefit of mentoring programs; young administrators learn how to lead from senior administrators. As noted throughout this review, there are numerous other values to be found in mentoring arrangements. However, learning the ropes will always be a benefit in a coaching or mentoring scheme.
>
> Finally, mentoring makes people feel as if they belong in their new settings. The fact that another, more experienced school administrator engages in behavior that signals care about another's personal and professional well-being is a powerful statement that suggests that a newcomer will be taken care of in the school or school district.

The internship has been found to be an excellent catalyst for this process. The student begins to develop this important mentor/mentee relationship and to understand its multiple benefits. The intern gets a head start on making the essential transition to successful administrator. At the same time, the mentor learns more about this process under joint direction with university staff.

In discussing the benefits of the internship and mentoring to the mentors, Daresh states, "Here, mentors find that grooming a promising new administrator is a challenging and stimulating personal experience. . . . One example of this is found when protégés are successful and perform their jobs well. Mentors also report a sense of satisfaction in seeing the values and culture of a school system handed over to a new generation" (2004, p. 504).

This also provides an important opportunity for interns to impress their mentors and to be identified and tapped for future school administration. Obviously, the attitude of the intern will influence the effort and satisfaction that occurs in this experience. If the internship is viewed as another hoop that the intern must go through, neither person will learn or gain much from the experience. If the intern exhibits energy and enthusiasm for the work, it will become contagious. "Mentors receive new ideas and perspectives by allowing protégés to add their own insights into the ways that organizational problems are addressed. Mentors who are attentive to the potential of those with whom they interact are able to capitalize on a new source of knowledge, insight, and talent, and they may be able to translate this into their own professional growth and advancement" (Daresh, 2004, p. 505). The interns themselves have a tremendous influence on the quality of the experience for both themselves and their mentors.

There are also a number of benefits that accrue to the school district where the internship occurs. The more obvious benefits are the availability of free labor to help out within the school. Other benefits are the development of more capable staff, development of lifelong learners and professional relationships, and greater productivity. The presence of an advocate and supportive colleague in a higher-level position enables the intern to make contributions more quickly, to avoid errors, to use knowledge more effectively, to take risks, to become more accomplished, and, most important, to accelerate the learning curve. Students with mentors have greater confidence, are more motivated, and are more willing to take risks (Wanous, 1983). In general, those who complete an internship working with effective mentors have considerably more success in completing their preparatory work and in their future careers. Murray and Owens (1991) identified increased productivity, improved recruitment efforts, motivation of senior staff, and enhancement of services as benefits of an internship and mentoring.

Much of the literature suggests that internships yield benefits for both the interns and mentors (Ehrich, Hansford, & Tennent, 2004). Some of the benefits found in such studies include:

- Clarified roles and technical expertise
- Career advancement
- Psychological support (satisfaction, reward, growth)
- Rejuvenation
- Increased confidence
- Personal fulfillment
- Assistance with work
- Collaboration
- Networking
- Reflection
- Incentive to work harder
- Professional development (skills and behaviors)
- Friendship
- Stimulated improvements
- Support for career aspirations

Figure 1.1 presents the most frequently cited positive outcomes from educational studies, according to Ehrich, Hansford, and Tennent (2004). Examination of this figure shows that 42 percent of studies indicated positive outcomes for the interns of support, empathy, encouragement, counseling, and friendship. Figure 1.2 presents the most frequently cited problematic outcomes from educational studies. According to Figure 1.2, the two most frequent problems identified with internship and mentoring were (1) lack of time and (2) professional expertise and/or personality mismatch. Of the studies reviewed, 35.8 percent reported only positive outcomes. Substantially more studies noted more positive outcomes for interns (82.4 percent) than for mentors. The authors suggested that this might be attributed to the fewer studies that sought opinions from mentors.

Their study "indicates not only many common themes and points of convergence but also that mentoring seems to offer considerably more benefits than drawbacks" (p. 503). Internships acclimate students to their future roles and provide an opportunity to develop needed confidence to leave the principal preparation program and go directly into an administrative position.

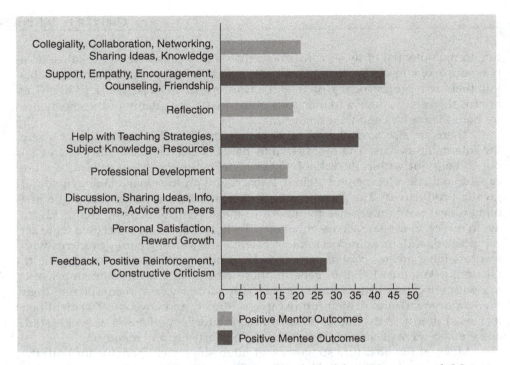

FIGURE 1.1 Four Most Frequently Cited Positive Mentor and Mentee Outcomes from the Educational Studies

Source: Ehrich, L., Hansford, B., and Tennent, L. (2004, October). Formal mentoring programs in education and other professions: A review of the literature. *Education Administration Quarterly, 40,* 4: 524. Copyright 2004 by Sage Publications. Reprinted by permission of Sage Publications, Inc.

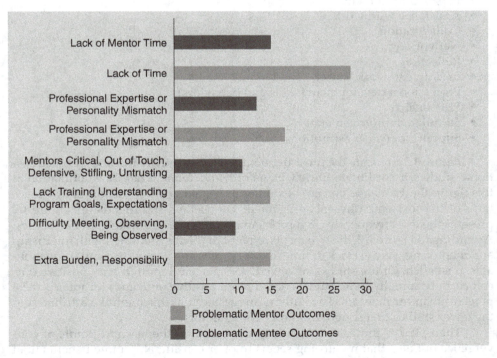

FIGURE 1.2 Four Most Frequently Cited Problematic Mentor and Mentee Outcomes from the Educational Studies

Source: Ehrich, L., Hansford, B., and Tennent, L. (2004, October). Formal mentoring programs in education and other professions: A review of the literature. *Educational Administrative Quarterly, 40,* 4: 524. Copyright 2004 by Sage Publications. Reprinted by permission of Sage Publications, Inc.

chapter 2

Internship Components and Course Scaffolding

It is difficult to talk about a single structure for the internship class because it takes on so many different forms at different colleges and universities. Perhaps it is best to discuss the internship in terms of the components that can be found in the variety of courses now offered. In this way, the intern can select and focus on the specific components that are a part of his or her program. One element of an internship that is often an essential part of all programs is *reflection* (Brown & Irby, 2001; Lester & Pascale, 2004; Sergiovanni, 2005; Schon, 1983; Williamson & Hudson, 2001). As a result, reflection on the internship will be developed as a separate chapter (Chapter 3).

Some key questions interns will ask themselves is when to participate in clinical experiences, how experiences will be arranged, how their knowledge and skill will intersect with real-world experiences, how experiences will be documented, how they will know their skills and abilities are being developed, and so on. Each university answers these questions uniquely using input from professional associations, state departments of education, foundations, surrounding school divisions, students, and fellow university instructors.

The answer to many such questions is partially found in the course materials provided by the education leadership faculties. This text/handbook complements these materials and shows how interns can best extract the important meaning, knowledge, and skills from their internship experiences. What is the process by which the internship can educe, and the intern can elicit, higher levels of meaning from experiences in which the intern is involved? How will your experiences gained during an internship be combined with the knowledge you have gained in preparation program course work? The answers to these questions are still emerging and are unique to each program as educational leadership staff continue to develop and refine clinical/internship experiences that occur within their programs. As a result, there is not a consistent template that each program follows.

University interns receive a course syllabus and/or internship course pack to guide them during their placement with a sponsoring school system. These guides provide specific information to help interns in planning, completing, and reflecting on the internship experience, and are focused on issues of documentation, reporting, and meeting course expectations. Interns are also guided by the policy, rules, and regulations of the sponsoring school district and state department of education. Your actual internship process and clinical components are based within the context of each state and university's requirements and regulations and those of accreditation agencies (Hackmann, Schmitt-Oliver, & Tracy, 2002). This text/handbook provides needed guidelines for completing a successful internship while fitting within the requirements of the diverse internship programs that exist at different universities. This chapter presents supporting assignments for the internship that are found at most universities now offering internships as part of an administrative and supervision preparation program.

COMMITMENT

An important element of all of this is that the mentor, the intern, the staff at the site, and the sponsoring school system have an attitude of commitment to your development as an intern. Of course, the single most important element is that the internship process is highly valued by the intern, mentor, and university supervisor and that they give the process their strongest effort and attention. Interns will waste everyone's time, gain little, and harm the process for future interns if they have little personal/professional motivation or interest in completing an internship. If the internship is nothing more than another painful hoop that the future educational leader must jump through to prepare for educational leadership, the intern should re-assess his or her desire to become an educational leader.

Another important element is that the intern be self-directed in his or her internship process. This is a time when you will be expected to express confidence and independence in completing internship experiences. The instructor and the mentor will facilitate the learning process, serve as resources, and ensure that growth has actually taken place, but they do not direct it; that is the responsibility of the intern. Interns will be expected to get help if they are unsure of what needs to be done or how it might be best completed, but this is not a time for a lot of hand holding. The intern uses self-support, self-confidence, and self-reliance in completing the work and related course assignments. It is a time of freedom to apply what is known and what has been learned in real-world settings, and to match what you want to learn with key activities and career aspirations.

Instructors and mentors ensure that interns are provided opportunities to discuss their development experiences in an atmosphere of collegiality and mentoring. This opportunity to share perspectives and seek solutions to common problems is extremely important to the long-term growth of educators (Cunningham & Gresso, 1993). In this way, interns serve as resources to each other. Reflection and periodic self-analysis are helpful for trying to see how things might be done differently the next time around, and for focusing on traits that you might want to change in order to improve professionally.

THE INTERNSHIP

The internship is designed to engage you, as a prospective administrator, in planned and coordinated authentic learning experiences in a real-world setting. You are provided opportunities to engage in clinical experiences in schools in order to make critical theory-to-practice transitions while gaining practical administrative skills. Through these internship activities, students gain first-hand experience in a relatively safe environment within a strong supportive culture. Interns gain important insights into the operation of schools as they develop their leadership skills by handling real-world opportunities. Use this time to apply the theories you learned in your program so you can figure out which theories will work for you in your particular school setting.

Goals

It is important that interns have a clear understanding of the goals of their internship and/or practicum program. Some possible goals of the internship might include:

- To allow the intern the opportunity to observe, over time, a variety of leadership styles practiced by experienced administrators in various situations at multiple levels in the organization.
- To help the intern gain self-confidence in administrative decision making through progressive opportunities to test knowledge and skills in diverse clinical settings.
- To provide the intern with the opportunity to interface with diverse publics in carrying out the day-to-day responsibilities inherent in school administration.
- To provide interns with an opportunity to practice their craft in a controlled situation with a safety net to help and protect them.
- To provide interns an opportunity to validate their knowledge, skills, philosophies, and values.
- To provide interns with the opportunity to explore authentic work and receive feedback in order to position them for the next stage of their professional career.

Each university program may have slightly different goals. However, the major theme is to prepare the future administrator to deal with the day-to-day expectations that leadership places on him or her.

Capasso and Daresh (2001) help to relate the internship experience to an individual's preparation program. They state:

Well designed programs offer participants many possible alternative goals:

1. Enable interns to develop administrative competence progressively through a range of practical experiences
2. Allow interns to apply knowledge and skills gained through universities in a practical setting
3. Enable interns to test their knowledge, skills, and personal commitment
4. Provide interns with an opportunity to gain insights into the preparation of a school, its goals, and how those goals may be achieved
5. Give interns insights into their progress toward personal and professional goals
6. Showcase the talents of interns as potential future school leaders. (p. 14)

You will want to make sure that you are clear on what your goals are regarding the completion of an internship experience.

INTERNSHIP PROCESS

It is important that the activities in which the intern is involved are broad in scope covering all standards (or assigned requirements) and the diverse areas of administrative responsibility. Student activities are typically planned by the intern and his or her mentor within the supporting school district, with the oversight of the university instructor.

Most students report that they work with their external mentors (a well-regarded practicing administrator, see Chapter 7) to develop opportunities in which they can engage in meaningful administrative responsibilities. It is also quite helpful for interns to have lots of opportunities for interactions with instructors, practicing administrators, and fellow students regarding specific internship activities. It is especially beneficial to glean information and insight from experienced leaders because the typical intern lacks such administrative experience. Research suggests that interns value the opportunity to learn and practice leadership with a mentor (Browne-Ferrigno, 2003).

Your university instructor typically approves activities and/or is involved in jointly planning the activities with the site mentor and you. Internship activities that are planned, scheduled, and structured have proven to be as beneficial as are random experiences. Random experiences, however, tend to be haphazard in regard to providing balanced experiences. It is also helpful to have an understanding, up front, of the different types of activities that might become a part of your internship experience.

For those preparing to be principals, there are a few advantages to having experiences at the central office level. The district-wide experience helps you to know the types of activities that occur in these offices and provides a range of people to be able to call on in the future when you need a resource to answer some questions or assist in an activity. Therefore, it is wise to include some central office administrative experiences as part of the internship (see Chapter 8, Planning Internship Activities).

Internship Course Components

You will typically be provided a course packet, an internship manual or brief handbook, and/or a course syllabus that describes the internship process and the guidelines for your internship in educational administration. These guides will spell out the specific requirements for your internship course. This text/handbook serves to complement these guides. This chapter provides information on the types of components that might be a part of the internship program. Some of these will be a part of your internship class, but by no means will all of these be a part of the course. This text/handbook provides a generic structure that will assist you in getting the most from your internship, in the most efficient and effective way possible. You will use your course syllabi, handbook, forms, and so on to determine which of the internship course components found in this chapter are relevant to your course of study.

The typical roles of course components are to help in the assessment process, to encourage reflectiveness, imprint details, increase professional involvement and recollection, increase successful solutions, and create a historical record of your work. Various forms of note taking and record keeping can make a vital contribution to improved understanding, communication, and development of practical knowledge. Although some of these forms are presented at the end of this chapter, many universities require students to use systems such as Excel, InfoPath, or Access to design and present the forms and information. These programs provide form design, information entry/collection systems, and data storage/transmission, all of which will be important tools once you become an administrator. You can learn more about these tools on the web at www.office.microsoft.com followed by /Excel or /InfoPath or /Access, respectively.

What follows are briefs of possible internship course components. As mentioned, no one program or internship experience would include all of these elements, but most programs use at least one or more. Each course component can stand alone or it can be combined with others in a complementary fashion.

Needs Assessment.   You will want to complete a professional needs assessment (see Chapter 8) identifying areas of need that might be addressed during the internship experience. Interns will seldom, if ever, be equipped equally with the repertoire of competencies, knowledge, and skills needed to perform effectively in all activities. The needs assessment begins to help interns to think through the types of activities from which they will gain the greatest benefit. They might design their internship to begin with activities with which they are more comfortable and to work up to the activities about which they know the least. According to Cordeiro and Smith-Sloan (1995), activities should be scaffolded—moving quickly from the simplest activities for individuals to complete to assignments of increasing complexity. As interns become oriented and gain confidence and skill with more familiar tasks, they should move to increasingly complex assignments in which they have the greatest need for professional development.

Each individual can be helped to develop an internship activity plan designed to prepare him or her for educational leadership by following ideas discussed in Chapters 5, 7, and 8. The most important aspect of the internship plan is the intern's reflection about the leadership abilities and the types of experiences that would be most beneficial. The internship plan helps to assure that interns will achieve their objectives.

You might begin by establishing a clear understanding with your mentor and your university supervisor as to what your expectations are and what their expectations are regarding your internship experience. The second step is to look at school division job descriptions, policy manuals, performance evaluations, school improvement plans, and other information that helps you to understand the expectations and practices of administrators in your district and school (see also Chapters 3 and 7). Next, you will want to participate in activities in which you can build good relationships so your mentor and other administrators feel comfortable around you and thus will be more likely to help you learn (see Chapters 5 and 6).

Certainly, observing how people do their work and interact with others will help you understand the school and district culture. You then need to determine how you can best fit into that culture so that people will be comfortable with and trust you. You will want to develop firm relationships and gain credibility within the work culture and with parents and administrators outside your work unit.

Internship Activity Plan. An internship activity plan categorized under appropriate standards (ISLLC, ELCC, state standards, or others) is normally maintained by the intern—in this case, the ISLLC standards are being used. Some internships do not use standards but instead use an administrative skills log or some other form or means to help interns organize their work. The log provides evidence of involvement in a meaningful and practical activity. The log documents the intern's work on the activity and includes artifacts related to the "contracted" activity. The artifacts should help to illustrate the intern's level of understanding, application, and growth. Artifacts are intern-made documentation—physical, intellectual, or behavioral creations that are produced as a part of the intern's efforts. The artifact is often produced as a response to a given need or activity. It is quite often the products that were produced during an activity in which you were involved.

Although the student's mentor and university instructor have key roles in matching internship activities to the self-assessment of needs, desires, background, and aspirations of the intern, the intern's active involvement in the planning process is key to a valuable internship experience. One of the first things in which the mentor and intern will be involved is discussing their individual expectations and the activities in which the intern will become involved. This may change somewhat as you become involved in administration at the site and identify new areas of opportunity and growth that might be of benefit. According to Milstein, Bobroff, and Restine (1999, p. 37):

> In the initial planning of any new program, representatives must interact as a
> group to define the purposes of the internship program. The next key step is to

design the operational procedures that will contribute to meeting the purposes. Key players need time to discuss the philosophies about what should occur in an internship program, build consensus about program expectations, and ensure the preparation of outstanding administrators. This contributes to building a foundation of communications on which to develop goals, objectives, and *activities*. It may also serve to facilitate discussions on how program expectations can be provided and the roles of the university and the school district.

The internship is a highly visible activity and will have a significant impact on your future promotion within the sponsoring district and probably those districts within the region. For this reason, it is important (far beyond the internship course) that you do a good job as an educational administrative intern. Your planning and internship experience proposal should not be taken lightly. A well-conceived, appropriate plan of internship activities will go a long way toward ensuring a successful internship (see Chapter 8).

The student is expected to use the information collected in the self-assessment (Chapter 8) and the school-assessment (Chapter 7) to develop an internship activity plan for the entire internship. This will be further discussed in later chapters. Although the plan is not written in stone, it will be the major guide as to what will occur during the internship experience, what support will be needed, and how it will benefit the intern. You should reflect on the standards, your self-assessment, your mentor's background, and the internship setting to determine what you need to know, the skills and knowledge you need to develop, and what will be possible for you to achieve at your internship setting. The activities listed in Chapter 8 should help you develop your internship activity plan.

Internship planning might include any readings, experiences, communication with individuals, meetings, support, and so on that might be needed. You might especially want to focus on the support that will be needed to successfully implement plans regarding each activity. You might develop your internship activity plan using a guidance sheet like the following:

Internship Activity Plan

Internship Plan for _____ Date _____

Standard _____

Activity No	Internship Activity	Knowledge and Support Needed	Needed Mentor Assistance	Skills to Be Attained	Timeline for Achievement
1					
2					
3					

This will help to ensure that you are clear regarding your responsibilities and know what you will need to do to accomplish the activity. This activity plan also helps you to understand the mentor's role in each of the intern's activities. The activity plan is meant to help the intern to think through activity responsibilities in order to mobilize individuals and achieve effective results.

Other information that you might want to report on an activity plan or as attached clarifying documents might include:

Trigger event(s): the occurrence(s) that made you aware that there is a situation requiring your attention

Goal(s) for action: what you will be trying to accomplish by your actions

Possible causes, school-based: the one or two factors within your school that seem likely to have caused the situation

Possible causes, administrative-based: the one or two aspects of administrative behaviors, beliefs, values, or attitudes that may have caused the situation to arise

Additional information: details gathered before taking action that seem to have a bearing on the situation

Planned solution: steps you plan to take to resolve the situation

Target date: the date you expect to have resolved the situation

Outcome: a brief description of the outcome of the resolution and what still must be done

Time: the number of hours spent on this activity (Sliver, 1986)

Work Logs.   In addition, combined or as a separate document, the work log can be used to record critical incidents, successes, plans, and problems of the internship experience, as well as feelings, impressions, and reflections on experience, and can be a place to note further research and inquiries on a periodic basis. The log should be kept in a spiral notebook that can be shared with the supervisor, peers, and the university instructor. A major purpose of a work log is to keep track of work on activities and the number of hours spent on each activity (see Form 2.1). Once the activities that cover a specific standard have been completed, the on-site supervisor signs the log sheet to certify completion. The university instructor usually also signs these sheets. The log sheets are used to determine and certify that all required internship objectives have been met and the intern has fulfilled all university and/ or state requirements.

The most important element will be the quality of the activities in which you are involved during your internship experience. Getting good experience is the only remedy for inexperience.

Seminars.   Opportunities for reflection time are vital for interns to learn from their experiences in the field. Milstein (1993) states, "the more students can explore meaning through reflection with peers and others, the more that they can make sense of their experiences. Experiences are accumulated with great rapidity at the field-based sites, so opportunities to share reflection should be provided with regularity" (p. 199).

Interns highly value quality interactions with practicing school leaders. Another important aspect is sharing their on-the-job learning experience with their cohort peers or fellow classmates so that they can learn from one another and discuss how their mentoring administrators address problems of practice (Milstein & Krueger, 1997). It is also very helpful to work with the university supervisor to link textbook and course learning to authentic practices. Interns also greatly appreciate the opportunity to develop lifelong networks with fellow interns—which is probably best supported by the classroom seminars in which students share their experiences.

Seminars provide a structured opportunity to converse with fellow interns who are having similar experiences and challenges in different education settings.

The opportunity to share and discuss your experiences, challenges, and frustrations with fellow students and your university supervisor helps to build confidence and self-reliance, and to dispel feelings of isolation. Seminars serve as support networks that may persist for the rest of your professional life. The goals of the seminar are: (1) to support and inform students about the program; (2) to enable them to analyze their practice and reflect on strengths and areas of needed improvement; and, most important (3), to provide opportunities for candid, encouraging, and focused discussions that support the interns in thinking through how they might or how they did approach their activities.

There are many possible topics for seminar classes. Interns can suggest topics or can present some of their best activities for the rest of the students to discuss. Discussions related to the reflective journal offer powerful topics for classroom discussion. Seminars can also be pre-structured on specific topics, and practitioners from sponsoring school systems can be invited in to discuss how various intern concerns might be handled. Some seminars are scheduled at internship sites, model schools, or even at school division and/or state headquarters. Experiences are discussed in relation to your knowledge and theory base, gained during your program of study.

You and your fellow interns will want to bring ethical dilemmas that each has confronted and resolved to seminar sessions for discussion and further analysis. This will provide a chance to confront multiple issues and discuss the ethical basis on which decisions are made. This is especially interesting when a number of core ethical values have come into conflict in some way, or when the ethical values of different groups are in conflict—individual versus community (see Chapter 5).

The seminar provides time to share field experiences, to discuss concerns, to provide ideas and assistance, and to network to build confidence and fine-tune responses to activities. Interns consistently value the opportunity for interaction with other interns, staff, and university instructors. Fellow interns are very important in dealing with the intensity of the internship experience. Fellow interns can be good listeners who provide encouragement as well as great ideas on how to handle various responsibilities. Seminars often develop into networks that continue long beyond the completion of the internship and into one's professional career (Restine, Kruger, & Milstein, 1990).

Supervisor Visits and Triad Meetings.   The university supervisor may visit your internship site to observe you in various administrative settings while you are engaged in contracted activities. The number and types of visits are specified by the internship instructor and educational leadership faculty at your university or college. The supervisor might discuss your performance and how to best develop needed skills. Meetings may be between the university supervisor and the student, or may also include the site mentor, becoming a *triad* meeting. Some universities have standard conference report forms that are completed by both the university supervisor and/or the site mentor and then discussed with the intern during the supervisor or triad meeting. The major focus of these visits is on sharing formative assessments and developing possible growth plans. The meetings are also used to correct any inappropriate or unproductive behavior by the intern and develop a plan of improvement if it is needed. In most cases, these visits will be beneficial to all involved.

The Interstate School Leadership Licensure Consortium (ISLLC), Educational Testing Services (ETS), and the Council of Chief State School Officers (CCSSO) came up with the most important dimensions of the job domain for the position of school administrator (Hessel & Holloway, 2002). There is a direct link between these educational leadership dimensions and the ISSLC standards and the SLLA. As a result, these dimensions were used to develop an intern assessment and conference form to be used in discussions with interns (Form 2.2). This is only one possible example of many of the forms that are being used for formative evaluation of the intern. For example, forms can be based on ISSLC, ELCC, or state standards.

Staff in many programs have designed their own forms; Form 2.2 provides an example of one form based on ETS job domains.

Project.   Some universities require a project to be completed as part of the internship experience. The project typically entails a major school issue that has been assessed as a needed area of analysis and response by the administrator. It is often much longer in duration than other activities in which the intern is involved, sometimes extending over the entire academic year. Documentation includes the issues, goals, relevant research, knowledge base, planning and decision-making process and how it was implemented, problems that developed and how they were solved, final outcomes, evaluation of results, needed followup, and a timeline for all of this. Interns might design, develop, implement, and assess such things as:

- After-school programs
- A math and science academy
- A fine arts academy
- A program for transition into the middle school or high school
- An inclusive curriculum model
- A teacher mentoring program
- A handbook for enriching instructional strategies
- An improved reading success program
- A program closing the achievement gap
- A crisis response plan
- A grant application
- An integrated technology pacing guide
- A new teacher academy
- An updated faculty or student handbook or the policy manual

The list is endless and is often determined by a combination of the needs of the intern and the school division in which he or she is completing the internship.

Culminating Report.   Some internship programs require interns to write a final report that discusses their field experience and provides an overview of the entire internship experience. The report often includes specificity regarding tasks; decisions and decision-making procedures; outcomes; a flavor of emotions, relationships, issues, and communication; and some reflection on the experience. There are some ethical considerations, for example, privacy, that must be reflected in any culminating report. The report often references related artifacts, articles, and other information, which are usually placed in an appendix to the culminating report.

What follows are some typical questions that you might be expected to respond to in your culminating report:

1. In what ways has the internship experience (or the activities participated in) clarified aspects of your previous knowledge or information about educational leadership and/or the ISLCC standards?
2. What kind of values, attitudes, beliefs, or feelings—professionally and personally—have the experiences produced?
3. Were the activities relevant to your academic experiences? How?
4. What surprised you?
5. What, in essence, has the field experience taught you?
6. Did you get the results you wanted?
7. What have you learned about your educational leadership knowledge base, your values, and the practice of school administration?
8. How might the internship experience assist you when you become a practicing administrator?

The culminating report could include a response on how you are adequately prepared to meet each standard (ISLLC, ELCC, or state).

PARTIAL SAMPLE OF A CULMINATING REPORT

I was heavily involved in our strategic goal to improve student achievement through the implementation of units of study using Understanding by Design as developed by Jay McTighe and Grant Wiggins. I know that this program was effective because our students are enjoying our lessons more and parents are seeing better unit test scores from many classes. Our community supports our efforts and parents have volunteered to make teaching aids and to type worksheets for us. We did recognize that not all teachers had implemented the plans and that others were slowly falling back into lecturing and away from differentiation strategies. I realize that you cannot let up when implementing new strategies and must figure out ways to reinforce strategic goals throughout the year. Our discussion of Michael Fullan's work in a number of classes, especially discussion of the planning process, was most helpful during my internship experience. We agreed that in November we would need to reinforce what had been presented in August and teach several more strategies. I also believe that it is the ethical responsibility of the administrator to hold teachers accountable for the implementation of strategic goals, particularly when they have a direct bearing on students' learning.

If I could improve my performance relative to the Understanding by Design training, I would not have all the exploratory and physical education teachers in one group. I did not realize how many people were in that group. I was trying to spread my presenters out equally, but that group did not get the best strategies for their needs. In November, I divided this group into two smaller groups—physical education, and technology and all other exploratory teachers.

If I could improve my performance relative to this sub-standard it would be to get our physical education staff more on board with differentiation strategies in their health lessons. They have been using the same lesson plans for years and their projects are not relevant to today's youth. I never see their classes in the computer lab or see students working together. The students are seated in rows and the teacher is in the front lecturing. I understand why students hate their health days and do so poorly on their health grades. Until our administration holds these teachers accountable like the rest of the faculty, they will not change.

I have learned that promoting a vision requires a great deal of networking and getting as many people aboard as possible. If your vision is not articulated clearly and effectively there can be misdirection, wasted time, and confusion. You must make the goals and strategies an important part of all school activities throughout the year and constantly reinforce all developmental activities. Although I learned about changing work cultures in my course work, I found it very difficult to change the attitudes and practices of teachers in physical education. I know that I need more work in this area and was not as well prepared for this type of challenge as I thought I was. I was surprised by this and realize that I need to focus more attention in this area before becoming an administrator.

I experienced a very difficult dilemma in one of my internship activities. I had to count all the textbooks and compare my numbers to the inventory sheets prepared by all the subject area coordinators. Many times my numbers did not coincide with theirs. Some of the teachers did not complete their textbook inventory sheets correctly and that made my job more difficult. I had to work directly with some teachers and have them come in after school to explain their accounting techniques. I discovered that the assistant principal in charge of textbooks had never required the faculty to fill out the forms correctly and that is probably why our numbers did not match.

Teachers do not understand that not following directions can cause major problems when final reports are due. I tried to get reports ready for Central Office and I did not have prior information that had been sent by our assistant principal. When we were given the past information, the numbers did not coincide with our information this year. It was very difficult to explain how we had too few textbooks in some subjects and so many more in others without finding fault with the assistant principal. He had been lax in his work for several years and seemed to be pushing his work on other members of his staff. He felt his only job was to supervise. This presented a difficult moral challenge, in that I had values that seemed to be in conflict. It also presented a political dilemma, in that I have to work with this assistant principal in the future. I decided that the best approach was to write guidelines that all teachers would use for accounting for textbooks and I placed the information in the teacher handbook.

This truly turned a losing situation into a winning one. I now believe more in Steven Covey's win/win philosophy. The principal, assistant principal, teachers, and even central administration were pleased with my efforts. There was some reference to the hopes that my work would end the "nightmares that had occurred in the past." This was a valuable learning experience that showed me that there are methods of turning a losing situation into a winning one and that the administrator's job is to find those solutions.

Administrative Platform.   The platform clearly espouses the basis on which you carry out your work, make decisions, and handle yourself as a leader. The concept is based on the political model, in which parties are expected to develop platforms to aid supporters and voters in understanding what they stand for so the people can make informed choices. The platform summarizes, in writing, a description of your core values, beliefs, and philosophies about educational leadership.

It is important that interns and those with whom they work have a clear understanding of the foundational principles, conceptualizations, philosophy, and values on which they base their judgments. Your style, beliefs, decision-making process, leadership style, and so on should be embodied in the platform on which you stand. Platforms "are made up of those basic assumptions, beliefs, attitude and values that are the underpinning of an educator's behavior" (Sergiovanni & Starratt, 2001, p. 84). Educational leaders carry out their work, make decisions, and plan instruction on the basis of such platforms.

The platform is a self-reflective document providing a framework for administrative action. It may have been developed throughout the administrative preparation program. It states the principles, ethics, and values that underlie a person's actions. Ultimately, it describes how their administrative practices and actions are related to these beliefs. It also helps to identify any inconsistencies among beliefs, values, practices, and knowledge. When one's platform and behavior are incompatible, the administrator decides which to alter.

Individual platforms should be in general agreement with the philosophy, mission, goals, and direction of the school system. The process itself is great for self-awareness and value clarification, can reduce or at least make conflict explicit, and can serve as a point of reference. The platform should be observable in the person's actions. Interns should compare their platforms to others' and reflect on areas of agreement or disagreement. The platform may become part of a culminating portfolio.

Culminating Portfolio.   A prospective administrator's professional portfolio is a collection of academic and work experiences and accomplishments that document his or her potential for management and leadership excellence. The portfolio details personal and professional qualities not presented in a typical resume or administrative application. It is a collection of an intern's work that tells the story of the efforts, progress, and achievement toward preparation to be an outstanding educational administrator. It is a history of the student's journey toward leadership. This should not be a scrapbook of everything the intern has done but a careful selection of important items that characterize the quality of the intern's work. A guiding theme might be "what best demonstrates what I know and what I am able to do" or "which are the most important works I have accomplished."

The portfolio, like the platform, focuses on the candidate's knowledge and beliefs (philosophy, ethics, and values) as a practicing administrator documenting relevant performances in which he or she has been involved. It provides an opportunity for the candidate to document learning experiences and reflect on professional growth. The portfolio showcases a sampling of the intern's best work.

It demonstrates the achievement of leadership standards, skills, and accomplishments. Artifacts are collected to demonstrate that the student has developed the needed background to become an effective leader. Thus, the portfolio is a systemized and organized collection of evidence to monitor the individual's knowledge, skill, and experience.

The professional administrative portfolio serves, along with the mentor summative assessment, as a summative evaluation tool to assure that each student meets the competencies for leadership in the major areas spelled out in the standards (ISLLC, ELCC, or others). The portfolio can be used for a final determination that each student has met the exit criteria adequately for graduation, licensure, and practice.

The portfolio can be organized according to three major sections: (a) introduction, (b) body (academic experience), and (c) appendix (work experience). The purpose of the first section, the introduction, is to present the author to readers and contains such items as a table of contents, introduction page, personal statement, professional goals and objectives, vita or résumé, statement of ethics, philosophy of education and philosophy of leadership, and other additions.

The second section, the body, is the substance of the portfolio and consists of subsections that correspond to each of the standards (ISLLC, ELCC, or others). The purpose of the body of the portfolio is to demonstrate the student's knowledge and understanding of the standards. Each subsection ends with a reflective statement that ties the student's academic and professional work to the standard.

It is the responsibility of each student to collect academic items for inclusion, determine the placement of selected items into the body of the portfolio, and write reflective statements describing how these items demonstrate the student's preparedness on each specific standard.

The final section of the professional administrative portfolio is the appendix. As such, its purpose is to *supplement* the body of the professional administrative portfolio. Artifacts in the appendix should be selected carefully and sparingly to avoid making the portfolio appear as a scrapbook rather than a unified presentation of one's professional self. (See Form 2.3, Professional Portfolio and Work Artifacts, for suggested artifacts for the portfolio appendix.)

These guidelines outline only one of many possible formats for the professional administrative portfolio. They provide a sampling of possibilities to assist authors in selecting items that reflect their knowledge and understanding.

Electronic Portfolios.   More recently, portfolios are being created in an electronic format that presents all of the student's information on a computer disk, zip disk, hard drive, DVD, or even web site. The intern scans the entire culminating portfolio and presents it on the computer. The electronic version allows for easy access and updating. It even can include video streaming, in which the intern verbally presents information or demonstrates competencies.

To create an electronic portfolio, first you will need to become familiar with the electronic equipment and software. The major steps for creating an electronic portfolio are planning, setting up templates, creating your individual portfolio (entering information), and finalizing the portfolio. There is a great deal of information on the internet to help you to design and create your electronic portfolio. For example, see www.essdack.org/port/index.html or Dr. Helen Barnet's web site at www.electronicportfolios.com.

Electronic portfolios can be created by the intern by setting up his or her own headings. They can also be developed under a menu that is provided by the university, or the intern can use one of the commercially produced electronic portfolios like Chalk and Wire's e-portfolio or College Live Text. Commercially produced portfolio servers vary in cost depending on the company and the services requested.

E-portfolio (www.chalkandwire.com/eportfolio) claims that a beginner can develop an electronic portfolio that is easily accessed and updated and looks as if it was created by a professional graphic artist and web designer. This system allows you to easily configure the entire system to meet your needs. It has unlimited storage space, state-of-the-art file back up, firewall protection, and virus scanning. The portfolio can be downloaded from the web at any time and you can burn a CD-ROM or DVD as needed.

Another system that is widely used is College Live Text (www.college.live text.com/college). This system claims to be a complete development, management, and assessment solution specifically designed for colleges and universities. The live text portfolio solution allows interns to customize their online presentations, add content online, and use a text editor. It provides access to potential employers, showcasing skills the employer wants to see, and provides instructor scoring and assessment capabilities using portfolio assessment tools.

The rewards of creating a professional portfolio lie in both the process and the product. The experience fosters

- Assessment of performance and reflection for growth
- Tracking professional progress
- Development of professional goals
- Visualization of accomplishments
- Highlighting of skills, talents, or qualities of character
- Unique presentation of accomplishment and style
- A sense of pride and self-esteem
- Documentation for employment interviews

Mentor's Assessment

Most programs require the mentor to assess the intern's performance and discuss the completed assessment form. This is done periodically throughout the internship as a formative assessment (see Form 2.2) and as a culminating activity or summative assessment (see Form 2.4). These forms are sometimes completed as a collaborative process by both the university supervisor and site mentor. The summative assessment entitled Performance Standards for Prospective Principals (PSPP) is an example of a summative assessment (Form 2.4) of on-the-job performance of internship students. The assessment categories are based on standards and sub-standards provided by the Educational Leadership Constituent Council (ELCC), and is aligned with the ISLLC standards. Your educational leadership program may have its own form(s) to be used for mentor summative assessment.

The scoring rubric for the PSPP based on ELCC guidelines follows. Based on the candidate's performance, candidates are rated as unacceptable, acceptable, or exemplary according to the following rubrics:

Unacceptable. The evidence is not conceptually related to the sub-standard, or it is unclear whether the intern was substantially involved in the activity represented by the evidence. Insufficient context is provided for a reviewer to interpret the evidence. Self-assessment lacks depth of analysis, or does not indicate concrete actions that can be taken to improve performance.

Acceptable. The evidence is clearly related to the sub-standard. Contextual information or the evidence itself indicates that the intern had a substantial role in the activity represented by the evidence. Self-assessment is rigorous, and indicates steps that will be taken to improve performance in the sub-standard domain.

Exemplary. The evidence is clearly related to the sub-standard. Contextual information or the evidence itself indicates that the intern had a leadership role in the activity represented by the evidence. Self-assessment is guided by both introspection and data collected related to the activity. Steps are provided for improving the activity/product and the intern's performance in the sub-standard domain.

Perhaps the most comprehensive discussion of educational leadership assessment appears in *A Framework for School Leaders: Linking the ISLLC Standards to Practice,* by Karen Hessel and John Holloway (2002). This resource provides a blueprint for the level of performance on most of the central themes of educational leadership "organized around the core proposition that the most crucial aspect of a school leader's work is the continuous improvement of student learning" (p. 2). These authors use four levels of performance in their Component Performance Table: rudimentary, developing, proficient, and accomplished, as presented in Form 2.2. These performance indicators are used by the mentor or university instructor to designate the intern's level of performance on each of the components of the dimensions of school administration factors.

The assessment provides an excellent opportunity for the external mentor to discuss your effectiveness during the internship experience, identifying areas needing further development. It also assists the classroom instructor in determining a grade for your internship class and in helping the instructor and the intern plan future development activity or preparation regarding the intern's professional leadership.

CELEBRATION

Celebrating key moments in an individual's life nourishes and feeds the spirit. The successful completion of all internship activities provides an excellent opportunity for a ceremony to commemorate your educational leadership accomplishments. Completing an internship is a significant achievement in an educational leader's career and is worthy of celebration. The intern has completed a transition from the "preparation for" to the "practice of" leadership and that is why the process can be called a rite of passage. Such changes in one's life station are typically marked with ceremonies of passage. You are celebrating the transition that has resulted in the emergence of a new person—an educational leader. You are celebrating the process of transformation and the realization that you are on a different life journey. Life transitions are signs that we will fulfill our destiny and the promise of our lives. Congratulate yourself and other interns.

•   **Form 2.1**   •

Work Log

Keeping a log of experiences during internship activities will help the intern to develop the skills necessary to become a reflective practitioner while documenting work efforts and outcomes, along with skills and knowledge required. The completed work log sheets should be signed by the intern's mentor. The sheets serve as both documentation and as a resource for the intern in future discussions, reflections, reports, and so on.

Work Experience Log

Intern's name _____

Time Period Being Documented _____   Total Contact hours _____

Setting _____   Cooperating Professional _____

ELCC, ISLLC, or State Administrative Performance Standard _____

_____

Objective, Purpose, or Outcome Sought _____

_____

Description of Activity(ies) _____

_____

_____

Work Completed _____

_____

_____

_____

Final Outcome (Attach Supporting Documents) _____

_____

_____

Reflections _____

_____

_____

Social Justice Reflections (Optional) _____

_____

Recommendations _____

_____

_____

Followup _____

_____

_____

_____

Mentor's Signature/Date

· **Form 2.2** ·

Intern's Formative Assessment and Conference Form

Intern's name_____   Site_____

Dimensions of School Administration	Rudimentary (Little or No Evidence)	Developing (Limited Evidence)	Proficient (Clear Evidence)	Accomplished (Consistent Evidence)
Leadership				
Evidence observed or not observed:				
Recommendations for improvement:				
Strategic Planning				
Evidence observed or not observed:				
Recommendations for improvement:				
Facilitating Student Learning				
Evidence observed or not observed:				
Recommendations for improvement:				
Implementing and Evaluating Curriculum and Instruction				
Evidence observed or not observed:				
Recommendations for improvement:				
Supervising and Evaluating				
Evidence observed or not observed:				
Recommendations for improvement:				

Dimensions of School Administration	Rudimentary (Little or No Evidence)	Developing (Limited Evidence)	Proficient (Clear Evidence)	Accomplished (Consistent Evidence)
Relations with Faculty/Staff				
Evidence observed or not observed:				
Recommendations for improvement:				
Professional Development				
Evidence observed or not observed:				
Recommendations for improvement:				
Community Relations				
Evidence observed or not observed:				
Recommendations for improvement:				
Management				
Evidence observed or not observed:				
Recommendations for improvement:				
Maintaining Security				
Evidence observed or not observed:				
Recommendations for improvement:				
Operations				
Evidence observed or not observed:				
Recommendations for improvement:				

Assessor's signature _____ Date _____

·   **Form 2.3**   ·

Professional Portfolio Work Artifacts

Check the items you have selected and collected or created for entry into the appendix of your professional portfolio. Place the items in the following order. No individual is expected to have experiences in all of these areas.

Portfolio Work Artifacts

❏ **Professional Development**
  ❏ List of courses, workshops and special training (transcripts)

❏ **Professional Involvement**
  ❏ Professional organizations
  ❏ Task force/committee service
  ❏ Special reports
  ❏ Mentoring or peer-coaching logs
  ❏ Published articles, books, video
  ❏ Leadership roles

❏ **Leadership Development**
  ❏ Administrative degree(s)
  ❏ Supervisory positions
  ❏ Other leadership roles
  ❏ Formal leadership training

❏ **School Involvement**
  ❏ School clubs, activities, projects
  ❏ Special "connections"
  ❏ Team sports or activities
  ❏ Summer school program

❏ **Community Involvement**
  ❏ Projects
  ❏ Partnerships
  ❏ Leadership roles

❏ **Professional Endeavors**
  ❏ Outstanding lessons/projects/areas
  ❏ Work samples
  ❏ Research
  ❏ Student work samples
  ❏ Photos
  ❏ Computer slides

❏ **Honors and Awards**
  ❏ Certificates
  ❏ Awards (letters)
  ❏ Acknowledgment in field (distinctions)
  ❏ Related photos
  ❏ Honors

❏ **Performance Evaluations**
  ❏ Selected observations
  ❏ Summative evaluation
  ❏ Reflections
  ❏ Letters of recommendation

❏ **Commendations**
  ❏ Letters from supervisors
  ❏ Letters from peers
  ❏ Letters from students
  ❏ Letters from parents or community
  ❏ testimonial letters

❏ **Professional Reading**
  ❏ Books, articles, videos, tapes

· Form 2.4 ·

Performance Standards for Prospective Principals

Mentor's Assessment Instrument
(summative evaluation)

To be completed by candidate's school-based mentor.

_____   _____
Intern (please print or type)   Date

_____   _____
Mentor (please print or type)   Mentor's signature

Mentor's Assessment

(This form uses ELCC standards but ISLLC standards could easily be substituted.)

Purpose

The *Performance Standards for Prospective Principals* serve as the culminating assessment of on-the-job performance for principal licensure candidates. The standards and sub-standards are based on those promulgated by the Educational Leadership Constituent Council, which approves principal preparation programs under the auspices of the National Council for Accreditation of Teacher Education (NCATE). The rubrics contained in the assessment instrument were developed locally, through focus group interviews and individual feedback from teachers, principal licensure candidates, and acting school administrators.

Scoring Guidelines for Mentors

Based on your knowledge of the candidate's performance, please rate the candidate as "Unacceptable," "Acceptable," or "Exemplary" according to the provided rubrics. You may leave an item blank if you have insufficient knowledge about the candidate's performance in a specific area. *A brief written justification should be provided for "unacceptable" and "exemplary" ratings.* The written justification should be appended to the assessment instrument.

Instructions
Please check the appropriate rating based on your knowledge of the intern.

Sub-Standard Performance Descriptors	Unacceptable	Acceptable	Exemplary
Standard 1.0: In the internship, candidates demonstrate that they are educational leaders who have the knowledge and ability to promote the success of all students by facilitating the development, articulation, implementation, and stewardship of a school or district vision of learning supported by the school community.			
1.1 Develop a vision	❏ Minimally participates in schoolwide strategic planning processes.	❏ Develops and maintains accountability plans that reflect the school's mission and goals.	❏ Provides leadership in formulating the school's vision and strategic direction.
1.2 Articulate a vision	❏ Has little impact on aligning the behavior of other stakeholders with the school vision.	❏ Uses a variety of strategies to communicate and build relationships with all stakeholders.	❏ Evaluates school programs, structures, and activities with reference to goals and vision.
1.3 Implement a vision	❏ Implements vision-related activities only as required.	❏ Works collaboratively with colleagues in planning for and implementing educational goals.	❏ Demonstrates the ability to direct and guide programmatic growth commensurate with established goals.
1.4 Steward a vision	❏ Exhibits behavior or language that is inconsistent with the school vision.	❏ Reinforces vocabulary and concepts related to vision. Publicly celebrates milestones and intermediate successes.	❏ Assumes a leadership role in regularly renewing the school's vision.
1.5 Promote community involvement	❏ Fails to acknowledge contributions of others in achieving goals. Tends to work in isolation.	❏ Shares successes with greater school community. Incorporates community resources into mission-related strategies.	❏ Directly engages the community in formulating and evaluating school or program goals and strategies.

Sub-Standard Performance Descriptors	Unacceptable	Acceptable	Exemplary
Standard 2.0: Candidates who complete the program are educational leaders who have the knowledge and ability to promote the success of all students by promoting a positive school culture, providing an effective instructional program, applying best practice to student learning, and designing comprehensive professional growth plans for staff.			
2.1 Promote positive culture	❑ Engages in language or behavior that undermines school values.	❑ Models expected behavior and recognizes others who exhibit desired behaviors.	❑ Creates opportunities to reinforce school values on a school-wide basis.
2.2 Provide effective instructional program	❑ Has limited understanding of the school's instructional program. Is not proactive in reviewing program effectiveness.	❑ Knows all domains of the school's instructional program. Uses student performance data to guide decisions about the instructional program.	❑ Systematically ensures alignment between curriculum, instruction, and assessment.
2.3 Apply best practice to student learning	❑ Does not actively seek current knowledge about best practices. Tends to be satisfied with the status quo.	❑ Has knowledge of current effective instructional methods. Utilizes a systematic approach to translating instructional initiatives into classroom practice.	❑ Develops or coordinates instructional programs that utilize best practices identified through research.
2.4 Design comprehensive professional growth plans	❑ Lacks knowledge of how individual professional growth plans fit into the larger framework of school needs.	❑ Has an effective working knowledge of the school division's professional development plan. Participates in developing professional development plans for other school staff.	❑ Assists staff in identifying and participating in professional development activities that are clearly linked to implementation of the school's strategic vision.

Sub-Standard Performance Descriptors	Unacceptable	Acceptable	Exemplary
Standard 3.0: Candidates who complete the program are educational leaders who have the knowledge and ability to promote the success of all students by managing the organization, operations, and resources in a way that promotes a safe, efficient, and effective learning environment.			
3.1 Manage the organization	❑ Fails to set appropriate goals or consistently fails to meet deadlines. Violates pertinent policies or inconsistently applies them. Communication oversights impede project coordination or implementation.	❑ Creates appropriate project timelines and accountability mechanisms. Is knowledgeable of and consistently adheres to pertinent laws, rules, and regulations. Communicates effectively with staff, students, and other stakeholders.	❑ Manages change in the school through modeling, consensus building, feedback, and accountability. Effectively accesses and coordinates resources to achieve goals.
3.2 Manage operations	❑ Significant operational difficulties go unnoticed or are not responded to in a timely and effective manner.	❑ Routinely monitors the school environment and instructional program. Solicits and responds to feedback from staff representing all operational areas of the school.	❑ Effectively focuses and coordinates staff from all operational areas on improving school culture and student performance.
3.3 Manage resources	❑ Oversights in planning or managing resources cause operational difficulties. Inappropriately manages or accounts for resources. Attributes poor personal or organizational performance to lack of resources.	❑ Ensures that staff and students have necessary materials and information for a safe, secure, and effective learning environment. Ensures that instructional programs are appropriately staffed and supported and that resources are properly accounted for.	❑ Proactively acquires additional resources to pursue mission-relevant goals. Develops and implements creative solutions to overcome perceived resource impediments.

Sub-Standard Performance Descriptors	Unacceptable	Acceptable	Exemplary
Standard 4.0: Candidates who complete the program are educational leaders who have the knowledge and ability to promote the success of all students by collaborating with families and other community members, responding to diverse community interests and needs, and mobilizing community resources.			
4.1 Collaborate with families and other community members	❏ Limited or passive involvement with families or community agencies.	❏ Develops and maintains positive relationships with families and community members. Helps families support children's educational achievement and social development. Uses a variety of strategies to communicate with various stakeholder groups.	❏ Provides leadership in establishing and maintaining home–school and school–community relations in a manner that supports the school's strategic goals.
4.2 Respond to community interests and needs	❏ Little awareness of or responsiveness to specific community needs.	❏ Understands how pertinent community interests and needs impact the educational program. Solicits feedback from the community regarding program development and school performance.	❏ Collects and analyzes data from community stakeholders or on community resources to support planning and program development.
4.3 Mobilize community resources	❏ Rarely seeks opportunities to involve the community in pursuing school goals.	❏ Utilizes a variety of community resources to enhance instructional and extracurricular programs.	❏ Establishes and maintains active collaboration with community members, businesses, and other agencies to enhance the instructional program.

Sub-Standard Performance Descriptors	Unacceptable	Acceptable	Exemplary
Standard 5.0: Candidates who complete the program are educational leaders who have the knowledge and ability to promote the success of all students by acting with integrity, fairly, and ethically.			
5.1 Act with integrity	❏ Engages in duplicitous behavior or covers up problems.	❏ Is honest, direct, and solution-focused. Acknowledges responsibility for actions.	❏ Influences others to be honest and accept responsibility for their actions. Confronts others' off-mission behavior in a constructive manner.
5.2 Act fairly	❏ Inappropriately favors some students or staff, makes belittling comments about others. Prejudges situations without collecting sufficient information.	❏ Uses sound, selfless judgment when rendering decisions that affect others. Openly solicits feedback from those who are affected by decisions.	❏ Recognizes and addresses policies or practices that adversely and unevenly affect the welfare of students or staff.
5.3 Act ethically	❏ Seems to be motivated more by self-interest than the school's mission. Violates school policies or circumvents established procedures.	❏ Consistently implements policies and procedures. Willingly shares time, information, and resources to help others achieve goals.	❏ Resolves ethical conflicts on the basis of ethical principles. Judgments reflect an abiding concern for students' well-being.

Sub-Standard Performance Descriptors	Unacceptable	Acceptable	Exemplary
Standard 6.0: Candidates who complete the program are educational leaders who have the knowledge and ability to promote the success of all students by understanding, responding to, and influencing the larger political, social, economic, legal, and cultural contexts.			
6.1 Understand the larger context	❑ Exhibits limited concern for or understanding of matters outside the immediate sphere of influence and activity.	❑ Knows stakeholders, influential community members, and the political structure of the school and community. Keeps informed about major trends in education and other fields.	❑ Has a comprehensive understanding of school mission and goals, and how external constituencies and broader trends impact the school's ability to meet its goals.
6.2 Respond to the larger context	❑ Rarely initiates change at personal or organizational levels. Stays in a reactive or maintenance posture relative to most responsibilities. Seems unaware of how actions are viewed by or influenced by external groups.	❑ Makes decisions that are sensitive to the social, economic, and cultural diversity of the school community. Adapts external mandates in a manner that ensures both compliance and the furtherance of the school's mission.	❑ Initiates change in response to changing external circumstances. Keeps close track of developments in policy circles and in the local community. Anticipates the need for change, and helps others recognize and adapt.
6.3 Influence the larger context	❑ Minimally participates in professional organizations, or in school division or state committees.	❑ Maintains active involvement in professional societies. Participates in school division, community, or state organizations that have direct or indirect effects on schooling	❑ Pursues changes in the community or policy context that further the school's mission.

Please provide additional information regarding the intern's strengths and areas that need further development (include any suggestions for further development). Append pages, if necessary.

Source: John A. Nunnery, Old Dominion University, © 2003. Reprinted by permission. The process of developing these rubrics was generously supported by the Wallace–Reader's Digest Fund's *Leaders Count* initiative.

chapter 3

Reflection on the Internship Experience

A study completed by Ehrich, Hansford, and Tennent (2004) confirmed that both mentors and—to a slightly less extent—mentees considered reflection to be an important part of the mentor/mentee process and fundamental to the overall development of an educator. This reflective process is described as a reappraisal of beliefs, practices, ideas, and values. Reflection was defined as taking time to personally consider actions, words, and thoughts from multiple perspectives in order to think about their meaning for continuous professional growth. Daresh (1988) stressed the importance of providing an opportunity for students to think about and reflect on their experiences and personal development. This is best supported when students are encouraged to raise questions, challenge existing practice, and influence their own evolution as a leader.

Cunningham (1998) found that learning in situations like the internship required an opportunity to reflect on and articulate personal learning experiences, and to direct one's own learning. Both active learning, as in the internship, and self-reflective learning were found to be complementary and to support one another. This process is greatly facilitated where an instructor helps to lead this process and when a social environment of warm and friendly relationships exists (Smith, 2003).

Williamson and Hudson (2001) suggest that the best way to stimulate reflection in the internship process is by providing forums for students to reflect on their experiences, leadership practices, and their own professional development. Seminars, site visits, networking, and reflective journals provide excellent means by which interns can process their experiences and think through alternative approaches. These researchers suggest, "these opportunities to critique, process, problem-solve, and dream helped make the internship the most meaningful aspect of the program for many students. The internship, complemented by the seminars, was the place where connections were made—between theory and practice, between the ideal and the real, between professor and students, and among one another" (p. 5). Students suggest that it is in processing of internship experiences, not the actual experiences, where meaning and understanding are developed.

Research suggests that sustained experiences are important, but not sufficient without opportunity and time to process and reflect on experiences. Including reflections in internship activities allows students to internalize their learning, to think through how it is relevant to their platforms and their future practice, to achieve an awareness of alternative approaches, and to develop the habit of seeing reflection as a process to improve practice in the future (Brown & Irby, 2001; Edmonson, 2002; Lester & Pasacale, 2004). The worth attached to the reflective process is infinite. Effective internships include an opportunity for interns to reflect on and articulate their personal learning experiences (Smith, 2003). Smith also found that when learners are isolated from instructors, mentors, and peers, the support for—and quality of—learning was reduced.

REFLECTION

Reflection is the key to truly getting all that you can out of an experience (Leithwood & Stager, 1986; Moller, 1996; Polite, McClure, & Rollie, 1997; Short, 1997). Once you have completed an activity, it will be valuable to sit down and write an analysis of what you learned. This analysis should be in first person and honest. It is advisable to get a journal or other type of notebook to keep these thoughts together so you may go back and read them as you need to. This is also an invaluable way to keep accurate records of your thinking, beliefs, responses, values, and so on related to your activities. If you felt that an activity was enriching and worthwhile, you should definitely write it down so you may remember later and recreate it as the situation arises. More importantly, however, if you find an activity to be disappointing or disengaging you should give a candid reflection of this as well. You should think through how you might approach an opportunity differently the next time. This is the only way to learn what works for you and in what situations. You should convey your thoughts and emotions in your reflection as well as a play-by-play of the activity.

Here is one caveat. Because the document includes your reflections on your experiences, you will need to consider confidentiality as you keep your reflective journal. The university instructor will typically want to see your reflective journal. There is also a chance that your school system mentor will know you are maintaining a journal and want to see it. If this person does not understand the purpose of the reflective journal, he or she may become offended by questions related to how things might have been done differently, concerned about questions related to your becoming an administrator, and so forth. Confidentiality may also be an issue because the journal can be an excellent source for discussions during reflective seminars, internship supervisor/instructor visits, and even discussions with on-site supervisors. This should not be a problem if everyone understands the purpose and confidentiality of the reflective journal from the beginning, and if all seminar classes are maintained confidential.

THINKING REFLECTIVELY

The reflective journal is somewhat similar to a diary. It is an opportunity to be very introspective regarding your professional behavior, how activities were handled, how activities might have been handled differently, your latest thinking regarding leadership and the job that you aspire to, and so on.

The purpose of the journal is to take time to step back and reflect and analyze the activities in which you have been involved, the decisions you have made, and the actions you have taken. You are giving free reign to your intuitive and perceptive mind, which works in patterns, instincts, feelings, insights, and enlightenments, to work with your more rational and cognitive mind—which works through reasoning, inquiry, rationality, and problem solving. You allow your experiences to incubate in your mind, and record the thoughts that emerge. Some thoughts bubble up from subconscious activity, providing a new perspective on the ways you and others have been doing things or an awareness of new ideas that were not present previously. This type of perception usually does not happen when we are busy or feeling a great deal of tension, so a reflective journal is best written in a quiet, peaceful, beautiful place where the mind is given greater freedom to be reflective.

Even before you begin the internship, you probably have had a number of thoughts that you have pondered regarding the experience. You will not have a clear understanding of what might occur during your internship experience and this will serve as a catalyst to certain reflections. What will I be expected to do as part of the internship? Will I be able to meet the expectations that will be placed on me? How can I impress everyone involved so that they will serve as references and mentors in helping me to get a promotion into administration? Sweitizer and King (2004, p. 84) provide a list of common concerns that interns have mentioned in "what if" statements. Here is a partial list.

What if:

A client insults me? A client becomes verbally abusive?

A client confronts me?

A client gets physical?

A client attempts to sexually approach/assault me?

My writing skills aren't good enough?

I don't learn quickly enough?

I can't handle all the responsibilities?

I make a mistake and something really bad happens?

People lie to me?

I lose my temper?

I don't have the answers?

I hate the job?

I get sued?

People resent, don't like, and/or ignore me?

Anxieties typically come out at the very beginning of the experience but quickly go away once you have begun working with your mentor. It is helpful to share anxieties and to reflect on them up front. If nothing else, interns are often surprised and relieved to learn that they are not alone in these concerns. In fact, these types of concerns often help us to better prepare for new experiences.

Reflection helps in human and professional development, in that it creates an equilibrium giving expression to a combination of rational, insightful, and inner wisdom to bring to the surface a more complete understanding of ourselves and our behavior. It typically allows us to see things in a new way, from different vantage points, and we can learn much as these vantage points add needed perspective. You then evaluate your reflective writing to see if it might help you in any way to better understand the organization and your professional responsibilities. Some experts suggest that it is recognizing the importance of perspectives, insights, and reflective thoughts that helps us become more in tune with a capable and competent self. Reflection is a process by which we can better develop ourselves to the fullest, and at the same time improve our capability and judgment (Cunningham, 1991).

The challenge is developing a greater awareness of yourself as a professional and the nature and impact of your performance as a leader. The internship provides an opportunity to revisit your leadership behavior and decisions in relation to the impact they have had in practice. Researchers (Brandt, 1992; Johnson, 1990; Schon, 1983; Sergiovanni, 2005) have documented the importance of reflection to improved performance. Those administrators who practice reflection on a regular basis are described as superior to those who do not practice reflection. It seems

REFLECTION: GETTING STARTED

I was a little nervous reading through the principal job description, the policy manual, and the school improvement plan. I knew that in one week I needed to know all the particulars for starting an internship at a school with over one thousand students. I did not know the majority of the faculty or my mentor very well. The meetings that I had with my mentor and all of the pre-planning helped me to feel more confident and to get off on the right foot. I realized how important good preparation, hard work, and self-assessment are to being an effective administrator. I learned that I did not have to be afraid to ask questions when I was in doubt. I learned that I needed a network to get needed information and the work accomplished. Collaboration is very important, particularly in the beginning. I decided the best way to learn is by total immersion into the job even though I did not totally understand the work that was necessary.

I decided to work very hard during the internship to be very positive and prepared. My mentor had explained that he would be sharing some confidential information and that integrity and confidentiality were very important. I quickly realized it is important to be well-versed in the regulations and to be able to work quickly. The number and speed with which things started to come at me was quite a surprise. You definitely need great decision-making, conflict resolution, and time management skills. It will take some time for me to comprehend the big picture and that is causing me some problems.

I tried to be fair and understanding but I can tell some teachers are testing me and I am afraid that if I am not authoritative I will become a doormat. I did not expect these feelings and wanted to be participative and facilitative. I find myself falling back too often to policy, rules, and procedures. I don't want to break them but I also don't want to stunt teacher creativity. This is a much more difficult balance then I ever expected.

wise to analyze your efforts and the effect they have had, and from that information to think through how you might improve your performance.

What follows are examples of some guiding questions that you might use for reflection:

- How clear is your vision for education and for yourself as an educational leader?
- Does your behavior match your philosophy of education and leadership?
- What actions support or contradict how your values guide your behavior?
- Where have your actions defined your role as an instructional leader?
- What seems to be the motivation for your actions?
- What are the measures of the quality of your performance and what are your strengths and weaknesses?
- Are you moving toward achieving your personal and professional goals and where do you see yourself on the road to being your very best?
- What road blocks do you face and how are you going to deal with them?
- What is your developmental plan for the immediate future?

THE REFLECTIVE JOURNAL

The reflective journal is maintained to record insights and learning. It is also used as a data-collection device, encouraging students to be observers and inquirers into their own organizational settings (Lester & Pascale, 2004). The reflective journal can be a personal record of practical experience and growth, feelings, and beliefs about how administrative responsibilities are handled, as well as a record of the integration of theory, research, and practice. The journal may be shared with faculty and peers. Journals may be used for occasional assigned reflection on internship topics. Journals are typically only reviewed by the university supervisor.

As mentioned earlier, one thing to consider in writing your reflection is the issue of privacy. Please consider sensitive matters and legal issues when using names in your reflection. In fact, it is probably better not to include specific names in your reflection. This may save you much heartache in the long run. Your reflection might address the following areas:

1. Description of the setting
2. Overview of the experience
   a. Functional details (problem analysis, information collection or analysis, implementation or delegation)
   b. Programmatic data (instructional, curriculum design; staff development)
   c. Interpersonal information (motivation; oral or written expression)
   d. Contextual details (philosophical, legal, political, or social issues; public/ media relations)
3. Your reflections on success and failure, what might be done differently, what you have learned, and so on
4. Artifacts that may help you recall the experience

The reflective journal is a highly personalized experience and often motivated by insights, enlightenment, and *ah-ha* moments. Thus, the form it takes is very personalized and determined by the intern who is involved in the reflection.

In discussing a model program, Tschannen-Moran (2005) stressed the importance of students being innovative and involved in a variety of reflective activities. The interns maintain a reflective journal that "captures the intern's analysis of the impact of the leadership skills observed within the educational setting and to speculate on alternative approaches" (p. 14). Interns meet weekly with their field

---

Reflective Journal Entry: Fiscal Stewardship and Stress

If I learned anything from my summer school experiences, I learned how an administrator must be accountable for school resources and must know how to manage big operations. The first day of registration was so hectic and parents were not happy waiting in long lines for registration, payment, and bus information. We tried our best to work quickly but so much information had to be received at each station. I was responsible for collecting the money. Parents tried to force me to allow their students to register without paying. Some wanted free payment but were not receiving free lunches. The parents who had to pay for two classes were upset. By noon, my nerves were shot and my responsibilities with the finances had only begun. I was not able to think as clearly or to work as effectively with parents because I was so upset. I was very worried about accurate records for the money received and the general accounting procedures and realized I

was not well enough prepared to handle money and accounting procedures. I do not want to find myself in this position ever again.

I quickly realized that I needed the advice of experts and used their skills to assist me. I need to understand the bookkeeping aspects of a school more. Our finance class did not give me the expertise I feel I need to be an administrator. I plan to take a higher level of finance class in the spring so I can learn more. I did read the Manatee Manual that gives very specific rules and procedures for accounting, but much of the manual I did not understand. I also looked at the Association for School Business Officials (ASBO) guidelines for managing money (www.ASBO.org). I plan to take a finance class in the spring to learn more about specific regulations about accounting in the school. I also hope the bookkeeper will be willing and have time to work with me on fiscal stewardship and bookkeeping.

supervisor for reflection and dialogues and have electronic conversations with their mentors. These and other experiences provide content in the writing of a culminating report, which captures the skills and experience gained during the internship and throughout the preparation program. The reflection serves as the preface for the student's portfolio.

Lester and Pascale (2004) offer a reflective scale designed to allow interns to holistically assess the degree of reflectivity occurring in their reflective journals. Their scale was adapted slightly for use by administrative interns and by others (such as instructors or mentors) who might be assessing the degree of reflection taking place. The scale, shown in Form 3.1 runs from 1 (not at all) to 7 (in great depth). This Reflectivity Scale can be used by the intern to give further thought to the type of information that might be included in a reflective journal.

Reflective Questions

Your reflections should help you to get in touch with your feelings, beliefs, values, and how they influence your behavior. Have your judgment and perceptions been influenced by your role as an intern, your new relationship with the principal or others, or the pressure from the responsibilities of the position? Are you responding to or missing important cues that can help you to make the right decision? Are you openly confronting or hiding from the natural confusion that you feel in this new role? Do you counter differences in thinking between yourself and others by trying to understand the reasoning of the other person or by discrediting or blaming the other person? What did you learn? Were there any *ah-ha* moments? What insights did you gain? Can you think of new applications for what you learned? Are there some concerns you need to address?

REFLECTIVE JOURNAL ENTRY: CUES, CONFRONTATION, CONFUSION, AND INSIGHTS

One of my guiding principles or values is to make decisions that are in the best interest of children. I never realized this might place me in conflict with staff; however, for some staff this seemed to be the case. I was responsible for the discipline in one of my activities and tried to do what I could to help these students to improve behavior and return to class. For example, one student was sent to the office for not paying attention and sleeping in class. The teacher stated that the student was unmotivated, lazy, and probably on drugs. When I talked with the student he did seem lethargic and his eyes were dilated, so I took him to the nurse for evaluation. She believed he was extremely depressed and underfed. The student said that he did not want to go back to class because the teacher and students hated him and constantly bullied him about his behavior, dress, and looks. His records showed that he was an intelligent student but an underachiever.

I decided to allow him to temporarily miss the math class for a few weeks and come to the office to do his work. I obtained worksheets and assignments from the classroom teacher and decided to mentor him personally, which made the math teacher furious. I did not ask the teacher to give this student any special favors, just to count the work he had done correctly and give him an opportunity to show that he had mastered the skills necessary to go to ninth grade math. The teacher did that but was unhappy about my decision. The teacher stated that the boy needed to learn a lesson about respect and better work ethics. The student's math teacher came up to me in front of several other teachers and told me that I needed a lot more practice being an administrator because I was too soft on kids. I had no business interfering with his student who was sleeping in class and was unmotivated. He should have been allowed to fail. When he left he was furious with me. My only comment to him as he left was to thank him for his work and to wish him well with his classes.

In a couple of other discipline cases I had to deal with parents who were difficult to handle.

Even though I realized the parents did not understand the policy, I believed that letting them vent their frustrations would get me further than trying to read them the policy. After their yelling and crying for twenty minutes, I gave these parents the written policy. I also called back and told these irate parents how the situation had been resolved. The teachers again felt that I had favored the students and their parents and not the teachers, even though the student behavior and parent support improved.

You have to be an advocate for the child and help the parent understand what can be reasonably done with the resources we have available. A listening ear and calm voice helps defuse the situations. You cannot make every parent, teacher, or student happy but you can care about the child and the situation. I know that I need more experience with dealing with difficult parents and diffusing anger. I hope we will be taught more about this in our administrative program. Parents do seem pleased that I care about their child passing. However, again, teachers thought I was much too lenient with these cases, tending to favor the parents and students over the teachers. Several of my teachers thought I took way too much guff from parents and should have sent these students home. I stood my ground and took the heat from a few teachers, and in the long run, I feel the students benefited from my caring. They passed their courses and many were able to work with their teachers and classmates after our special times together.

I am a little confused, however, and look forward to discussing this problem with others and to see what they do. I learned a great deal about myself from these experiences. I cannot please everyone and sometimes I must do what I feel is the right thing to do no matter what others might think. I felt I made good decisions with these students but I am troubled by the teachers' reactions. I am so glad that I did not respond to teachers in a negative manner. I acted professionally. It did shake me up and I am now more confused than before about a balance between teachers' and students' needs.

Another activity that surprised me was interviewing prospective teachers and staff members. We each had a chance to ask questions and to record our impressions on a score sheet with ratings from 1 to 5. I did realize that having a secretary write down answers for later discussion is quite helpful and I will certainly have a secretary present if I have to lead interviews. I feel having a group discuss the candidates is very fair and each of us see qualities the others might not witness in the interview. I was so glad that my mentor felt my input was important in his decision. I was treated very professionally by the administrators. My mentor had me score first. He and the others thought I was a little hard on the candidates since I did not score as high as they did, but sometimes I would defend my score by repeating an answer that was given by the candidate that seemed weak or vague. I was especially interested in teaching strategies that the candidates found successful in their classrooms. It was difficult to select from some of the candidates the best choice for our needed positions.

I need more practice with interviewing potential employees. I seem too serious with my questioning and had trouble putting the candidates at ease. I was especially concerned about being too tough on teacher candidates, since my relations with some of our existing teachers, during discipline situations, had become strained. I want to really become very introspective about my attitude toward teachers. Perhaps my expectations are too high or I have an inappropriate disposition—possibly a lack of respect—toward teachers? I definitely plan to follow up on these concerns but I don't know exactly how. I look forward to discussing this with my university instructor and fellow interns.

Your ability to be reflective has a bearing on the success you will have as an intern and administrator. Reflection will help you to put your best foot forward and to present yourself in the best possible way. It will help to prevent you from making the same or similar errors in the future. It will help you see your strengths—which you might build on in the future. It will help you to see what works and what is getting in the way. Reflection begins with taking stock of your thinking and behavior and focusing on discrepancies between them, and on your impact on others. When you have questions you will want to seek out the help of mentors, instructors, and colleagues who can help provide perspective and possible alternatives. You are not a finished product, you are growing, developing, and learning. That is what the internship is all about and that is why reflection is so important.

Reflectivity Scale

Instructions: This scale is designed to holistically assess the degree of reflectivity displayed in the intern's journal. The scale can be adapted and modified to encourage and/or assess reflectivity for specific internship goals or objectives. The scale includes eleven components of reflectivity, each rated on a scale of 1 to 7. The interns themselves or the assessors indicate the rating assigned to the intern's reflection by circling the appropriate number. The ratings should be made after having reviewed the entire reflective journal and should provide a general evaluation of reflectivity. Referring often to the journal being rated is recommended. The scale can be used to rate the level of depth that the intern displays in his or her journal.

1. Identifies consistencies, inconsistencies, similarities, and/or differences in the intern's interactions with teachers and others.

Not at all		Moderate degree			In great depth	
1	2	3	4	5	6	7

2. Relates actions and/or interactions to theories or theorists either by name or description.

Not at all		Moderate degree			In great depth	
1	2	3	4	5	6	7

3. Relates actions and/or interaction to the current methodologies, strategies, models, techniques, tools, and/or materials (either by name or description).

Not at all		Moderate degree			In great depth	
1	2	3	4	5	6	7

4. Hypothesizes about the causes of actions and interactions.

Not at all		Moderate degree			In great depth	
1	2	3	4	5	6	7

5. Evaluates the appropriateness of strategies in terms of the intended objectives.

Not at all		Moderate degree			In great depth	
1	2	3	4	5	6	7

6. Evaluates the appropriateness of the content and materials in terms of the intended objectives.

Not at all		Moderate degree			In great depth	
1	2	3	4	5	6	7

7. Evaluates the appropriateness of the content and materials in terms of the student (e.g., age-appropriate, culturally relevant, etc.).

Not at all		Moderate degree			In great depth	
1	2	3	4	5	6	7

8. Judges the extent to which intended outcomes were achieved.

Not at all		Moderate degree			In great depth	
1	2	3	4	5	6	7

9. Relates personal, affective reactions to the actions and interactions in the school.

Not at all		Moderate degree			In great depth	
1	2	3	4	5	6	7

10. Speculates about alternatives and/or formulates possible plans for future action.

Not at all		Moderate degree			In great depth	
1	2	3	4	5	6	7

11. Reports on-the-spot change of direction based on identification and analysis of events.

Not at all		Moderate degree			In great depth	
1	2	3	4	5	6	7

Source: Lester, Paula E., and Pascale, Isabel D. (2004). *Field-based learning for school administrators.* Reprinted with the consent of ProActive Publications, Lancaster, Pennsylvania.

chapter 4

Standards and the Internship

A driving force for the improvement of administrative preparation programs and, more specifically, internships is the *standards* movement. Preparation programs across the United States are guided by a set of standards that have been widely enforced by university instructors, practitioners, professional associations, and policymakers. Hessell and Holloway (2002) suggest, "if we are to improve the quality of schools of America then the standards encompassing the requisite knowledge, skills, and dispositions of the principal must be clearly defined." The Interstate School Leadership Licensure consortium crafted standards in 1996. The ISLLC standards have become the model in nearly forty states and have become a powerful stimulus for universities to revise their administrative preparation programs and internship activities in school administration.

The Council of Chief State School Officers (CCSSO) and The National Policy Board for Educational Administration (NPBEA) worked together to create and later support the work of the ISLLC and the standards they were asked to develop. The purpose of the standards was to inform educational administration preparation programs as to what was important content that future educational leaders needed to know. The CCSSO also envisioned an assessment tool that could be incorporated for awarding advanced certification. ISLLC drew on the previous work of the educational leadership professional associations and the standards movement to develop six ISLLC standards that focus on the knowledge, performance, and dispositions of school leaders.

The ISLLC Standards for School Leaders were developed by key personnel from twenty-four states and nine associations representing the educational administration profession in order to improve policy, practice, and research throughout the country. The standards are focused on what the committee called "the heart and soul of effective leadership." All standards support the essential importance of the learning environment. Each of the standards places special emphasis on vision and promoting the success of all students.

Certainly the ISLLC standards provide a very solid foundation for planning the internship. There are many other standards, however, that can be used, and the ideas presented fit the internship courses that occur throughout the United States, not depending on any one set of standards. The ISLLC standards are only used to exemplify the structure of the internship course. You will need to check with your university department policy and internship instructor to determine what standards are being used in your program.

The ISLLC standards also became the basis for the Educational Testing Services School Leaders Licensure Assessment (SLLA), which has been adopted in thirteen states as part of their licensure process (see Chapter 14 for more information). In addition, the National Council for Accreditation of Teacher Education (NCATE) and the Educational Leadership Constituent Council (ELCC) aligned their standards with the ISLLC standards. According to NCATE Program Standards (standards for School Leadership are available at www.ccsso.org/content/pds-slis11cstd.pdf):

> The internship is defined as the process and product that result from the application in a workplace environment of the strategic, instructional, organizational and contextual leadership program standards. When coupled with integrating experiences through related clinics or cohort seminars, the outcome should be a powerful synthesis of knowledge and skills useful to practicing school leaders.
>
> The internship includes a variety of substantial concurrent or capstone experiences in diverse settings planned and guided cooperatively by university and school district personnel for credit hours and conducted in schools and school districts over an extended period of time. The experiences need to provide interns with substantial responsibilities which increase over time in amount and complexity, and which involve direct interaction and involvement with students, staff, parents, and community leaders. Ideally, an internship should include some work with social service organizations involved with inter-agency activities affecting schools.

Various possible standards are presented below to provide a good idea of the various views and the similarities of the different standards. In addition, the ELCC standards, which are based on ISSLC, standards, can be found on the ELCC/NCATE web page.

ISSLC FRAMEWORK

ISSLC provides one possible framework for the scaffolding on which the internship is constructed. These standards also incorporate a set of indicators of performance needed by school leaders in the twenty-first century. There are 183 indicators that accompany the six ISLLC standards. They spell out the minimum knowledge base, the dispositions, and the performance indicators that are embraced by the standards. The indicators are broken into forty-three that describe the knowledge needed by school leaders, forty-three that address the dispositions of the school leader, and ninety-seven that spell out the specific performance expected of the school leader. The performance indicators provide a list of the types of skills and abilities that interns should develop as a part of their preparation program and during their internship experience.

What follows are the six ISSLC standards along with a sampling of the specific performance indicators related to the standards (Council of Chief State School Offices, 1996).

ISLLC Standard 1

A school administrator is an educational leader who promotes the success of all students by facilitating the *development, articulation, implementation, and stewardship of a vision* of learning that is shared and supported by the school community. The administrator facilitates processes and engages in activities ensuring that:

- The vision and mission of the school are effectively communicated to staff, parents, students, and community members.
- The vision and mission are communicated through the use of symbols, ceremonies, stories, and similar activities.
- The core beliefs of the school vision are modeled for all stakeholders.
- The vision is developed with and among stakeholders.
- The contributions of school community members to the realization of the vision are recognized and celebrated.

- Progress toward the vision and mission is communicated to all stakeholders.
- The school community is involved in school improvement efforts.
- The vision shapes the educational programs, plans, and activities.
- An implementation plan is developed in which objectives and strategies to achieve the vision and goals are clearly articulated.
- Assessment data related to student learning are used to develop the school vision and goals.
- Barriers to achieving the vision are identified, clarified, and addressed.
- Needed resources are sought and obtained to support the implementation of the school mission and goals.

ISLLC Standard 2

A school administrator is an educational leader who promotes the success of all students by *advocating, nurturing, and sustaining a school culture and instructional program* conducive to student learning and staff professional growth. The administrator facilitates processes and engages in activities ensuring that:

- All individuals are treated with fairness, dignity, and respect.
- Professional development promotes a focus on student learning consistent with the school vision and goals.
- Students and staff feel valued and important.
- The responsibilities and contributions of each individual are acknowledged.
- Barriers to student learning are identified, clarified, and addressed.
- Diversity is considered in developing learning experiences.
- Lifelong learning is encouraged and modeled.
- There is a culture of high expectations for self, students, and staff performance.
- Technologies are used in teaching and learning.
- Student and staff accomplishments are recognized and celebrated.
- Multiple opportunities to learn are available to all students.
- Curricular, co-curricular, and extra-curricular programs are designed, implemented, evaluated, and refined.
- Curriculum decisions are based on research, expertise of teachers, and the recommendations of learned societies.
- The school culture and climate are assessed on a regular basis.
- Student learning is assessed using a variety of techniques.
- A variety of supervisory and evaluation models are employed.
- Pupil personnel programs are developed to meet the needs of students and their families.

ISLLC Standard 3

A school administrator is an educational leader who promotes the success of all students by ensuring management of the organization, operations, and resources for *a safe, efficient, and effective learning environment*. The administrator facilitates processes and engages in activities ensuring that:

- Knowledge of learning, teaching, and student development is used to inform management decisions.
- Operational procedures are designed and managed to maximize opportunities for successful learning.
- Emerging trends are recognized, studied, and applied as appropriate.
- Operational plans and procedures to achieve the vision and goals of the school are in place.
- Collective bargaining and other contractual agreements related to the school are effectively managed.

- The school plan, equipment, and support systems operate safely, efficiently, and effectively.
- Time is managed to maximize attainment of operational goals.
- Problems are confronted and resolved in a timely manner.
- Financial, human, and material resources are aligned to the goals of schools.
- The school acts entrepreneurially to support continuous improvement.
- Organizational systems are regularly monitored and modified as needed.
- Responsibility is shared to maximize ownership and accountability.
- Effective problem-framing and problem-solving skills are used.
- Effective conflict-resolution skills are used.
- Effective group-processes and consensus-building skills are used.
- Effective communication skills are used.
- There is effective use of technology to manage school operations.
- Fiscal resources of the school are managed responsibly, efficiently, and effectively.
- A safe, clear, and aesthetically pleasing school environment is created and maintained.
- Human resource functions support the attainment of school goals.
- Confidentiality and privacy of school records are maintained.

ISLLC Standard 4

A school administrator is an educational leader who promotes the success of all students by *collaborating with families and community members, responding to diverse community interests and needs*, and mobilizing community resources. The administrator facilitates process and engages in activities ensuring that:

- High visibility, active involvement, and communication with the larger community is a priority.
- Relationships with community leaders are identified and nurtured.
- Information about family and community concerns, expectations, and needs is used regularly.
- There is outreach to different business, religious, political, and service agencies and organizations.
- Credence is given to individuals and groups whose values and opinions may conflict.
- The school and community serve one another as resources.
- Available community resources are secured to help the school solve problems and achieve goals.
- Community, youth, and family services are integrated with school programs.
- Diversity is recognized and valued.
- Effective media relations are developed and maintained.
- A comprehensive program of community relations is established.
- Public resources and funds are used appropriately and wisely.
- Opportunities for staff to develop collaborative skills are provided.

ISLLC Standard 5

A school administrator is an educational leader who promotes the success of all students by *acting with integrity, with fairness, and in an ethical manner*. The administrator facilitates process and engages in activities ensuring that:

- The leader examines personal and professional values.
- The leader demonstrates a personal and professional code of ethics.
- The leader demonstrates values, beliefs, and attitudes that inspire others to higher levels of performance.

- The leader accepts responsibility for school operations.
- The leader uses the influence of the office to enhance the educational program rather than for personal gain.
- The leader treats people fairly, equitably, and with dignity and respect.
- The leader protects the rights and confidentially of students and staff.
- The leader demonstrates appreciation for and sensitivity to the diversity in the school community.
- The leader recognizes and respects the legitimate authority of others.
- The leader examines and considers the prevailing values of the diverse school community.
- The leader expects that others in the school community will demonstrate integrity and exercise ethical behavior.
- The leader opens the school to public scrutiny.
- The leader fulfills legal and contractual obligations.
- The leader applies laws and procedures fairly, wisely, and considerately.

ISLLC Standard 6

A school administrator is an educational leader who promotes the success of all students by *understanding, responding to, and influencing the larger political, social, economic, legal, and cultural context.* The administrator facilities process and engages in activities ensuring that:

- The environment in which schools operate is influenced on behalf of students and their families.
- Communication occurs among the school community concerning trends, issues, and potential changes in the environment in which schools operate.
- There is ongoing dialogue with representatives of diverse community groups.
- The school community works within the framework of policies, laws, and regulations enacted by local, state, and federal authorities.
- Public policy is shaped to provide quality education for students.
- Lines of communication are developed with decision makers outside the school community.

Certainly no one will perform at the same level on all performance indicators. Also, it will be impossible to focus attention on all aspects of the standards in a single internship experience. If the six ISSLC standards are used, the intern, with the help of advisors, will need to select the components of professional practice on which they want to direct their attention (see Chapter 8). This process begins by becoming very familiar with the standards on which your internship program will be based.

STANDARDS OTHER THAN ISLLC

As mentioned before, this book has been designed to function as a textbook/handbook for all internships regardless of the specific structure of the internship course. Although many internship courses are designed around the ISSLC and NCATE/ELCC components discussed above, that is not true of many other internship courses. However, most of the standards other than ISSLC have the same focus and relatively similar outcomes and leadership tasks as do the ISSLC standards. Although it would be impossible to review the foundations for all internships, in all education administration preparation programs, in all states, two other collaborative efforts at developing standards will be reviewed. Each adds greater clarity to the expectations for the professional development of our educational leaders. Each intern will want to determine the set of standards on which his or her internship experience is constructed.

The Administrator Credential Assessment Program

The Administrators Standard Working Group (ASWG) was formed in the northeast to establish standards for educational leaders and develop an assessment tool. This group was made up of representatives from the New England states, New York, Pennsylvania, and the Relational Laboratory for Education Improvement of the Northeast and Islands. As this effort grew it became known as the Administrator Credential Assessment Program (ACAP). ACAP evolved into a set of guidelines for training and assessing school-building and district office administrators and to guide internship experiences.

The items within the framework suggest requirements regarding the knowledge and skills necessary for effective job performance. The ACAP standards are as follows:

Framework I—Providing Visionary Leadership
- Working with the community for shared vision
- Encouraging and promoting positive change
- Embracing and supporting diversity
- Using interpersonal skills to address needs
- Collaborating in the fair use of resources
- Using organizational decision-making and problem-solving skills
- Collaborating with the community to achieve a shared vision

Framework II—Providing Instructional Leadership
- Promoting the development of children
- Applying knowledge to enhance learning and instruction
- Facilitating the improvement of curriculum and teaching practice
- Encouraging the use of assessments vis-à-vis student growth and program effectiveness
- Promoting professional development
- Modeling high professional standards and ethical practice

Framework III—Providing Administrative Leadership
- Applying knowledge of human resource management
- Managing the operation of the facilities
- Monitoring school budgets
- Ensuring compliance with mandates and polices

This framework is still being refined and incorporated in leadership training programs (Lester and Pascale, 2004).

Southern Regional Educational Board Leadership Initiative

The Southern Regional Education Board, with support from the Wallace foundation, organized the SREB Leadership Initiative to work with states in the southeastern part of the United States to redesign leadership preparation and certification programs to focus on core functions of schooling. In 2001, the SREB organized a small network of universities from eleven of its seventeen member states to collaborate on research, design, and demonstration based on sets of conditions and standards of improved preparation.

A primary focus of this effort was on the improvement of principal preparation with a major focus on the internship. They first defined critical components of an internship experience and then a set of essential competencies for improving schools and raising student achievement. Some of the core components of an internship according to this initiative are:

- Collaboration between the university and school districts that anchors internship activities in real-world problems principals face, provides for appropriate structure and support of learning experiences, and ensures quality guidance and supervision
- An explicit set of school-based assignments designed to provide opportunities for the application of knowledge, skills, and ways of thinking that are required to effectively perform the core responsibilities of a school leader, as identified in state standards and research, and incorporated in the preparation program's design
- A developmental continuum of practice that progresses from observing to participating in and then to leading school-based activities related to the core responsibilities of school leaders, with analysis, synthesis, and evaluation of real-life programs at each level
- Field placements that provide opportunities to work with diverse students, teachers, parents, and communities
- Directing principals who model the desired leadership behaviors and who know how to guide interns through required activities that bring their performance to established standards
- Rigorous evaluations of interns' performance of core school leader responsibilities, based on clearly defined performance standards and exit criteria and consistent procedures (SREB, 2004)

According to Kathy O'Neill, Director of the Leadership Initiative,"effective internships require that university and districts collaborate to design programs that are supported and supervised by well-prepared mentor principals and university faculty and include a strong evaluation component."

The SREB also included a set of essential competencies that they believed were needed for improving schools and raising student achievement. The essential competencies were developed from a prior SREB research study on essential knowledge, skills, and disposition of successful principals who are to lead school improvement (SREB, 2004). Activities and field experiences were described in regards to knowledge and skills related to the essential components that are being used in some internship programs. The essential components and related field experiences follow.

1. **School leaders are able to create a focused mission to improve student achievement and a vision of the elements of school, curriculum, and instructional practices that make higher achievement possible. Field experiences require:**
   a. Working with teachers to implement curriculum that produces gains in student achievement as defined by the mission of the school
   b. Working with the administration to develop, define, and/or adapt best practices based on current research that supports the school's vision
   c. Working with the faculty to develop, define, and/or adapt best practices, based on current research, that support the school's vision
   d. Assisting with transitional activities for students as they progress to higher levels of placement (e.g., elementary to middle, middle to high school, high school to higher education)

2. **School leaders are able to set high expectations for all students to learn high-level content. Field experiences require:**
   a. Developing/overseeing academic recognition programs that acknowledge and celebrate student's success at all levels of ability
   b. Providing activities resulting in raising standards and academic achievement for all students and teachers
   c. Providing authentic assessments of student work through the use and/or evaluation of rubrics, end-of-course tests, and projects

3. **School leaders are able to recognize and encourage implementation of good instructional practice to motivate and increase student achievement. Field experiences require:**
   a. Using a variety of strategies to analyze and evaluate the quality of instructional practices being implemented in a school
   b. Working with teachers to select and implement appropriate instructional strategies that address identified achievement gaps
   c. Working on a school team to prioritize standards and map curriculum in at least one content area across all grade levels of the school
   d. Working with a group of teachers to unwrap adopted standards and develop assignments and assessments aligned with the standards
   e. Working with a school team to monitor implementation of an adopted curriculum
   f. Being involved in the work of literacy and in numeracy task forces
   g. Working with curriculum that is interdisciplinary and provides opportunities for students to apply knowledge in various modalities across the curriculum

4. **The school leader is able to create a school organization where faculty and staff understand that every student counts and where every student has the support of a caring adult. Field experiences require:**
   a. Working with staff to identify needs of all students
   b. Collaborating with adults from within the school and community to provide mentors for all students
   c. Engaging in activities designed to increase parental involvement
   d. Engaging in parent/student/school collaborations that develop long-term educational plans for students

5. **The school leader is able to use data to initiate and continue improvement in school and classroom practices and student achievement. Field experiences require:**
   a. Analyzing data (including standardized test scores, teacher assessments, psychological data, etc.) to develop/refine instructional activities and set instructional goals
   b. Facilitating data disaggregation for use by faculty and other stakeholders

6. **The school leader is able to keep everyone informed and focused on student achievement. Field experiences require:**
   a. Analyzing and communicating school progress and school achievement to teachers
   b. Gathering feedback regarding the effectiveness of personal communication skills

7. **The school leader is able to make parents partners in their student's education and create a structure for parent and educator collaboration. Field experiences require:**
   a. Working in meaningful relationships with faculty and parents to develop plans for student achievement

8. **The school leader is able to understand the change process and have the leadership and facilitations skills to manage it effectively. Field experiences require:**
   a. Working with faculty and staff in professional development activities
   b. Inducting and/or mentoring new teaching staff
   c. Building a "learning community" that includes all stakeholders

9. **The school leader is able to understand how adults learn and knows how to advance meaningful change through high-quality, sustained professional development that benefits students. Field experiences require:**
   a. Conducting study groups, problem-solving sessions, and/or ongoing meetings to promote student achievement
   b. Scheduling, developing, and/or presenting faculty with professional development activities that positively impact student achievement

10. **The school leader is able to organize and use time in innovative ways to meet the goals and objectives of school improvements. Field experiences require:**
    a. Scheduling classroom and/or professional development activities in a way that provides meaningful time for school improvement activities
    b. Scheduling time to provide struggling students with the opportunity for extra support (e.g., individual tutoring, small-group instruction, extended-block time) so that they may have the opportunity to learn mastery

11. **The school leader is able to acquire and use resources wisely. Field experiences requires:**
    a. Writing grants or developing partnerships that provide needed resources for school improvement
    b. Developing schedules that maximize student learning in meaningful ways with measurable success

12. **The school leader is able to obtain support from the central office and from community and parent leaders for his or her school improvement agenda. Field experience require:**
    a. Working with faculty to communicate with school board and community stakeholders in a way that supports school improvement
    b. Working with faculty, parents, and community to build collaboration and support for the school's agenda

13. **The school leader is able to continuously learn and seek out colleagues who keep them abreast of new research and proven practices. Field experience require:**
    a. Working with faculty to implement research-based instructional practices
    b. Working with professional groups and organizations

Some states, such as Texas, have their own educational administrative standards that are often used to plan internship activities. Some universities use skills such as those presented in Chapter 8 around which to organize internship activities. A number of professional associations have developed skills of effective school leadership which can be used for designing internship experiences. Probably the primary example of this is the NPBEA *Principals for Our Changing Schools: Knowledge and Skill Base,* which was written by a number of teams under the direction of Wayne K. Hoy. Some university educational leadership faculty have also created their own unique ways for organizing internship activities and reports. The information presented in this text/handbook will fit the skills, standards, or other approach that is used at your university. The ISLLC or the ELCC standards are used in all examples throughout this text/handbook. If necessary, you can simply substitute the standards being used in your program for the ISSLC standards.

chapter 5

Ethical Belief Systems

In preparing for your internship, it is important to establish, or re-establish, a set of philosophies or values of leadership and education. The internship provides an opportunity to re-affirm your code of ethics (see your administrative professional association web page for their code of ethics) in leadership. It is important to have a strong set of ethics and philosophy from which to work in the highly charged, legally binding, very political world of school leadership. In order to solidify your philosophy, values, and platform, you must focus on the changes you would like to make and determine which ones will be most important during your internship experience. It is advisable to consult your mentor, instructor, and/or graduate advisor to reflect on whether your philosophies, values, and vision are on target toward success in educational leadership. Throughout your internship, return to these foundations and make sure your dispositions and behaviors are inline with them.

The internship provides an excellent opportunity to examine and explore the moral dimensions of leadership and to support the ongoing refinement and reconstruction of your professional identity. Foster (1986) stated that this examination and exploration "questions the framework of the way we organize our lives or the way our lives are organized for us" (p. 72).

This is why a collaborative of educational professional associations believe that professional leadership requires the administrator to maintain standards of exemplary professional conduct. As a result, the professional associations have developed a common set of ethical standards to which they subscribe. Beyond these there are additional standards of good practice that can serve the intern quite well. Although we should continuously explore and question the values operating at any given time, there are some foundational principles related to the internship that are quite widely accepted. What follows is a discussion of some very basic areas of good practice. These and other values and beliefs will become very important. You will want to consider them and refine your ethics and belief system throughout your internship experience.

WORK ETHICS AND OTHER POSITIVE VALUES

Educational administrators are expected to come from their administrative preparation programs and system-wide orientations ready to take on the responsibilities of the job. Once you are hired, there will be an expectation that you already know how to do the work. In fact, expectations are so high that results will be expected immediately. There is no time for on-the-job training in education. School divisions are not going to hire you so you can follow someone around for a year, to watch and then imitate what they do. For this reason, the internship is invaluable. Therefore, you should use the internship to learn as much as possible so you will be better able to handle the responsibilities of the first year as an educational administrator.

The internship also provides an excellent opportunity for the school district to observe your administrative work, as an intern, prior to making a decision to promote you into a full-time administrative position. If you put in a poor effort and are ineffective as an intern, it will lower the probability of your being promoted to an educational administrative position. You will be less likely to be hired because you do not seem to have the background, knowledge, ability, or work ethics that it takes to do the job effectively.

So, you can breeze through your internship and be behind the pack, or you can give it your best effort and have an internship experience worthy of the position for which you will be vying. When you ask yourself, "Why should I do an internship?" the answer should resonate in your head, "To obtain needed background knowledge and to highlight my work ethics."

Certainly you would not be involved in education or an internship if you did not have a strong work ethic. There are a great many expectations placed on educators, and in today's world, you cannot succeed or even survive unless you can get a lot done and get it done well. This is the gold standard of being able to roll up your sleeves and get the job done. It is celebrated in people like Cal Ripken, a baseball player for the Baltimore Orioles, who appeared in over 2,500 consecutive baseball games, performing well in almost all the games. It is one of the first things mentioned by business leaders who have worked themselves up to the top of their organizations.

Work ethics stress quality, but they also stress effort, dedication, a can-do spirit, and a don't-let-it-fail, whatever-it-takes attitude. If the mission is worthy of pursuing, then it is worthy of being achieved. People with a strong work ethic do not lack attention to an ethical code and appropriate standards, but focus on effective and efficient performance. The focus is not on speed, but more on the deliberateness with which work is done. This is the person that is known as the one you can count on to get the job done. Effective leadership requires a willingness to dedicate one's professional life to getting important goals accomplished and getting them accomplished well.

In today's world, customers want good service and they want it in a reasonable period of time and at a reasonable price. That requires committed, hard-working, empowered staff. Terms that revolve around a strong work ethic are *strive, sacrifice, effort, performance,* and *accomplishment.* A strong work ethic requires an organization that clearly values its employees as the most important assets.

The work ethic encompasses a value of always striving to do better. What makes life fun is a constant movement upward. In the end, it is often the energy put into the activity that is the most important element related to life's final success. Of course, the activity must be worthy of the energy. The easiest way to practice work ethics is by really loving the work and gaining great personal satisfaction from the results. The motivation for work ethics is important and can have negative consequences if that motivation is a compulsive behavior to keep busy—to escape personal problems, avoid going home, boost self-esteem, and so on.

Like almost all things in life, the work ethic can be taken too far. You must always save some energy for yourself, your family, and the significant others in your life (see Chapter 10 on time management). It is both unhealthy and unproductive, over the long term, to work too hard for too long a time. Everyone needs time away to re-energize and re-charge. This can be difficult with the present-day pace of life and the challenge of resolving competing demands of work, family, and friends. As an intern, you must realize that there are times when it is best to leave an activity and take some personal time. In this way, when you return, you will have a new perspective and be better able to accomplish the work.

REFLECTION: DOING THE WORK AND FOLLOWING POLICY?

I am very intimidated to go into these situations not knowing what will come out of them and being able to fit all of my internship experiences into a certain time frame. When I was confronted with how much work was entailed in the short amount of time, I got really scared and not sure of how to handle my time management. Would I have to let something go or provide a lackluster performance? I also don't want to step on any administrators' toes. Teaching everyday is a major task to accomplish. How am I going to handle my duties as a teacher and be able to handle my duties as an internship student? I have no idea! My university supervisor told me it is the reality of the job, but I am not convinced. I am usually good at time management, so I am hoping that I will be able to manage my time in this experience as well.

I am completing my internship under a controlling style of leadership. I have always had a "dictator-like" approach to situations, big or small, so I am comfortable with this style. Ethically and morally, I am afraid that it will get in the way as I try to complete these experiences and I am hoping that I will be able to change my ways a bit, being influenced by research, classes, and outstanding educational professionals supporting more collaborative approaches. I am not sure if my belief system is appropriate for administration.

Right off the bat my first experience was very upsetting to me. I found that it was going to be difficult for me to act as an administrator and not as a concerned teacher. A student had been sent to the office for a discipline problem. I just wanted to sit down and talk to him, not to punish him, but there were consequences to his actions. I felt this was probably more difficult for me because he is a former student of mine who made straight As. How could this happen? My mentor was helping me in this case and he was very stern with the student. I was glad to hear that ten days of OSS would be reduced to five and that he would have to go through a substance abuse program. My mentor handled the situation without any problem and maintained professionalism and followed the appropriate policy. He expressed to me that this is a difficult part of the job when you want to help them but that you cannot ignore the policy for one student and follow it for another, because of the way you might feel about the students. I agree this will be a challenging part of my job as an administrator because I believe you should give a student the benefit of the doubt in special cases and try to help them and not discipline them.

Professionalism

You should consider yourself employed as an administrator during your internship. This will keep you mindful of the standards under which you are being assessed. You will want to begin by getting off to a good start. You need to consider such characteristics as your dress, your hygiene, your language, your demeanor, and your attitude. Think of how you perceive your principal or other administrators you have worked for. Did he or she dress impeccably or shabbily? Did he or she speak intelligently? If it was a man, was he freshly shaven with a clean haircut? If he had a beard was it well maintained? If it was a woman, was she gaudy or overly made up? Did she dress appropriately for the workplace? All of these things are important; other people's first perceptions of you are usually based on how you look and act.

Since an administrator is highly visible in the school and in the community, it is necessary to portray professionalism at all times. Your clothing should always be professional and impeccable. If you are unkempt your audience will first notice your dress and form an opinion. You want to start off on the right foot by making a good first impression. This will improve the probability of later success. You might ask your mentor to critique you in that area. You might think that this is not a problem for you, but it may be for someone.

Of course, dress is only the most immediate and visible professional issue that you will be facing. Many of these professional issues are covered throughout your administrative preparation, so only a few will be touched on here. As a professional, you have a responsibility to confront situations that are inappropriate, unethical, or unsuccessful. There are a number of improprieties that are important to guard against, such as being sexually intimate with a subordinate or student; being libelous or slanderous in your communication; behaving in a threatening or assaultive manner; purposefully misrepresenting a situation or suppressing important information; failing to use reasonable precautions to protect school employees, students, and parents; and being dishonest or fraudulent in your actions, to name a few. Besides the limits of appropriate behavior you should not go beyond the limits of your role and responsibilities or the policy and procedures of the school system without express written permission. You should maintain the highest standard of ethics regarding stewardship responsibilities and in dealing with contractors and suppliers and related regulatory requirements. Obviously, you should not be involved in criminal activities or corruption. This is never excusable.

You should always honor the grievance process and confront unethical and illegal behaviors. You should honor diversity and be socially and culturally aware. You should always act with integrity and competence. Finally, you should disclose your status as an administrative intern when dealing with others. The potential for liability is very real, and as a general rule, your behavior will typically be tested against the community standards and expectations and the standard for your profession. Ultimately, ethics are rooted in morality (Sweitzer & King, 2004).

In addition to taking care of others, a part of professionalism is taking good care of yourself. First of all, do not place yourself in a position where you can be physically, emotionally, professionally, or ethically injured. Do not place yourself in a long-time position that will most likely damage your health. Eat good foods, get needed rest, and do not allow yourself to get out of shape. As Steven Covey would suggest, be of sound mind, body, spirit, and heart. Do not criticize, complain, compare, or compete, just serve your way to greatness. Take time to address your own physical, mental, social, emotional, and spiritual needs. Celebrate life. Enjoy your family and friends. Be optimistic and have a positive outlook on life. Remember your altitude is often determined by your attitude.

Attitude

A good attitude and the use of good vocabulary are also indispensable during your internship and in your future career. First impressions will be made on appearance, but lasting impressions are made by hearing you speak and watching you carry yourself through different situations. It is good practice to use proper vocabulary and to carry an attitude of humility; after all, you are the intern. The internship is like an extended job interview. Put your best attitude and behavior forward, and make this a habit. You would not use unprofessional vernacular in an interview. You would not come to an interview acting overconfident. You would not be critical, angry, or dejected. These are behaviors that would turn people away from you in professional settings. Knowing this, you should not demonstrate these behaviors during your internship, either. Be positive and look on the bright side.

Now is the time to mentally prepare yourself for the true rigors of the job. Request a copy of the Policies and Procedures Manual, Student Handbook, School Improvement Plan, and any other pertinent information that helps you to understand and be prepared for the professional behavior that will be expected from you. It is essential for you to know the rules of the school and school division in order to operate efficiently. Every school district has different procedures for different situations. It is even possible for different schools within a district to have slightly different procedures. Your actions will be very difficult to defend if you have not followed approved policy and procedures. There may even be some unspoken rules. Ask your mentor if there are protocols to follow that may not be written in the manual. Learning the ropes early will be a credit to your dedication and desire to become an administrator.

Confidentiality

The need for confidentiality should be obvious without being mentioned. However, let's face it—sometimes you will hear something that may be too good to keep quiet. Keep it quiet anyway! No excuses! Remember that there are very strict laws about confidentiality, especially when it comes to children, families, and employment. Since you plan on being a leader and an employer, it is best that you pass up the opportunity to gossip about any story that is too good to keep quiet. Careers may be made on gossip but they will certainly also be broken on it. Not to mention the fact that you are held by law to not speak about incidents that have happened in your presence. Consider what you will be expected to maintain confidential. In this way, you will be much less likely to accidentally tell someone the wrong thing. (See number 62 on the Possible Activities for Internship experiences in Chapter 8.)

Following Policy

As mentioned, one way to ensure a successful internship is to abide by university and school system policies and procedures. All universities with internship programs have guidelines for candidates to follow. You can usually acquire these guidelines from your university's web page, your graduate advisor, or your internship instructor. It may be required for you to gain experiences from different levels of education. For instance, some universities may require you to perform activities at the elementary, middle, and high school levels. Some programs may require you to have an external experience (e.g., social services, the judicial system, housing, health, business, military) or a central-office experience. It is up to the university to decide the types of settings for the internship. Programs also typically dictate the number of hours and types of experiences necessary for licensure.

You should be familiar with school division policy and procedures. When you wander very far from policy you are pretty much on your own and typically on fairly thin ice. The policies have been approved and when you follow policy you are on very safe ground regardless of the outcome. Certainly, the goal of leadership is not to be on safe ground, but it is probably good advice for you as an intern and a neophyte in administration. As you get your wings, you will be able to be more innovative and experimental.

ETHICS AND THE INTERNSHIP

Ethical decision making consumes a great deal of time in a typical workday. These are the types of issues that typically get administrators into the greatest amount of hot water. Educational administrators have been fired for trying to get a relative or friend a job, for not releasing information and trying to cover up problems, for using school system money in a way that seems to be for personal use, for treating students differently for the same infraction, for exerting poor stewardship regarding resources and construction, and for mistreating employees. It is quite important that you as an intern have an opportunity to confront ethical issues in your practice through a combination of professional development experiences and discussions with mentors, instructors, and colleagues. It is important that interns develop an ethical frame of reference so when they are confronted with ethical dilemmas, they have an ethical framework and map for reference. (For more information on ethics see www.globalethics.org.)

ETHICAL DILEMMAS: A PRICE TO PAY

An effective administrator must act ethically—with integrity and fairness—because he or she is the leader of the school. My mentor asked my opinion about some situations concerning several faculty members who she suspected of grade changing to meet the grade point average to play fall sports. My mentor wanted to know what I would do as an administrator of the school. These were two of the star players on a team that was supported, almost adored, by the community, parents, and teachers. Both were being scouted for university scholarships. I told her that we must act ethically and investigate our suspicions. Every child must be treated fairly and must meet the grade point requirements. I firmly believe that rules should be followed to the letter. This rule is very clear and all coaches and teachers understand it. I did realize that this would be a very unpopular decision and could generate a lot of concern and press coverage. It might not be supported by a large number of people, including a majority of the school board.

My mentor agreed with me, and following an investigation that proved noncompliance with policy, these two teachers were dismissed from our school division. They are awaiting an appeal and there has been a backlash from the community. I admire my mentor for taking this position, but we both underestimated the public relations problem this has caused for my mentor. If she had looked the other way as had been recommended, no one would have known about the grade changes. Now the players' families were considering suing my mentor and the district, the coach requested a transfer to another school, the faculty were split regarding what had been done, and many community, board members, and parents considered the principal to be a traitor. In hindsight, I can see it is often very difficult to stand up for one's values and ethical beliefs even when they are supported in policy. Without the policy providing support, I know my mentor would be fired. Her job is probably tenuous as it is, and she is scheduled to be transferred.

Interns must understand the different perspectives on ethics and will need a strong ethical compass to guide their decisions. This is absolutely necessary in order to be able to confront the multiple competing claims and ethical paradigms with decisiveness, competence, and balance. You will be required to adequately explain and support your decisions if you are to avoid charges of unethical behavior. This is especially important in those cases when you decide to bend the rules or policy slightly due to some extenuating circumstances.

Self-Assessment of Key Educational Values

Certainly moral stewardship and the development of core values is a clear foundational imperative. Values are a central element in the achievement of important educational outcomes. This is where a common shared purpose is developed and where meaningful outcomes are defined. These values are anchored in issues such as justice, equity, community, trust, respect, service, participation, alignment, ownership, accountability, performance, excellence, and integrity. This is where individual and collective power evolves through commitment and passion in the achievement of a shared set of desirable outcomes.

Planning, decision-making, and day-to-day organizational operation is seldom value free. That is because at all levels and in most all decisions, except highly rational activities like mathematics, there are discrepancies between two or more ideas. These discrepancies typically occur because those parties are operating with differing information and/or they have different values in the given situation. Certainly one's ethical beliefs run to the very core of decision making. In fact, values and ethical beliefs are so important because they have a significant influence on the way one thinks, which influences everything one does. Issues such as morale, politics, social status, culture, technology, and economics play an important role, but how one thinks about such issues is influenced by a set of ethical beliefs or values. Certainly professional common sense is important, but so is a clear understanding of the values that influence thinking. As a result, interns have the responsibility for contemplating their ethical values as they confront and deal with the complexities marked by educational leadership (Bull & McCarthy, 1994; Heslep, 1997; Rebore, 2001).

Core Values

A primary or foundational belief system for all educators is the focus on promoting the success of all students. This is an essential lens through which everything is more clearly seen. Everything that you do as an administrator and all decisions that you will make should be assessed in regards to how you are helping students to achieve their full potential. These beliefs or lenses through which you recognize what is important, what is right, and what is to be done, have been called dispositions. Your dispositions are what you as a school leader value or believe in—your values. This means that your interests, values, dispositions, beliefs define your purpose and all that you do. Therefore, it is essential that you be aware of the implicit core beliefs that shape your behavior as an educational leader.

In fact, one of your major roles as an educational leader will be to help individuals to achieve a consensus on what the core beliefs or values of the organization should be. This core belief serves as a guidance system for those working within the organization and provides the glue that allows people to work together within a common framework. A number of core values have gained wide acceptance and have become the foundation for the development of standards and assessments in the educational administration profession.

Interns will want to reflect on the values that have been put forth as important (see the ISLCC standards in Chapter 4, for example). The intern will want to determine how these values (ISLCC, ELCC, state) are or are not being practiced during the internship experience. Interns can use these disposition statements to experience and reflect on the moral aspects of leadership in a more systematic way. Hopefully, this process will sensitize interns to the moral and ethical issues that will confront them as leaders.

Form 5.1 provides a list of some of the generally held dispositions or beliefs that typically guide the work of educators (based on ISLLC and the SLLA). This is not a comprehensive list; however, it does bring out some of the core beliefs about education. They are the values that will assist you in knowing what to do and how to assess your work regarding what are successful outcomes. Check your own assumptions against this list and consider what seems to be the assumption existing within your internship site. Which of these assumptions do you disagree with? Which do you feel run counter to what exists at your internship site? Discuss disagreements with your instructor, classmates, and internship mentor.

Give some thought to how what you agree or disagree with might influence your behavior in your internship. You might want to discuss this with your instructor, mentor, and/or fellow interns. You might have others complete this form and then provide feedback to one another.

The greater the agreement between your assumptions and those of the profession and organization that you have been assigned to, the greater the probability of success of having a satisfying experience. Of course, you will want to look at other information regarding your preparation for completing an internship experience. This will help you to refresh your memories about values, philosophy, knowledge, and experience related to becoming an intern. A platform and/or portfolio can be a rich source for such a review. Make notes on your strengths and weaknesses and be prepared to discuss these with your instructor, mentor, and classmates.

You might ask yourself value-laden questions such as the following:

1. What leadership strategy will you use and how will you know if it is successful?
2. How will you incorporate your knowledge of research and best practice in what you do?
3. How will you confront conflicts that develop and how will you know if that approach is successful (see Chapter 13)?
4. How will you work with your instructor and mentor and how can they best help you (see Chapter 7)?
5. How will you plan needed activities, facilitate their implementations, and assess results (see Chapter 8)?
6. What are your beliefs about bringing about needed change (see Chapter 12)?
7. How will you establish relationships and communicate to other professionals and clerical helpers on the staff (see Chapter 12)?
8. How do you want to be seen by others? Is that a realistic expectation?
9. How do you want to be perceived as an administrator?
10. What types of activities will benefit you the most from your internship experience (see Chapter 8)?
11. Who will be your cheerleaders, who will push you to get more involved in your internship experience (see Chapter 7)?

Self-awareness might be the critically most important factor to your success as an intern. The key to your success is your behavior. Your behavior comes from your knowledge, beliefs, values, and dispositions; so the more you get in touch with these the better your will understand your behavior as an educational leader.

Within an educational organization, ethical professionalism is exemplified by promoting success for all students, acting with integrity and fairness, following professional codes of ethics, and developing and following ethical practices. You will want to begin by making a habit of asking student-centered questions and deciding on the basis of whether your decisions will help or hurt students. What message will my actions send concerning the importance of student learning? The educational leader demonstrates a professional code of ethics by being involved in service to the educational community, fostering trust, and through ethical behavior and decision-making that promotes the good of all students and a professional learning community over personal desires. Remember, ethical school leaders have a primary responsibility to ensure that they make a positive difference in the life of each student.

USEFUL PROFESSIONAL WEBSITES FOR EDUCATIONAL INTERNS

What follows is a list of sites for a number of educational leadership professional organizations. These sites are loaded with very useful information for educational interns and help to complement this and the next chapter. These professional organizations are:

- Council of Chief State School Officers (CCSSO), www.ccsso.org; state superintendents
- National Association of State Boards of Education (NASBE), www.nasbe.org; state school board members
- National School Board Association (NSBA), www.nsba.org; school board members

- American Association of School Administrators (AASA), www.aasa.org; superintendents
- Association of Supervision and Curriculum Development (ASCD), www.ascd.org; central office personnel and supervisors
- National Association of Secondary School Principals (NASSP), www.nassp.org; high and middle school principals
- National Association of Elementary School Principals (NAESP), www.naesp.org; elementary school principals
- National Association of Middle School Principals (NAMSP), www.namsp.org; middle school principals
- School Leadership Series of Assessments for Licensure (ETS), www.ets.org; information on SLLA

The ethical standards promoted by many of these organizations follow.

STATEMENT OF ETHICS FOR SCHOOL ADMINISTRATORS

Issue

An educational administrator's professional behavior must conform to an ethical code. The code must be idealistic and at the same time practical, so that it can apply reasonably to all educational administrators. The administrator acknowledges that the schools belong to the public they serve for the purpose of providing educational opportunities to all. However, the administrator assumes responsibility for providing professional leadership in the school and community. This responsibility requires the administrator to maintain standards of exemplary professional conduct. It must be recognized that the administrator's action will be viewed and appraised by the community, professional associates, and students. To these ends, the administrator subscribes to the following statements of standards.

The educational administrator:

1. Makes the well-being of students the fundamental value in all decision making and action
2. Fulfills professional responsibilities with honesty and integrity
3. Supports the principle of due process and protects the civil and human rights of all individuals
4. Obeys local, state, and national laws
5. Implements the governing board of education's policies and administrative rules and regulations
6. Pursues appropriate measures to correct those laws, policies, and regulations that are not consistent with sound educational goals
7. Avoids using positions for personal gain through political, social, religious, economic, or other influence
8. Accepts academic degrees or professional certification only from duly accredited institutions
9. Maintains the standards and seeks to improve the effectiveness of the profession through research and continuing professional development
10. Honors all contracts until fulfillment, release, or dissolution mutually agreed upon by all parties to contract

· Form 5.1 ·

Ethical Statements Underlying Current Thinking and Practice

Please indicate your agreement or disagreement with the following statements:

Standard 1: Development, Articulation, Implementation, and Stewardship of a Vision

Agree **Disagree**

❑ ❑ All students can and will learn.
❑ ❑ Everything that occurs in the school should be focused on student learning.
❑ ❑ It is important to work with all groups, including those whose opinions may conflict.
❑ ❑ Students should be actively involved in the learning process.
❑ ❑ The overarching concern is to ensure that students have the knowledge, skills, and values needed to become successful adults.
❑ ❑ A key responsibility is to promote success by facilitating the development and implementation of a vision of learning.
❑ ❑ It is highly unlikely that success will occur unless those involved buy into and share the vision.

Standard 2: Advocating, Nurturing, and Sustaining a School Culture and Instructional Program

Agree **Disagree**

❑ ❑ Decisions should be based on research and best practice considerations.
❑ ❑ All decisions should be focused on student learning.
❑ ❑ It is essential that students and staff feel valued and important.
❑ ❑ Curriculum and instructional decisions should be based on a variety of ways in which students can learn.
❑ ❑ Professional development is an important part of school improvement.
❑ ❑ It is important that the leader has knowledge of learning theory and principles of effective instruction.
❑ ❑ A variety of supervisory models should be employed.
❑ ❑ Primary focus is on the design, implementation, evaluation, and refinement of curriculum and instruction.
❑ ❑ It is important for students to demonstrate successful application of knowledge and skills they have acquired.
❑ ❑ All barriers to student learning should be identified, clarified, and addressed.

Standard 3: A Safe, Efficient, and Effective Learning Environment

Agree **Disagree**

❑ ❑ It is important to appraise effectiveness and manage decisions to enhance learning and teaching.
❑ ❑ It is important to establish good and respectful relationships with colleagues, students, parents, and the community.
❑ ❑ An effective leader must trust people and their judgments.
❑ ❑ An important focus of leadership effort is the effective resolution of conflict.
❑ ❑ It is important to align resources to the goals of the school.
❑ ❑ It is as important that the school plant operates safely and efficiently as it is that the curriculum and instruction are in place.
❑ ❑ It is important to set high expectations.
❑ ❑ Leaders need knowledge of measurement, evaluation, and assessment strategies and should use multiple sources of assessment data.
❑ ❑ Schools should be places where children feel safe and protected from harmful activity.

Standard 4: Collaborating with Families and Community Members and Responding to Diverse Interests

Agree Disagree

❏ ❏ Diverse stakeholders should be treated equitably.

❏ ❏ It is essential to involve families and other stakeholders in school decision-making processes.

❏ ❏ It is important to give credence to and incorporate individuals whose values and opinions may conflict.

❏ ❏ The school operates as an integral part of a larger community.

❏ ❏ Families are partners in the education of their children.

❏ ❏ Resources of the family and community need to be brought to bear on the education of students.

❏ ❏ It is very important that the public be informed about what is occurring within their schools.

Standard 5: Acting with Integrity, Fairness, and in an Ethical Manner

Agree Disagree

❏ ❏ Schools should be freely open to public scrutiny.

❏ ❏ It is important that you clearly examine and understand your personal and professional values.

❏ ❏ The right of every student to a free, quality education should be a primary value of all educators.

❏ ❏ All decisions should be based on the inherent worth and dignity of all.

❏ ❏ It is important to apply policy, procedures, and laws fairly, wisely, and consistently.

❏ ❏ A leader should accept the consequences for upholding one's principles and actions and not try to blame others.

❏ ❏ The leader should use all the power of his or her office to constructively and productively serve all students and their families.

❏ ❏ The leader cannot favor either instruction or operations when planning his or her work efforts.

Standard 6: Understanding, Responding to, and Influencing the Larger Context

Agree Disagree

❏ ❏ It is important to address information about family and community concerns and expectations.

❏ ❏ Programs and activities should recognize a variety of ideas, values, and cultures.

❏ ❏ It is important to address emerging trends that support school goals.

❏ ❏ A very important role of leadership is to actively participate in the political and policy-making context in the service of education.

❏ ❏ You must work within a framework of laws to protect student rights and improve student opportunities.

chapter 6

Practitioner's Advice for the Intern

A significant amount of advice has been accumulated from mentors and mentees regarding how to have a successful internship experience. These are more word-of-mouth suggestions then ideas that have come from research or philosophy. This personal style of advice has grown out of experience and has been handed down from mentors, university supervisors, fellow interns, and administrators for the purpose of encouraging a successful experience. They are not the main core elements of the internship, but suggestions that can make the work go easier and keep the intern out of troubles that could have been easily avoided.

Certainly you will get a lot of advice that will not cost you anything, until you begin using it. Much of that advice is based on experiences in which someone learned about ways of doing the internship that worked well, and they believe these ways should be practiced and others should be avoided. Of course, advice should always be well thought out and carefully considered before being put to use. It is hoped that some of the suggestions found in this chapter will be helpful.

UNWRITTEN DISPOSITIONS

There are certain unwritten dispositions regarding administrative approaches or behaviors that need to be known. Dispositions are typically defined as one's beliefs and values, but can also include certain personality and behavior patterns that influence an individual's success or failure. Certainly fairness, equity, dignity, respect, integrity, confidentiality, professionalism, and work ethics are important dispositions, but so might a positive outlook, a good sense of humor, courage, and consistency be some important dispositions to success. These may be dispositions that will be key to helping interns to get through the experience and to be effective and successful over the long haul.

Humor

It is an asset to be able to see humor in life's problems. Humor refreshes and recharges batteries. Humor has a way of lightening and humanizing a situation. Humor can neutralize a conflictual, highly charged situation. Humor is a powerful tool in gaining acceptance. It can also help when you are treating a delicate subject, but you must be very careful not to offend. Even laughter can be out of place in certain situations. Remember that insensitive or misguided humor may upset others' emotional well-being, but done well, humor helps us to realize our concerns or positions may not be quite so important in relation to larger issues. Why be harsh, when you can quip? "This diet is horrible" becomes "We're on such a strict diet; we can't even listen to dinner music." You can answer a supervisor's question regarding failure, "You should have been a better influence on me," or "I'm like Sears and Roebuck, I'll take back anything." With humor you can capture attention, create a mood, release tension, and establish rapport.

Not everyone has the special gift of humor. However, if you don't have a natural ability to make jokes on the spot, you can at least find some good jokes or funny stories and practice using them. It will help if you look at joke books or write down great jokes and lines that you hear. Comedians say an ad-libber (someone who speaks spontaneously) is a person who stays up all night to memorize spontaneous jokes. Good humor is often the result of planning and preparation. Work on your humor and use it, and quips will spring to mind more naturally.

Mark Twain suggested "Let us live our lives so that when we come to die, even the undertaker will be sorry." A good source of humor is in the incidents of life that are occurring around you everyday. "You are such a nice guy that when you are telling offensive people to go to hell, they look forward to the trip." When you read magazines and newspapers, look for unintentional humor. Humor is also found in hobbies, sports, and business practices. In trying to motivate people to follow a project through to its final success, a manager stated, "Getting to the one-yard line doesn't add a thing to the score." A humorous way of saying "I know you are tired but you can't quit now, keep working." Remember, only use humor because it is fun and improves your relations with others while getting good messages across to people. As Will Rogers said, "An onion can make people cry, but there has never been a vegetable invented to make them laugh."

Positive Outlook

Although this was mentioned as an important value in Chapter 5, your outlook is quite often mentioned by practicing administrators as the make or break element of an effective intern. A positive outlook toward the people with whom you come into contact and those who must do the work, along with the work itself, is essential to sustainable success. You cannot have sustained success unless you like the work and the people you are working with. Everything flows more smoothly when the group shares a positive outlook regarding the work and they enjoy working with one another.

You as a leader have an important role in modeling this behavior and serving as a catalyst for commitment, enthusiasm, pride, and loyalty about and for the work and the work group. This is sometimes described as collegiality, which is a closeness that grows out of believing the work is important and also from caring for one another. Group members feel comfortable enough to express themselves frankly. For this to occur, there needs to be a level of trust and mutual respect so that each member feels comfortable with the work and his or her superiors and subordinates. The vision for the organization is mutually owned and not fragmented into "I'll do my thing and you do yours." Group members have a professional interest in working together. There is group solidarity in sentiment and belief. "I believe even more in myself because others believe in me." "We will continue to feel a sense of importance and closeness which will enable us to continue to draw upon each other for support and advice." A positive outlook enables us to energize ourselves and others.

Courage

Always do your best and do not fear failure. Fear can keep you from having a good experience. You are brand new to the position, so you should obtain advice when needed; however, this can be overdone. Do not be afraid to make intelligent guesses and make your own decisions. You will make some mistakes. Without failure, you will not learn important lessons and you will not push yourself beyond your basic skills.

Without supervision and guidance, you will be afraid of making mistakes and will tend to avoid the types of activities from which you will benefit the most. Interns in this situation become tentative, insecure, indecisive, and anxious. Timely, continuous, and systematic support, encouragement, and guidance add substantially to the intern's confidence, knowledge, and leadership ability.

Having the opportunity to intern is the perfect way to further develop and test your leadership style. You should be willing to try several styles to determine which works best for you. You are relatively free to test the waters within the realm of professionalism, legality, ethics, and best practice. The point is to use this time, and the expertise of those in place, to guide and allow you to spread your wings and expand your range of knowledge. You cannot fly too high if you fly on your own wings. The point is to use this time to put the theories you have learned into a practical setting without risking more than needing your mentor or instructor to come in and bail you out or help you to alter course. The point is to utilize your safety net.

This point can be overstated; in some cases, interns become overeager and too willing to jump in and assume a role for which they are not ready. You must learn to walk before you can run. Take an approach that progresses from less demanding roles to those requiring greater and greater skill. Don't make the same mistake when there are so many to choose from. Learn with each activity and go onto a more demanding one. By beginning with an activity you are not ready for you can end up falling on your face and being put in your place—not a good start in administration. The problem, however, that is more often seen is the lack of courage to take on the daunting tasks of leadership.

As mentioned earlier, all administrators are going to make mistakes, even seasoned administrators; however, it is best to avoid mistakes in the first place, if at all possible. Practicing the belief that being forewarned is being forearmed, here are some common mistakes made by new administrators (McAroy & Rhodes, 2003):

1. Not notifying your immediate supervisor
2. Not respecting established policies and procedures
3. Being out of touch with reality
4. Having a lackadaisical attitude, especially toward discipline
5. Not practicing effective internal communication
6. Neglecting to follow through
7. Neglecting your teachers
8. Being too demanding
9. Overspending the budget
10. Lacking balance in your life

One mistake that is hard to discourage because it is really a positive attribute is being overly optimistic about what can be achieved in an internship. It is, however, important to make sure that your expectations are realistic. Make sure you understand the effort that will be required to complete the activity you are planning to schedule as part of your internship. Identify what you do have control over, where you share control with others, and what you have no control over. If someone tells you "that job is tougher than it looks," believe them. Don't get discouraged when you realize that it is much tougher than expected. This may be a sign that it is time for your work ethic to kick in and get it done, or it might be a sign of something you should not have undertaken in the first place. Situations like these should be discussed with your university supervisor.

Listening

Be a great listener. Listen, listen, listen; then listen some more. You need to begin with patient listening to understand the other person's thinking and position on an issue. You will quickly find yourself in trouble if you ignore what people are saying or simply pretend or feign listening. To avoid problems and failures down the line, it is essential that you practice active listening or even empathetic listening. Active listening is when you test your understanding of what was being said by summarizing what you heard or verifying in some way that you did understand what the person was saying. Empathetic listening is when you listen to what is being said from within the frame of reference of the other person (see Chapters 12 and 13).

In almost anything you do in life, it is best to bury your crystal ball. Don't assume; ask, listen, and observe. However you try to guess another person's motives or intentions, over 90 percent of the time you are wrong. You cannot guess what the other person is thinking. Steven Covey (1989) states, "Seek first to understand, then to be understood." Establishing mutual understanding in what is being done and why goes a long way in building trust, and ultimately in successful leadership. Not only do you empathetically listen but you explain your ideas clearly and logically in the context of the other person's viewpoint. Discuss the needed information that will allow a productive future to evolve (see Chapter 12, Effective Communication). This will go a long way in helping you to avoid future mistakes.

REFLECTION: TROUBLING TEACHER CONFERENCE

I had a very frustrating teacher observation and post-conference activity. My intentions were good, but my results were not. I chose to evaluate a very experienced teacher who was very kind to allow me to do an evaluation on him. He had very nice rapport with his students and they responded well to him. The lesson objectives were posted and he referred to them during instruction. The pace of the teacher's lesson was very slow and the teacher provided very few opportunities for the students to talk. Only one objective—cause and effect—was covered during the entire lesson. Students were continuously leaving the class to go to the bathroom, which presents a liability issue, disruption, and these students do not do well when an adult is not present. They also took five minutes to throw away trash and sharpen pencils without permission, which resulted in lots of side conversations. He formed groups during the last 20 minutes of the lesson but failed to visit with any of these groups. Students had nothing to do once they completed their work and there was a great deal of talking, moving about the room, and disruption. I was shocked at what was occurring during this experienced teacher's class.

During the post-conference, I went into great detail on all the inappropriate behavior and poor teaching that existed in the class. The teacher listened quietly, but seemed very frustrated. He became very resistant and complained about all the accountability and questioned my motives. The person quickly left the conference with hard feelings, said things that led me to

believe he was sorry he had ever gotten into education and wondered why he was staying. I was very discouraged and wished I had never gotten involved in this activity myself.

In hindsight, I realized that I had approached this experienced teacher incorrectly. I did not set a climate where we could both discuss what had occurred during the lesson. I had come to realize his expectations were too low for present-day requirements; however, that is often the case. My mentor suggested that I should have honed in on one key area—classroom management—and worked with the teacher to figure out some new ideas. He also suggested that I should have allowed the teacher to talk more. It shocked me that my mentor would not have gone into detail on all the problems existing in the class. Later, I realized my mentor was right; I had not really communicated with the teacher, which resulted in discouragement for all involved. The next time, I will be more supportive, provide lots of opportunities for the teacher to talk, focus on no more than two areas for improvement, and propose lots of suggestions, such as providing guided readings, having work for the students after they finish their assigned work, being clear on what they do when they complete their work, quickly correcting misbehavior, and working with the reading resource teacher on use of guided reading time. I will be supportive throughout the entire process. I generally need to work on communication skills when I am trying to correct problems or inappropriate behavior.

Do not underestimate the importance of secretaries, who can provide important information, support, and loyalty. They can help to make the work easier, more pleasant, and more satisfying. They have a very good understanding of the activity and culture within the school. They can help take care of you and keep you informed or they can leave you out of the loop and gossip behind your back. Remember, they typically have daily contact with most of the big players within the school and cannot help but know a lot about what is occurring within the school and providing key pieces of information to others. Of course, secretaries are not the only unrecognized support for the intern. Guidance counselors, teachers, maintenance staff, coaches, department heads, and many others can provide assistance and support to the intern.

Networking

The ability to network will be an asset for any school leadership candidate. When it comes to finding an educational leadership position, it is as much about who you know as it is about what you say and do. The knowledge you have acquired through your years of experience and academic study will be essential once you are known by the people who will be doing the interviewing and hiring. You have to establish visibility before you will be taken seriously and provided the best opportunities. Volunteer for any job that brings you out of your building. The more time you spend on committees and other special projects the more people get to know you and your skills and you get to know them. This also provides a great opportunity to learn and develop your knowledge and ability. It is a wonderful way to gain visibility and build relationships. Let people who can help you to get an administrative position know what you have learned and what you can handle.

Use professionalism at all times to maintain a positive rapport with those with whom you come into contact—central-office staff, other school administrators, mentors, other faculty and staff members, parents, students, and community members. All deserve and expect respect. As an intern, it is your responsibility to produce a feeling of respect and rapport with all whom you come in contact with during your experiences. It does not matter if the person is a custodian, a secretary, a librarian, or the superintendent—they deserve to be treated as if they are important and they matter, because they are and they do. This will help you build a reputation of decency and trustworthiness. These are two very significant qualities, indispensable for a future school leader. These relationships may develop into lifelong networks of people with whom you can associate and obtain advice throughout your career.

Dos AND DON'TS

There is always some danger in talking about having great experiences in the internship. It can look like the major objective of the intern is having a good experience, as opposed to practicing good leadership. This of course is not the case; however, if you do not enjoy your internship in administration it is unlikely that you will be a good administrator. As a result, seasoned administrators have passed down their wisdom regarding how to have a good and successful experience. There is not a long enough list, however, to keep you from making some mistakes and having a few bad days. Such lists are helpful, just the same, in that they can provide warning signs so that you can recognize problem areas before they get out of control. Certainly your philosophy, values, platform, and vision will help you to avoid missteps, but so can an awareness of some of the dos and don'ts of effective leadership. Following is a partial list (Lemley et al., 1997; Lovely, 2003; Lovely, 2004).

Dos

- *Obtain the support of those above you.* On controversial issues make sure you have the support of immediate supervisors so they will be able to support your decisions.
- *Show that you are a trained professional.* Present yourself as a professional at all times in your dress, behavior, decisions, and actions.
- *Chose wise advisors.* Talk to administrators, university professors, friends whom you trust and respect. The job is too burdensome to be carried alone.
- *Set priorities.* Make sure you do the most important things first and when your energy level is the strongest (see Chapter 12).
- *Balance your life.* Spend time with your family and friends. Reflect, exercise, and take care of yourself (see Chapter 12).
- *Be a hard worker.* Don't be afraid to work long days when needed; just make sure it is not needed everyday.
- *Be prepared for resistance.* Improvement, increased expertise, development, and so on require raising the bar and greater risk. Staff resistance comes in many forms including isolation, attacks, subversive activity, power plays, and basic insubordination (see the section on professional proximity beginning on p. 68). Know how to deal with conflict, political activity, and subversive behavior in as positive a way as possible (see Chapter 13, Conflict Management).
- *Enlist partners.* Building relationships will increase your political power base in a given situation. Don't depend on rational thinking, evidence, and logic alone to carry the day. Alliances add more voices to advance the proposal and provide key support and serve as advocates.
- *Maintain confidentiality.* Do not violate confidentialities or get involved in idle gossip.
- *Provide a sense of mission.* Articulate the purpose, vision, policy, procedure, and values of the school in terms of positive student outcomes.
- *Ask to do more.* You want to develop skills in many different areas, so take on as much as you can, effectively, to learn more and to demonstrate your ability.
- *Be positive.* Your enthusiasm will be contagious. Model the type of behavior you want to see from your staff. Behavior has symbolic value; what you do and how you project yourself impacts what others feel and do. Don't underestimate the impact that you, the leader, have on others. Capitalize on the symbolism of your behavior—greeting teachers and students; providing professional literature; creating bright, clean, and inviting buildings; celebrating successes; and so on. Do not think in symbolic or substance terms but realize that they can go hand-in-hand.
- *Establish a routine.* It is important to establish a routine that allows you to effectively complete your internship and to complete the internship documentation. Waiting until the last minute will not result in effective learning and will not encourage reflection.

Don'ts

- *Never leave rules to chance.* Have clear and precise rules for adults as well as students. It is best to follow policies and procedures; otherwise, it will be very difficult to obtain support if things go wrong.
- *Be consistent.* Don't play favorites. Apply the rules fairly and consistently.
- *Avoid the rumor mill.* Don't be sidetracked or misled by workplace gossip.
- *Don't be cynical.* Take the high road with your staff.
- *Don't be defensive.* Don't let yourself be backed into a corner trying to explain or justify a decision.

- *Don't assume others will give you feedback.* Let the staff know what you're working on and ask for their feedback about the issue or your performance.
- *Never lose sight of the need to plan and organize.* Poor organization undermines your effectiveness, so adhere to time schedules, have agendas for meetings, and keep track of everything.
- *Don't try to do everything yourself.* Empower others to take responsibility and make decisions. Learn to delegate.
- *Avoid change for the sake of change.* Change only those things that detract from the school's mission and goals.
- *Leave your previous school culture behind.* Don't try to transfer your old culture to your new school. Incorporate changes slowly.
- *Don't get carried away by the power of your position.* Keep in mind that leadership is exercised, not enthroned.
- *Don't get involved in ideological disputes.* Focus on shared values and shared purpose in your work with your staff.
- *Don't let your ego get in the way.* A theme in administration is "cool your ego." Do not worry about who gets the credit when you succeed. Rein in characteristics like pride, arrogance, self-grandization, and bragging.
- *Don't make snap decisions (practice patience and persistence).* You will be in more hot water from quick, ill-informed, rash, wrong decisions than from slow, correct decisions. Good decisions are often not immediate decisions. Be careful of the pressure to be decisive even when ill-informed. This is a delicate balance, however, because indecision and paralysis through analysis in leadership is deadly.
- *Don't own someone else's problems.* Problems that people are having at work or at home are under their personal control and should not be taken personally by the administrator. You will not help by feeling the pain and anxiety of those who might need your assistance or support.

These lists are by no means complete, but they may help to stimulate thinking about effective and ineffective administrative behaviors. This is why reflection is such an important part of the internship experience (see Chapter 3).

In summarizing the professional qualities of an effective mentor, Browne-Ferrigno and Muth (2004) believe that

> a mutually beneficial mentoring relationship requires special skills and attitudes for the aspiring or novice principal. To benefit from effective mentoring experiences, a mentee needs to have (a) a basic understanding of the nature of work and leadership in schools, (b) skills in listening and communicating, (c) an attitude of openness and collegiality, and (d) a personal commitment to the mentoring experience. (p. 489)

There needs to be a desire for multiple opportunities to engage in school leadership activities with practicing principals and to customize developmental activities to fit professional needs. The intern must have a desire to develop his or her leadership capacity through these activities.

PROFESSIONAL PROXIMITY

The internship provides an opportunity to make the transition from an existing, known role and to experience the uncertainty and challenges of taking on a new, unknown role—becoming an administrator. It is fairly common for interns to experience some feelings such as frustration with assignments or relationships, concerns about professionalism, and/or uncertainty about expectations, assignments, work structures, and so on.

It is always difficult to let go of previous professional identities and responsibilities while learning new ones, especially in those instances when you are completing an internship at the school in which you are or were a teacher. The internship serves as a catalyst for the development of a new professional identity and should be viewed in this way. You can incorporate background from previous roles, but your challenge is to learn to become an administrator. In a way, you are negotiating and integrating previous roles, experiences, and knowledge in order to create a revised self-identity—that of an educational leader. How successful you are in this process will affect your chances of future promotion in this highly visible position of an intern. This is typically more difficult when you complete your internship at your own school; however, that may be the only option that is pragmatic (see Chapter 7).

As interns make adjustments in their roles and responsibilities, they are also altering social relationships with teachers and others. Interns struggle as they relinquish the comfort and confidence of a known role, such as being a teacher, and experience discomfort and uncertainty in a new, unknown role as principal (Brown-Ferrigno & Muth, 2001, 2004). This can be a perplexing challenge. In these new roles, interns are being challenged to establish somewhat different relationships within a particular school setting. These new and evolving relationships can create some discomfort until a new set of norms and understanding evolve. This process is actually made more difficult as friends and colleagues no longer know how to relate to the person in this new role. This can result in periods of isolation until the transformation is complete. This transformation and socialization process is another goal of the internship experience.

Isolation

One of the first feelings that you may sense as an intern is that of isolation. You are truly in a transition period like the caterpillar that is not yet a butterfly; however, without the cocoon for protection. You are not a teacher, counselor, or dean, but you are not a principal, supervisor, or central-office administrator, either. You are in a transition role. It is not uncommon for teachers and other colleagues, even those who are your friends, to distance themselves from you during your intern experience. Since most everyone wants to be accepted and perhaps even liked, this is a particularly difficult challenge for the new intern.

Even though teachers may know you as a colleague, when you become an administrative intern, a tension develops. You are now viewed as an administrator—one of "them." In extreme cases the faculty attitude can develop into resentment, rejection, anger, or even rebellion. The good news is that these feelings tend to be short-lived once the intern is recognized as competent and shows that he or she has the best interest of the students, teachers, and profession in mind (Daresh, 1993).

The isolation that the intern feels can result in a sense that there is no one within the school with whom they can discuss problems, challenges, issues, or misgivings in a free and open way. This is a new experience, but you as a professional may not be able to call on your colleagues for assistance. This is why you have a university instructor and advisor and a school system mentor. Part of this sense of isolation from past colleagues is part of the territory of leaving your present position and becoming an educational leader.

Professional Identity

This process of developing a new professional identity while learning the roles and responsibilities of administration is made easier through a nurturing and supportive environment. Awareness, support, and effective strategies help interns deal with the multiple dimensions and challenges that they face during their internship experience and to foster healthy modes of adjustment. It is important that interns be aware of the challenges of their role transition and be prepared to deal with the multidimensional growth process that they face as they develop their professional craft.

The internship is sometimes described as an administrative appreciation process. Most interns are shocked by the magnitude of the responsibility and the challenge of the rather large, some might say overwhelming, number of expectations that are being placed on educational leaders. It is almost as if students, teachers, parents, fellow administrations, and community members are looking for a super hero rather than an administrator. As a result, things may not be what you really expected. This can be disappointing but it is part of the reality of administration. The situation may not be what you thought it would be; however, you have to believe that you can and will get the job done and will gain much from the experience (Capasso & Daresh, 2001; Martin, Wright, & Danzig, 2003; McCreight, 2004). This is not a time to second guess yourself and wonder what you are doing. Give your internship and administration a chance.

You will want to complete a "reality check" before you get started. This is where you might begin to realize that you may not be able to "save the world" this year or maybe even in the next five years, but that does not mean that you cannot have a big impact this year. In doing the best you can in the areas in which you have some control and responsibility, you will have an important impact, and the world is made better by the sum total of all our efforts. This is what might be called "possibility thinking." What can I get done and how can I best get it done? You begin to change unrealistic possibilities into successful realities. You move from what is beyond reach to a vision of what is realistically possible and manageable.

chapter 7

Successful Site and Mentor Selection

Interns either select or are assigned to practicing educational administrators who serve as their mentors. Mentors are experienced administrators who share their professional expertise with less experienced interns to help them get an effective start in their professional careers. The origin of the word can be traced back to the Greek poet Homer. In Homer's book entitled *The Odyssey*, King Odysseus sets out on an adventure to fight Trojans and entrusts his house, possessions, and his son, Telemachus, to the care of his good friend, Mentor. The elderly Mentor taught young Telemachus the knowledge and skills he would need to meet the future challenges he would face; thus the word mentoring.

Principal mentors are asked to work with interns to develop their knowledge and skills regarding effective educational leadership, while allowing their schools to be used as laboratories to provide opportunities for interns to apply and hone their skills and to become effective educational leaders. The intern's experience is greatly influenced by the quality of interaction that occurs with his or her mentor and with others in the workplace (Billet, 1996; Smith, 2003). Feedback on the intern's work from such an expert is extremely useful to the intern. Working alone with little or no feedback is not a favored approach to completing an internship. Therefore, there is a need to give thought to the selection of an effective mentor and to prepare the intern (mentee) for the interaction, assistance, and feedback that occur in high-quality experiences. This chapter focuses on providing interns the structures, understanding, and attitudes that are needed in order to have a high-quality intern/mentor relationship.

There are a number of considerations in effectively engaging the assistance of a mentor. Foremost is the importance of site selection, mentor selection, role assignments, and participant attitudes. One of the primary causes of failure of an effective internship experience is a lack of mutual agreement about mentoring and the mentoring process (Mertz, 2004). It is important, therefore, that mentors and mentees share common perspectives, perceptions, and dispositions about their roles and relationships. Certainly, primary to this is the willingness of the mentor to see that the intern gets real and significant experiences, to provide the time for assistance, support, feedback and all the other tasks so important to completing an effective internship. The mentor will allow the intern to be a part of the administrative team. Problems can be minimized by taking time to understand the roles and responsibilities of all parties in designing, planning, and completing a sound internship experience.

Some internship courses have training programs or an induction process for mentors; however, this does not exist in a majority of the programs (SREB, 2004). It is important that interns know the responsibilities and expectations for their mentors so that they can build important relationships and relay needed information.

MENTORING DEFINED

The mentor is a person who serves as a guide and an assistant as the mentee takes on new roles, new job identities, and school system and university expectations. The mentor helps facilitate the application of knowledge, skills, and behaviors the intern needs to achieve success on the activities for which the intern is responsible (Ashburn, Mann, & Purdue, 1987). Wasden (1988, p. 17) describes mentoring as "The mentor is a master at providing opportunities for the growth of others, by identifying situations and events which contribute knowledge and experience to the life of the steward [mentee]. Opportunities are not happenstance; they must be thoughtfully designed and organized into logical sequence. Sometimes hazards are attached to opportunity. The mentor takes great pains to help the steward recognize and negotiate dangerous situations. In doing all this, the mentor has an opportunity for growth through service, which is the highest form of leadership" (p. 17).

Crosby (1999) suggests that a mentor is "a trusted and experienced supervisor or advisor who by mutual consent takes an active interest in the development and education of a younger, less experienced individual" (p. 13). A more inclusive definition of mentoring (Muse & Thomas, 1988, p. 11) states that, "The primary purpose of mentoring is to prepare a new generation of educational leaders who will enter their first administrative position, confident and capable because of their extensive practical experience with outstanding mentor principals. The mentoring relationship between an experienced principal and an aspiring principal is built upon trust, respect, and caring, allowing the intern to learn how to be a professional administrator in a non-threatening, real-life setting. . . . Mentors provide opportunities for interns to discuss their administrative experience in relation to the classroom theory they learn in a university setting."

The mentor helps the intern to learn his or her new job while promoting socialization into the professional community. Mentors can assist interns in improving on the way they apply their knowledge and experience to problems of administrative practice by encouraging them to reflect on their practice. The mentor is a resource person who can answer the intern's questions regarding activities, skills, and best practice. The relationship between the mentor and mentee works best when it is based on mutual trust and a safe environment.

Regardless of the role description for the mentor, the actual relationship between the mentor and mentee will be as varied as the people who are in the roles. It is just human nature that some unevenness will occur among various internship experiences. The time spent with the mentor will vary greatly, as will the assignments and activities the mentor might arrange or support. Certainly, careful selection and development of a mentor will improve the probability of a quality experience, but there is a little luck of the draw in all of this. Some interns will have better experiences, guidance, and support than others. Some will develop a lifelong relationship, while others may never develop any type of relationship with their mentor.

Obviously, a lot of this will be up to the intern, but some of it will also be controlled by the mentor. Regardless, it is expected that you as an intern will take a great deal of responsibility for creating an effective partnership with your mentor. This means carrying out all activities to the best of your ability and obtaining assistance when it is needed. It means effectively communicating with your mentor, letting your mentor know the progress you are making, and asking the mentor for input. Do not gossip or grumble about your assignments with other interns and always be professional. Respond quickly to any problems and discuss them with your mentor and your university supervisor.

Roles of the Mentor

The role of your mentor is to help prepare you to go into your first professional position with competence, capability, and confidence. How each mentor principal fulfills this responsibility depends on the commitment, energy, time, and personal style of the mentor as well as the type of relationship he or she establishes with the intern. According to Browne-Ferrigno and Muth (2004, p. 489):

> Effective mentors give aspiring principals significant responsibilities to perform and opportunities to take risks without fear of reproach (Williamson & Hudson, 2001). They are available to provide constructive guidance, willing to engage in reflective dialogue, and able to communicate honestly and openly about their expectations for their interns (Cordeiro & Smith-Sloan, 1995; Crews & Weakley, 1996; Southworth, 1995). Mentor principals who are committed to supporting aspiring and novice principals are respected for the guidance that they give the next generation of school leaders (Merriam, 1983) and valued for their contributions to the field (Clutterbuck, 1985).

Both the mentor and the mentee are engaged in reciprocal professional development.

The mentor takes on many different roles according to Kram (1985), who includes terms like sponsorship, coaching, role modeling, overseeing, counseling, and even friendship. The mentor does not tell the intern how to do things, but helps the intern learn how to do things as the intern develops and refines his or her own personal knowledge, skills, and style. Other roles of the mentor are teacher, host and guide, developer of skills and intellect, patron, and sometimes even parent. Crosby (1999) added the importance of career-enhancing functions to any definition of mentoring.

According to Muse and Thomas (1988), the role of the mentor is:

Advising: responds to requests for information from the intern.

Appraising: involved in formal and informal evaluation of the intern throughout the internship experience.

Coaching: demonstrates the skills required for good job performance as a school administrator and allows the intern to practice those skills in a nonthreatening setting while providing feedback.

Communicating: opens lines of communication through which the intern's concerns, problems, and questions can be discussed honestly and effectively without destructive criticism.

Counseling: provides emotional support in stressful times, giving empathetic understanding and helpful concern to the intern.

Guiding: orients the intern to the unwritten rules, norms, and mores of educational administration.

Motivating: provides the encouragement and impetus for the intern to take action to achieve goals.

Protecting: serves as a buffer for the intern's risk-taking by providing a safe environment where the intern can make mistakes without danger and without losing self-confidence.

Role modeling: serves as a person the intern can emulate.

Skill developing: assists the intern in the learning of skills and tasks of school administration and instructional leadership.

Sponsoring: promotes the intern and advances his or her career. The mentor tells the intern of position openings, writes letters of reference, and recommends the intern for available positions, making the intern visible within the school organization.

Supervising: delegates tasks to the intern and takes time to analyze the intern's performance and provide feedback.

Teaching: instructs the intern in the specific skills and knowledge necessary for successful job performance.

Validating: evaluates, modifies, and finally endorses the intern's performance, goals, and aspirations (1988, pp. 14–15).

Muse and Thomas go on to describe the progression of these roles through the various stages of mentoring presented in Table 7.1. The mentor helps the intern to gain the confidence and skills to become a professional, contributing leader for the

TABLE 7.1 **Progression of Roles through the Stages of Mentoring (M = mentor, I = intern)**

FUNCTION	BEGINNING STAGE	DEVELOPMENT STAGE	SEPARATION STAGE
Advising	I learns of background, competence, experience of M	I seeks information from M based on M's knowledge, competence, expertise	I adapts advice from M to become effective faster
Appraising	M and I discuss methods of evaluation to be used	M discusses evaluation criteria with I, keeping I informed of M's judgment of I's performance	M provides I with final written evaluation after discussing it with I
Coaching	M demonstrates tasks; I observes demonstration	I practices the skills under direction of and with feedback from M	I is able to perform tasks competently and confidently
Communicating	M puts I at ease by friendly discussion of non-threatening topics	M provides opportunity for open discussion; listens to I and offers suggestions without destructive criticism	I and M communicate openly as professional colleagues
Counseling	Mutual trust and respect established by I and M	I brings problems and concerns to M, who listens, providing suggestions and support	I resolves concerns autonomously
Guiding	M tells I of the most obvious organization norms and politics	M and I discuss politics and professional standards to avoid violating norms	I fits into the organization and meets professional expectations
Motivating	M and I discuss dreams, goals of I	M encourages I to act to achieve goals and dreams	I takes direct action to fulfill goals, dreams
Protecting	M observes I's strengths and weaknesses	M serves as buffer against foreseeable problems and unjust criticism; I performs in safe environment	I is able to take risks in appropriate way
Role Modeling	I observes M's actions as a professional	I consciously and unconsciously imitates M's professional behavior	I adapts M's professional style to own style
Skill Developing	M and I discuss skills to be developed	M assigns tasks of increasing complexity to I	I has achieved competency in assigned tasks and skills
Sponsoring	M and I discuss career plans of I	M promotes I, writes letters of reference, makes I visible, recommends and introduces I	I is selected for professional position
Supervising	M gives direction, assigns simple tasks to I	M gives feedback; M and I analyze I's performance; more complex tasks assigned	I performs complex tasks autonomously; mutual dialogue of practice and theory
Teaching	M instructs I while I listens	I asks questions; M gives more complex instructions	I is able to instruct M and apply knowledge to performance
Validating	M and I discuss I's goals and aspirations	I modifies goals as M evaluates and confirms the goals	I achieves the goals confirmed as worthy by M

Source: Muse, I., and Thomas, G. (1988). *Mentoring: A handbook for school principals.* Provo, UT: Brigham Young University. Reprinted by permission.

school district and education in general. For important professional growth to occur, the mentor challenges the intern and serves as a catalyst for development.

The important understanding between the mentor and intern is sometimes complicated by this myriad of roles, which at times are confusing, contradictory, and require a herculian individual to cover them all. As a result, Mertz (2004) proposed a conceptual model to help unravel the "confusing, conflicting definitional threads" (p. 556) that relate to the mentoring process.

Figure 7.1 presents a continuum of mentor relationships visualized as a pyramid to reflect the increasing involvement and intensity required and the change in primary intent (Mertz, 2004). The level of effort, involvement, and intensity increases moving from the bottom (Level 1) to the top (Level 6) of this pyramid. This point is worth repeating: Congruence of expectations is very important to the completion of a successful intern experience.

Mentor/Intern Planning

After you have been oriented to the organization, policies and procedures, and expectations, you will be assigned to various activities (see Chapter 8). Your mentor may start you doing simple activities that allow the two of you to become acquainted and gain confidence in each other. You will then be given tasks of increasing difficulty. The mentor should include you when any opportunity for learning occurs. There are a number of things that the mentor can do to frame the opportunity so that it will be a high-quality learning experience. As this relationship reaches the

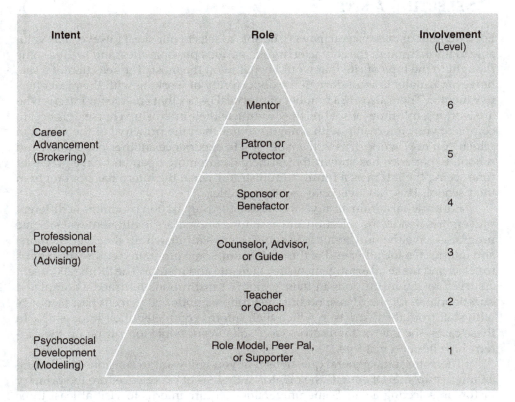

FIGURE 7.1 **Supportive Work Relationship Arranged Hierarchically in Terms of Primary Intent and Level of Involvement**

Source: Mertz, Norma T. (2004). What's a mentor anyway? *Educational Administration Quarterly, 40,* 4: 551. Copyright © 2004 by Sage Publications. Reprinted by permission of Sage Publications, Inc.

top of the pyramid, the mentor will give you opportunities for increased visibility and assist you in obtaining your first position in educational leadership.

Hopefully, mentors and interns will share learning opportunities, provide helpful feedback, and offer each other a sympathetic and confidential ear. This provides an opportunity for both to reflect on behaviors, to discuss latest research in the light of practical demands, and to influence each other's practice. This can become a very rewarding relationship that has the potential to become part of your lifetime professional network that will be so important to your future success.

Sharing experiences and obtaining other perspectives and new vantage points to think about your work is an essential element for avoiding the stress, chaos, anxiety, and disappointment that often occurs in the swim-or-sink, you're-on-your-own approach to mentorship practiced by some mentors. Therefore, a very important element of the internship process is the creation of a support network in which ideas can be exchanged, the work can be evaluated, best practices can be considered, assistance can be found, and, ultimately, important doors can be opened. You will enjoy and learn much by having an experienced administrator share her or his personal experiences relevant to the work, in a collegial environment.

There are an infinite number of opportunities to have very different internship experiences and it is in the planning phases that the myriad of possibilities are narrowed down to a specific site, mentor, and set of activities. Of course, no plan is written in stone and plans change as new opportunities present themselves.

SELECTING A SITE

For a number of reasons you may not be able to select your site. However, it is valuable to think through the characteristics of various possible sites, and to give some thought to the type of site that would benefit you the most. The selection of a site, however, usually is secondary to the opportunity of working with the most effective mentor. There also are a number of practical issues that emerge for interns who are working full-time jobs while they complete their internship course. It is best to complete your internship with a mentor other than the principal of the school in which you now work. This will enable you to experience another population and school. Experience has shown that principals are more open and have an easier time seeing the intern as a future administrator when the intern has not taught in their school. This, however, may not be possible.

Educational administrative and leadership preparation programs at different universities handle the selection and assigning of mentors in different ways. Some programs have the university or school system staff match up the sites, mentors, and interns. On the other end of the continuum, some programs require the interns to select and make all arrangements for their site and mentor. The SREB (2005) sent a survey to 156 institutions in their region; 61 institutions returned a completed questionnaire. Of the 61 responding institutions, under 50 percent had meetings with staff from the districts in which their interns completed their internships. In these cases, the interns themselves were soley responsible for setting up their internship sites and mentors.

There are some general questions that you will want to consider in selecting an internship site. Of course, the mentor and types of experiences are the primary factors in selecting a site. Some universities require interns to visit at least three different sites before choosing a site and mentor for their internship experience. In high schools, particularly, but also in middle schools you may end up with multiple mentors, as the principal has you work with a number of assistant principals. Your primary mentor, however, should be the principal. What characteristics of a site might be taken into consideration in planning your internship experience? These may already be spelled out in the university program or even a state endorsement policy; however, they will influence the type and quality of your experiences.

The site must provide the types of opportunities for development and growth that will best prepare you for your work as an educational administrator. There is some debate whether the intern should be placed in one that is most efficient for the intern who works full time, one that allows the intern to experience diversity, or one that fits some other criteria. The idea is that each site is somewhat different and can be best understood by looking at some of its characteristics.

The characteristics of the site itself will influence the types of experiences that you will have as an intern. Form 7.1, General Characteristics of the Site and Administrator, provides an opportunity for you to think about some characteristics of the work setting as you plan your internship experience. You may not have much control over site selection; however, you can use this instrument to think about the characteristics of the site where you will do your work and to think about complementing the experience with activities or visits to sites that are very different. It may be advantageous to select more than one site in which to complete your internship experience so you have an opportunity to experience different settings.

Every organization has a context in which your leadership will be situated. Duke (1998) states "One clear message from the presiding review of recent scholarship is that leadership is situated. It cannot be understood, in other words, apart from context. The context of leadership, however, may be characterized in various ways" (p. 182). You cannot understand what is occurring apart from that context. There are a number of size, gender, race, ideological, social, political, and economic dynamics that will influence the approach that might be most successful. The history, composition, and culture provide an important contextual understanding for the way things are being done. The structure of the organization explains how it is set up to accomplish its goals. There are also a number of instructional indicators, financial indicators, discipline/attendance indicators, guidance indicators, and miscellaneous indicators (see Form 7.4) that have a significant influence on "How things are done around here."

Management style as well as organizational politics will be essential elements about which to learn. When you are looking into politics, you are examining the coalitions made up of different groups and individuals who have power and influence. This type of information as well as much more that you will learn during your internship experience will help you to better understand your placement and to be successful in completing your internship experiences.

SELECTING A MENTOR

The mentor is influential in determining the types of activities the intern will be involved in as well as the productivity of the learning experience. Of course, the intern must work with the mentor to arrange excellent experiences (see Chapter 8), find time to be available to complete activities, earn the trust of the mentor, and be highly motivated to take on greater responsibility. The intern's experiences are greatly influenced by the quality of the relationship between the intern and the site mentor. Poor relationships usually result in poor internship experiences.

In selecting a mentor, you should determine what you most need to learn, then try to pair up with a mentor who has those skills and talents in a setting that provides the characteristics from which you will gain the greatest benefit. It is important that the person who serves as your mentor is willing to support and guide your development through the transition and challenges of becoming an effective leader. Not all leaders make suitable mentors. However, effective mentors take this role seriously, are committed, and set aside enough time to carry out the role.

Mentors should be experienced leaders who are visible and who maintain a high level of expertise. They should be active listeners who are responsive to the needs of others. Some of the more practical considerations are proximity, feasibility for the mentee, common planning times, and work load of the potential mentor. Mentors who have received training and/or served as mentors in the past are more likely to have the attitudes and skills necessary for effective mentoring.

It is probably best not to choose someone who is overloaded and has very limited time or who wants to pass you on to others for help. Potential mentors should be willing to pre-plan mentoring activities carefully, to follow up and discuss activities you have completed, to complete an assessment at the conclusion of the internship, and to help you in your job search. The person you select should have some interest in serving as a mentor (see Form 7.1).

There should be some level of compatibility between the mentor and mentee. This can be in areas such as personality, values, beliefs, philosophy, areas of expertise, and so on. The relationship will be difficult if the two of you cannot establish some rapport. You will need to be able to converse comfortably and to receive assistance with problem areas. An intern looks to the mentor as an advocate when challenges, needed information, and important problems arise.

Mentors not only can provide good answers—they are also able to ask the right questions of interns in order to help them to find their own right answers. Good mentors are flexible and able to see various effective ways of completing the work and can accept other ways of doing things. They don't require people "to do it their way or the highway." They are interested in pushing their interns to achieve practice beyond their present level of performance. They are also able to help their interns to read the social and political realities of the school division and the site in which they are completing their work.

Characteristics of Mentors

Capasso and Daresh (2001, pp. 103–104) have identified characteristics in the literature and research related to people who are effective mentors:

> . . . Your mentor should match some of the following characteristics, which have been identified in the literature and research related to people who are effective mentors of aspiring and beginning school administrators. Effective mentors:
>
> 1. Have experience as practicing school administrators, and they should be regarded by peers and others as effective
> 2. Demonstrate generally accepted positive leadership qualities, such as (but not limited to) the following:
>   a. Intelligence
>   b. Good oral and written communication skills
>   c. Past, present, and future understanding of the context
>   d. Acceptance of multiple alternative solutions to complex problems
>   e. Clarity of vision and the ability to share that vision with others in the organization
> 3. Ask the right questions of aspiring administrators and interns and not just provide the "right" answers all the time
> 4. Accept alternative ways of doing things and avoid the tendency to tell beginners that the way to do things is "the way I used to do it"
> 5. Express a desire to see people go beyond their present levels of performance, even if that might mean that their protégés are able to do some things better than the mentors can

6. Model the principles of continuous learning and reflection
7. Exhibit an awareness of the political and social realities of life in at least one school system; they must know the "real ways" that things get done

In addition to the characteristics of effective mentors noted above, other skills and abilities are often used to describe ideal mentors. Typically, these individuals demonstrate:

- Knowledge, skills, and expertise in a particular field of practice
- Enthusiasm that is sincere and convincing, and most important, the ability to convey this feeling to those they are mentoring
- The ability to communicate to others a clear picture of personal attitudes, values, and ethical standards
- The ability to communicate in a sensitive way the type of feedback needed regarding another person's progress toward goals, standards, competence, and professional behavior
- The ability to listen to colleagues' ideas, doubts, concerns, and questions
- A caring attitude, a belief in their colleagues' potential, flexibility, and a sense of humor

Mentors must have a willingness to invest time and energy in the professional development of their colleagues. They must have confidence in their own abilities. They must possess high standards and expectations of their own abilities and of the work of their colleagues. They must believe that mentoring is a mutually enhancing professional development opportunity in which both partners will achieve equal satisfaction from the relationship. In addition, there are other important considerations that will need to be made in arranging your field assignment. Pounder and Crow (2005) suggest:

> The participating school must agree to or negotiate the nature of the projects and a host of related practical issues—for example, the length of the project; the permission or cooperation of various entities, such as the school site council, the faculty, the teachers' union, the principal, the district superintendent, the school board, and students' parents; ethical principles that might constrain the project; and ways of managing the assignment or project that will not unduly interfere with other school processes. (p. 58)

The mentor must be able and willing to help you make all needed arrangements as well as develop your administration and leadership skills. This requires a willingness to commit time to you, and an understanding that (1) you are an inexperienced person who will need assistance and guidance on challenging assignments, and (2) you should not be assigned only menial tasks or passed off to other people for them to supervise and guide.

Few—if any—potential mentors will possess all of the above characteristics, but as more of these qualities show up in their administrative practice, the more likely they are to make excellent mentors. You may not have the luxury of selecting a mentor who has a number of these positive characteristics. If that is the case, you will observe some things at your internship site that are almost certainly not consistent with your belief systems, core values, or sense of best practice. You can still learn a valuable lesson in such cases, even though it will not be as valuable as observing behaviors and conditions that you want to emulate. Therefore, you will need a critical lens to be able to question what is being done, to ensure that it is in the best interests of all involved and meets standards for appropriate practice. Some interns become downright incredulous at what they see; however, it is a learning experience to be able to handle themselves and recognize what they would do differently.

Regardless of the ability of your mentor, you should always reflect on the way things are being handled at the internship site. Hopefully, you will be in a position to both observe effective practice and to be able to implement best practice when you are assigned duties at the site. There are times, however, when you may be asked to do something that runs counter to your style, philosophy, or values. In these cases you must balance the knowledge that you are operating in another individual's cultural, philosophical, and values system and you are there as a guest and only temporarily. You can learn from these situations. They may challenge your beliefs and ethics to the point where you feel very uncomfortable. You then must evaluate the ethical and political (your mentor may be able to influence your promotion) considerations to decide what you will do. You should always consult your instructor and other trusted individuals before challenging things that you have been asked to do or approaches you have been told to take, or before doing something you believe is unethical.

Mentor/Mentee Problems to Avoid

Everyone would like their internship experience to be ideal. However, the real world never seems to operate that way. This is often a bitter pill for the intern to swallow. Interns are in a situation where there are many hard-to-control dynamic variables that will influence the type of internship experiences they will have and what they will learn. This is why the internship is so important because the intern is thrown into the real-world environment where very little is a given. Students often find themselves in swampy situations.

Experience suggests that it might be wise to give thought to some possible problems that might develop as part of the internship experience (Milstein, Bobroff, & Restine, 1991; Smith, 2003; Williamson & Hudson, 2001). These problems do not occur for most students, but you may be one of the unlucky few who do have some problems. As they say, forewarned is forearmed. Here are some issues that have occurred during internship experiences.

Busy Work.   Part of what the intern will experience during the internship experience might be described as nuts-and-bolts or busy work. That is not to say that such work is not important to the learning experience or to the school. It is, in fact, a part of the job that the intern must understand. The challenge to the intern is to effectively deal with the routine and recognize its importance to the effective and efficient operation of the school. You will need to know how to operate the bells and clocks, supervise a school activity, even put stamps on envelopes, file papers, and answer telephone calls—as well as how to improve the learning systems and respond to legal and ethical issues. Part of doing routine work is an understanding that the intern will also be assigned some challenging activities that will provide significant learning opportunities. It is the old "If you scratch my back, I will scratch yours." If I do some of your busy work, you will see that I get some great learning experiences.

Lack of Supervision.   Interns work with very busy mentors who sometimes cannot seem to take time to provide for even weekly advisement, formative feedback, or evaluations. In addition, your university supervisor may only visit your site a few times during your experience and does not always understand the unique nuances of each school. Other mentors and supervisors may or may not be trustworthy regarding confidential discussions—and they may not have your best interest at heart. Along these same lines, you may not be kept informed regarding an issue or matter and may be operating with insufficient information. This is not necessarily done purposely, but because there was not sufficient time to share all the information and the intern is out of the loop regarding some of what occurs at the school.

The more you can be involved with your supervisor, the more you attend meetings and are in the loop, receiving systematic and timely feedback and guidance, the better you will be able to perform as an intern. Hopefully, by studying the information provided by your administrative preparation program, advisor, internship instructor, and this text/handbook, you will be able to minimize such problems.

The other side of the coin is for you to make sure that you are not too needy, demanding more attention than can be provided reasonably. Be sure to express appreciation for the time the mentor does provide to you.

School Supervisor Unwilling to Share Duties. Some administrators refuse to allow an intern to have any important administrative role within the school. Perhaps they are unwilling to run the risk of the intern mishandling an activity and negatively impacting students, teachers, and/or the community—getting the administrator in trouble. This may also reflect a quality of their administrative style—perhaps they have trouble delegating responsibilities. They also may lack confidence in the intern's ability to handle more than very routine, minimal tasks and they may feel they are protecting the intern from making mistakes. Or, they might be concerned that the intern's abilities will challenge theirs and it will develop into a competitive situation. (In a few cases, a highly effective intern may actually threaten an insecure or inexperienced assistant principal. Jealousy and other hostile feelings can develop, making for a challenging relationship and menial assignments.)

There are many possible explanations. However, the bottom line in such situations is that interns do not get very good experience. Every intern is expected to perform some routine tasks that are a part of administration, but you should not have a total internship of such tasks. Obviously, it is important to select mentors who are able to delegate and who are secure in their positions.

Poor Relationships. These can develop for many reasons. The intern may simply want to jump through the internship hoop totally unaffected and minimally involved, course credit being the major motivation. The mentor may have a preconceived notion about the intern and exactly how the intern should behave. Unproductive feelings can develop, such as envy, rivalry, disappointment, favoritism, or betrayal—with the end result being that people feel threatened. Relationships may become too close. One person or the other may loose objectivity, resulting in interns placed in situations for which they are not prepared. Another problem may result when an intern becomes so dependent on their mentor that they are unable to progress in their careers or to separate themselves from the mentor. Mentors can be idealized to a point where the intern becomes discouraged at the thought of living up to the ideal. On the other hand, if the mentor does not live up to the ideal, the intern can become disillusioned.

The crown prince/princess syndrome can cause arrogance, inferiority, or expectations of adulation. Problems can also develop around stereotypes regarding male/female intern/mentor relationships, such as when the rumor mill questions the time that mentors and interns spend together. This can result in rumors of favoritism, or sexual or intimate improprieties. Also, stereotyped attitudes might cause male mentors to overprotect female interns. Poor "chemistry" can result in friction if the mentor and intern just naturally do not seem to get along. There are endless reasons for poor relationships. The intern should do everything possible to avoid them.

Teacher Unions. In some school districts, the intern might be an active member within a teacher union. Administrators usually have a different view of teacher unions than teachers and interns themselves. Due to the union's advocacy role for teachers, administrators can find themselves in conflict with teacher unions and therefore resent teacher union involvement. Teacher unions often back teachers against administrators and provide a force that will support teachers in lawsuits and grievance cases. Unions are often called upon with great expectancy when there are questionable administrative actions.

The intern who is active in a teacher union may be crossing an unseen line that has been drawn and may have to contend with an administrative mentor who is bitter about the intern's involvement in the teacher union. The mentor may have difficulty trusting the intern because of stereotypical concerns regarding people who are active in teachers' unions. This may be a problem that you will have to work out with your mentor, or you may have to think about leaving the teacher union to become an administrator.

Loose Lips. The mentor/intern relationship can be seriously damaged if either person criticizes or compromises the other in any way—in conversation or writing. The mentor particularly may be sensitive to any reflections that might question why they did something or what the intern might have done differently. This can be a problem if the mentor asks to look at the intern's notes or journal, where the intern might have questioned a behavior or an approach taken by someone in the organization, even if it is simply part of a reflection about the activity (see Chapter 3). No one can guarantee total confidentiality for any documentation you might supply or anything that might be said in a class seminar or other setting. Some mentors are more sensitive than others and care must be taken in questioning the effectiveness of a mentor's approach or what might have been a better approach, even though this is an important part of your reflective analysis.

Certainly there are other problems that can develop. Hopefully, however, you will not have to deal with any of these situations. If you do have a problem, your university advisor and the instructor for the observation, practicum, or internship class are there to provide help. Certainly, the probability of any of these problems occurring is significantly lowered by your carefully selecting a mentor and behaving very professionally.

GETTING STARTED ON THE CORRECT FOOT

The most important beginning for the mentoring process is a warm greeting by all involved. A number of steps help the intern get off to a good start. You may use Form 7.2, Getting Started Checklist, to complete the needed steps.

It is very helpful for interns to be included in planning any activity in which they will be involved. One of the problems mentioned is being left out of the loop on something that concerns you. It is important for you to be a part of the decision-making process for issues that you have been assigned the responsibility for implementing. It is more difficult when you think or feel as if others are ordering you around. However, you really have limited control over this, and that is another reason why it is so important to select an effective mentor.

Most interns say they want their mentors to "give me a task, give me direction, and give me room to work." Other statements about how mentors are helpful include, "is a good role model and provides career counseling," "shows support and appreciation for my dedication and hard work," and "encourages my professional development." Procedures and relationships that support good communication and allow flexibility and autonomy are essential. Good communication and access to the mentor are critical factors for success.

Form 7.3 provides a checklist of steps that will help the intern get off to a great start. You will want to discuss these items with your mentor during your initial meeting. Answers to this checklist will begin to predict the level of commitment that will be provided to you and the seriousness that the school district and mentor assign to internship experiences.

Orientation to the Site

It is important to understand the formal organization chart. However, power and authority do not always follow this formal chart. Watch how decisions are being made, who communicates directly with the principal, and who the teachers seem to respect and listen to. Frequently the best way to get things done as an administrator is through the informal channels based on relationships and informal power. A key part of orientation is gaining an understanding of the informal power structure within the school. Who will require stroking, who will need support, and who will require independence? Who will need to be on board if the plan is to ever be approved and implemented?

Another key element in your orientation is to learn how people within the school treat one another and work together to improve the quality of instruction and learning. These are the basic operating principles, work culture, and foundations of behavior within the school. This provides a basic understanding of how the employees within the school do their work and relate to one another. Some examples of the types of questions that will help you to understand the foundational work culture that exist are listed below (Bond, 2004).

- If staff members are having problems with one another, do they complain to others or do they discuss it with the person with whom they have the complaint?
- Do the same few people tend to dominate most group situations?
- Is it fairly common practice for the staff to have gripe sessions?
- Are most of the teachers' ideas and suggestions evaluated based on how successful they will be for all students?
- Does the staff follow up and evaluate the effectiveness of decisions made?
- Does the staff freely share their opinions and input in appropriate ways, and do they listen with respect to ideas of others?
- What are the operating principles that guide how decisions are made and work gets completed?
- What are the espoused official, formal, public mission, vision, values, and beliefs? (To determine this, see manuals, handbooks, newsletters, speeches, and, so on.)
- How do educational professionals get along with parent organizations?
- Are the resources of the organization adequate?
- How clearly are expectations defined?
- How do people get information in this organization?
- How well is the organization achieving its mission?
- Do people contribute their best efforts?
- Do staff receive recognition for outstanding work? (See Chapter 12.)
- How satisfied are most individuals in the organization?

Site Demographics

There is a significant advantage to becoming as familiar as possible with the school prior to beginning your internship experience. Knowledge of the school, students, and community helps you better understand the issues, expectations, and scope of responsibilities that entail the administration of this school or unit. The more you know about the school and community, the technical expertise, school system–specific procedures, and the demographics, the better you will be prepared to deal with the unique challenges of the school. Much of the first few weeks of your internship experience will be trying to learn the ropes.

Although all schools are similar in many ways, each school is unique and distinctive in important ways. You can learn a lot about your site by looking at some of its demographic characteristic indicators. The demographic indicators provide a portrait of the school as it exists at any given point in time. If you are an administrative intern, you will want as complete and accurate a portrait of the organization as is possible. The numbers may not always be easy to interpret, but they will help you begin to ask the right kinds of questions and to better understand what efforts are needed and why they are important.

Demographic indicators help the administrator to keep both feet firmly planted in reality. You might see that the dollars allocated for instructional materials have increased and assume that more instructional materials are being purchased. After examining the records, though, you might find that much less instructional material is being purchased but the costs of the instructional materials have risen sharply. Even though the dollar amount is increasing, the school is losing ground in this area. Comparisons with other schools will show how your school is doing on these indicators relative to those other schools.

Indicators can also be used to test thinking and plans against demographic indicators, to help determine whether the planned directions seem compatible with the indicators or if the organization is capable at this point in time of moving in the planned direction. Indicators can often be used to clear up any misconceptions that exist regarding the present state of the organization and what might be needed in the future. The data provide a tool to counter many arbitrary, prejudicial, and inaccurate statements that are made by teachers, parents, students, or even other administrators. These indicators tend to be the hard data that present facts that can be commonly known and understood. Form 7.4, Internship Site Demographic Indicators, provides an example of the hard data at the high school level that might help to provide an accurate portrait of the school.

Information is critical to carrying out internship activities successfully and providing sound support for what you are doing. Hard, quantitative data is not the only type of information you will want to collect, but it helps. Such data will help to educate you and others about your internship site. The data will help you to get a handle on the size and scope of the site to which you have been assigned. It will allow a way to check and balance beliefs and attitudes with the hard formal data. Interns should not begin their internship until they have collected some hard data regarding their internship site. The time taken up-front can do wonders—improving the quality of intern decisions and decreasing the likelihood of making blunders.

· ☐ **Form 7.1** ☐ ·

General Characteristics of the Site and Administrator

Characteristics of the Site

What type of school district? ☐ Urban ☐ Suburban ☐ Rural

What level? ☐ Elementary ☐ Middle School ☐ High School ☐ Special School
☐ Central Administration ☐ External Experience

Educational conditions: ☐ Implementing new initiatives
☐ Monitoring successful school
☐ Turning around failing or problematic school
☐ Other _____

Ethnic mix of attendees: ☐ American Indian or Native Alaskan (___)*
(what percentage) ☐ Asian ( ) ☐ Black ( ) ☐ Pacific Islander ( )
☐ White ( ) ☐ Other _____ ( )

*( ) percent of total population

Locate the policies and procedures manual, organizational chart, school improvement plan, PTA minutes, school demographics, district-wide data on the site, census data, and historical description of the site for more information.

Characteristics of the Leader

Distinguishing abilities of the leader: ☐ Manager ☐ Instructional leader
☐ Politician ☐ Visionary planner
☐ Financial expert ☐ Culture builder
☐ Disciplinarian ☐ School and community
☐ Technologist relations builder
☐ Other _____

Gender: ☐ Male ☐ Female

Job Experience: ☐ New administrator ☐ Mid-career administrator
☐ Seasoned administrator

Leadership Style: ☐ Autocratic (task focus) ☐ Participate (team building)
☐ Situational ☐ Cultural ☐ Transformational ☐ Servant

Obtain administrator job description, evaluation instruments, memos and directives, and meeting minutes for more information.

Form 7.2

Getting Started Checklist

Date Completed   **Activity Description**

_____   Have an "Internship Meeting" with the mentor before planning internship activities. This will help in determining the kind of activities in which you will be able to be involved.

_____   Obtain a text/handbook like this one to help to think about how to develop and implement an effective internship experience.

_____   Discuss and think through the timeline (monthly calendar), expectations, and logistics regarding the internship experience.

_____   Develop goals, select activities, and complete needed planning for conducting a quality internship experience. Include a schedule of meetings.

_____   Meet the staff and see that the intern's role is clarified and well understood.

_____   Review ethical considerations like confidentiality, professionalism, written and unwritten policy, rules, procedures, and expectations.

_____   Discuss the role of the university supervisor, the school system, mentor, and fellow interns.

_____   Discuss the evaluation process and documentation requirements.

_____   Discuss office procedures, use of equipment and materials, access to information, and so on (see Form 7.3).

_____   Complete the Internship Site Demographic Indicators (Form 7.4).

_____   Establish procedures for needed followup, reporting problems, and sharing escalating problems (what to do if you get into a jam).

· Form 7.3 ·

Preparing for a New Intern

✓ = Done **Activity Description**

❑ Has office space been made available for the intern?

❑ Are keys to the building, office, classrooms, etc., ready to give to the intern?

❑ Has a telephone been made available to the intern to use for school business?

❑ Have plans been made to give the intern a tour of the school?

❑ Will the intern have access to a computer, copy machine, intercom, and be informed of the procedures for using this equipment?

Has a plan been made to introduce the intern to the

❑ Faculty?

❑ Custodians?

❑ Secretaries?

❑ Lunchroom workers?

❑ Other staff members?

❑ Students?

❑ PTA and other parent groups?

❑ Have tasks been jointly planned with the intern to accomplish the first week?

❑ Has a yearbook or other collection of student pictures been arranged to share with the intern?

❑ Have a policy manual, organizational chart, teacher handbook, and student handbook been made available for the intern?

❑ Has the school calendar been copied to give to the intern?

· **Form 7.4** ·

Internship Site Demographic Indicators*

Instructional Indicators	Current Numerical Responses
Number of students in school (total)	
African American	
Asian/Pacific Islander	
Native American or Alaskan	
Hispanic or Latino	
White	
Number of teachers (total)	
African American	
Asian/Pacific Islander	
Native American or Alaskan	
Hispanic or Latino	
White	
Number of students held back	
Number of advanced placements courses	
Number of teachers participating in inclusion	
Number of seniors not graduating	
Average number of students in a class	
Number of teachers not certified/endorsed	
Number of administrator's supervising visits to the classroom	
Number of non-returning teachers	
Number of teachers sharing classrooms	
Average years of experience for teachers	
Average age of teachers	
Number of students in AP courses	
Number of students in honors courses	
Number of teachers with master's degree or higher	
Number of special education students	
Average amount of homework given a night in minutes	
Number of days tutoring is available (total for all departments)	
Number of class periods/day	
State assessment test scores	
Social studies	
Math	
Science	
English/language arts	
SAT—verbal	
SAT—mathematics	
Number of students completing SAT	
ACT score	
Number of students completing ACT	
Teacher attendance	
Finance Indicators	
Dollar amount school receives from vendors	
Dollar amount earned from sports	

Amount of money spent yearly	
Number of students on free/reduced lunch	
Dollar amount spent on instructional needs and supplies	
Amount of money spent on school and office supplies	
Amount of money taken in by the school (all programs together)	
Amount of money received from community/business partners	
Amount of money spent for classroom supplies	
Amount of money spent for classroom books	
Amount of money spent for library books, periodicals, other media	
Discipline/Attendance Indicators	
Number of discipline infractions for students (total)	
African American	
White	
Asian	
Hispanic	
Other	
Number of referrals written in the most recent year	
Number of tardies	
Number of absences	
Number of students suspended for more than five days	
Number of dropouts	
Guidance Indicators	
Number of students guidance sees per day	
Number of guidance counselors	
Number of students accepted to college	
Number of students who join the armed forces	
Number of students who enter the working world	
Number of students with no plan for after graduation	
Miscellaneous Indicators	
Number of parents in PTSA	
Teachers	
Students	
Number of faculty meetings/year	
Number of custodians	
Number of security guards	
Number of community/business partners	
Number of technology resource people	
Number of nurses	
Number of secretaries	
Number of school clubs	
Average number of evening events/month	
Number of computers used for	
Instruction	
Administration	
Number of computers with access to the Internet	

*Look at the organization's demographic profile and computerized information provided to central administration and to the state department of education for some of this information.

chapter 8

Planning Internship Activities

Internships throughout the United States are designed in an infinite variety of formats that involve interns in a great variety of activities. Perhaps the one common element is that they involve interns, as much as possible, in the daily administrative life of the school. The idea is to immerse the intern into the breadth, depth, and rigor of school administration. You are expected to take an active role in school leadership with a clear expectation that you will be responsive to multiple constituencies. You will be expected to take on increasingly more complex demands as you gain experience from preceding activities.

Once all of the internship policies and practices are understood, the correct mindset has been established, the mentor and site have been selected, and thus, the needed scaffolding to carry out the tasks are in place, it is time to begin to plan the specific activities in which you will be involved. Key elements in choosing activities are the knowledge, ability, skills, and behavior of the intern in relation to standards. The planning of the internship activities is an introspective experience where the intern, mentor, and university instructor/supervisor reflect on the intern's preparedness and needs in the development of an internship plan. Some of the conditions used to evaluate the internship plan are whether the plan:

1. Requires the intern to assume responsibility for real or authentic opportunities or tasks
2. Requires the intern to develop knowledge and skills that are applicable across diverse settings
3. Includes practice-based experiences that are aligned to cover one of the ISLLC standards or the standards being used in the intern's program of study
4. Connects theory and practice in a realistic and efficient way
5. Is feasible and sustainable within all parties' work schedules
6. Recognizes that activities assigned are more self-directed, field-dependent experiences with mentor and supervisor support
7. Provides openness and access to whatever is needed to complete the activity
8. Ensures that activities prepare interns to assume administrative roles with competence and confidence (Browne-Ferrigno & Muth, 2001; Smith 2003; Williamson & Hudson, 2001, 1999).

Planning is made easier when you complete a self-assessment as to your personal learning goals. Possible sources of data include the portfolio, professional standards, intern assessment, school work tasks, and so on. This information is used to design a planned set of activities that will cover your learning goals, the university expectation, and that will benefit the school or school district. In this way, activities are mutually beneficial to the intern, school, and university program. Some university programs also require the intern to take on a more demanding, larger-in-scope school improvement project. This requires taking an idea from inception through implementation to evaluation, including the collection and analysis of data about the project (Tschannen-Moran, 2005).

The intern will seldom be equipped with the full compliment of competences, knowledge, and skills needed to effectively perform all duties related to any given activity. This, however, should not be a reason not to choose or assign that activity. This is part of the normal growth process. In a way, you want to test the limits of your own competence and determine what you still need to learn. It is difficult to determine when you have exceeded your level of competence and you must obtain assistance from your mentor and university supervisor. In cases of deficient knowledge and experience, you will need to think about learning objectives, sources of learning, and needed support in order to carry out the activity.

INTERN'S SELF-ASSESSMENT

When completing self-assessments, think about areas of growth, and potential activities that might support that growth, in preparation for meetings with your university supervisor and/or external mentor. You will want to examine your values, skills, needs, and the types of activities in which you would like to be involved. This is the first step toward developing a plan for your internship experience. This initial information will allow you to give some systematic thought about yourself and the type of internship experience that you would like to have and that would benefit you most.

An assessment is based on being able to describe what you should know and be able to do. This information comes from your administrative preparation program, standards for your profession, performance appraisal systems, job descriptions, and other descriptive materials for successful school leadership. Administrative preparation program course content stresses research, knowledge, and understanding. Internships stress skills and capability—the ability to effectively apply knowledge, theory, and research to specific problems or practices. The second element is a self-assessment of what you know and what you are and aren't able to do in the practice of school leadership. This will allow you to determine the types of experiences from which you will gain the greatest benefit and for which you are prepared to take on responsibilities.

It is recommended that you complete a self-inventory of administrative skills (see Form 8.1) to serve as a guide, along with a Value and Belief Statement (see Chapter 5), portfolio, and other self-assessments for use in planning the activities in which you will be involved during the internship. Assessment is a critical component of planning an effective internship. Determining the areas in which you will gain the most benefit from an internship activity will be important regarding the leadership preparation you gain from completing your internship experience.

Perhaps one of the most widely accepted sets of self-assessment skills is the ten dimensions provided by the National Association of Secondary School Principals, which can be used to identify an educational leader's developmental needs. Each of the ten NASSP criteria serves as a skill that is either possessed by a potential leader or could be developed. The National Policy Board for Educational Administration published a framework for skills assessment entitled *Principals for Our Changing Schools* that describes twenty-one knowledge and skill bases needed for successful administrative practice. Form 8.1 provides a self-assessment of the intern's present level of performance regarding the selected seventeen skills that appear on this form. These include the ten current NASSP skills plus seven additional skills which are considered important for effective leadership in today's world. The headings and decriptions for the ten NASSP skills found in this form come from the NASSP *Selecting and Developing the 21st Century Principal* skills dimensions.

The self-assessment and culminating internship activities should be planned, meaningful, based on standards, and they should include essential knowledge and skills needed for successful practice. Well-planned internships that are conceptualized, based on a careful assessment of student abilities and needs, and are structured around standards have proven to be the most successful (Hackmann, Schmitt-Oliver, & Tracy, 2002; Hessel & Holloway, 2002; Lester & Pascale, 2004; Morgan, Gibbs, Hertzog, & Wylie, 1997; Morgan, Hertzog, & Gibbs, 2002). The assessments and standards discussed in previous chapters can serve as a guide during self-assessment and in cooperatively planning your internship experience. It will be very important for both you and your mentor to use self-assessment information to plan the types of experiences in which you will gain the greatest benefit. Once you have completed a self-assessment, the information can be used to begin to select the type of internship activities that will be most beneficial for you.

PLANNING POSSIBLE ACTIVITIES

What are the types of problems, issues, and activities that you will want to be involved in and from which you can gain the most skill and confidence? Ultimately, you will be expected to match your own desires to those of your university supervisor and your mentor and sponsoring school district. But, you will want to take some time to assess the types of activities from which you believe you will derive the greatest benefit. This analysis helps interns to be better prepared for discussions with their mentors and university supervisors and for the types of detailed finalized planning needed to complete an effective internship.

Pounder and Crow (2005) stress the importance of systematically addressing the types of experiences that an intern receives. They believe that such efforts by all those involved will contribute "to a stronger pipeline of effective school administrators." They suggest that such experiences "should familiarize aspiring leaders with various administrative responsibilities and provide leadership experiences with corresponding opportunities for structured reflection"(p. 57). They suggest that such experiences might include:

- Chairing standing committees or special task forces
- Coordinating school-level initiatives
- Leading whole-school planning
- Monitoring, analyzing, and reporting students' learning outcomes
- Participating in school–parent–community groups and related outreach efforts
- Supervising teachers and others
- Addressing school effectiveness and equity of access and outcomes
- Participating in school leadership teams

There are many potentially strong learning experiences for you as an administrative intern. Form 8.2 provides a worksheet where you can begin to give consideration to the types of activities from which you will gain the greatest benefit. You should only pencil in an X next to activities that you are interested in at this point in time. You will be able to put it in ink once you have discussed this tentative plan with your university supervisor and external mentor. Much more complete descriptions of each of the activities presented in Form 8.2 appear in the following section, Selecting Activities. The worksheet is provided to help you to pre-plan activities that might be beneficial and to help you to think through the type of responsibilities that exist in educational administration.

It is not easy for interns to accurately identify activities from which they will gain the greatest benefit. Interns are not even sure what activities might present themselves, or which ones their mentors might approve. The purpose of pre-planning is to improve the quality of the discussion with mentors and university supervisors regarding the types of experiences that will provide you the greatest benefit and assist you in identifying, selecting, and finalizing activities. This is important because your mentor and/or university supervisor need some guidance from you regarding the types of experiences that you want to have and why you believe these experiences are important.

Although the activities have been categorized under the ISLLC standards, few administrative responsibilities fit neatly into any one standard. Framing activities around the standards, however, provides a common, well-accepted language and foundation on which programs and assessments can be discussed and designed. Again, many standards parallel the ISSLC standards and might be easily substituted.

Selecting Activities

The intern's preparation will influence the level of complexity and challenge that he or she will be prepared to handle. However, you will want to become involved in activities that are challenging and from which you will gain the most knowledge and skill. The important factor is that each intern has a diverse set of high-quality activities allowing them to assume a leadership role in planning and implementing administrative action over the duration of the internship.

Factors to be considered are the site's needs, the student's previous experience and self-assessment, and the opportunities to experience genuine responsibility for a variety of leadership activities. The following list of "Possible Activities for Internship Experiences" (beginning on p. 94) is provided to help the student and mentor who are ultimately responsible for developing an internship plan. You may use Form 8.2 to check off the activities that you will be able to complete during your internship experience that seem to best meet your needs. The descriptions beginning on page 94 will help you to understand the purpose and expectations regarding each of the activities. This information is provided to help you to plan the best possible internship experience. These descriptions, which parallel Form 8.2, will help you to understand the objective of the activity, the activity itself, and possible artifacts that might be used to document completion of the activity.

The purpose of the pre-planning worksheet (Form 8.2) and Possible Activities for Internship Experiences is to help in identifying and selecting activities that will result in the intern being well prepared to take on the responsibilities of educational leadership. This is by no means an inclusive list, and you and your mentor may have other activities in mind. The list provided here is simply to be a catalyst for thinking about possible activities, based on standards and previous interns' experiences. The final activities selected will be influenced by your university program and instructor and by your mentor and sponsoring school district. But, within these parameters, you will have a great deal of freedom. Hopefully, all the planning regarding your internship will greatly improve your internship experience.

What follows is a list of many different activities; it is important to choose activities from this list that will provide opportunities for diverse experiences that meet the needs of your self-assessment and internship course. However, activity 62 deals with establishing important internship ethical standards. It is a highly recommended activity and should be completed prior to work on any of the other activities.

The list of activities provides brief answers to three questions regarding each activity. The three questions are:

- What will be learned by my involvement in this activity?
- What will I need to do to implement this activity?
- How will I document my work regarding this activity? (These are the artifacts that will appear in the culminating portfolio, culminating report, or other documentation.)

The suggested activities are as follows:

Possible Activities for Internship Experiences

A = Objective   B = Activity   C = Documentation (artifacts)

ISLLC Standard I: The Vision of Learning

❑ **1. Principal for a Day**
   A. The intern will be able to comprehend the various roles, obligations, time commitments, and issues in a single day in the position of a principal.
   B. The intern must meet with the principal and agree on a scheduled day to "take over" the principal's agenda and tasks for a full day (evening included).
   C. Depending on the events that day, the intern will submit all paperwork generated from the day's events, if applicable (e.g., discipline referral, letters of complaint written by parent, faculty meeting, in-house school concert).

❑ **2. Analyze Testing Data to Improve Instruction**
   A. The purpose of this activity is two-fold: to work with the school improvement team to suggest best practices and strategies to improve instruction based on standardized testing data, and to work with data to comprehend the challenges for students in various areas of instruction.
   B. The intern will obtain state standards data from the current year (or the most recent available) and target challenges in student achievement and instruction. The intern will research and suggest best practices and lesson plan ideas for teachers and subject areas, based on the data analysis of the test scores.
   C. Documentation to include will be summarized results of the current state standard scores (or most recent available), including the intern's paraphrasing of the data, as well as a list of best practices and suggested lesson plan activities for teachers and subject areas as created by the intern.

❑ **3. Redefine the Mission/Vision of the School**
   A. The purpose of this activity is to revisit the mission and vision of the school based on the changing needs of the student body, the environment, and educational legislation.
   B. The intern will analyze and review past mission and vision statements. The intern will assess the school's climate, needs, and the current educational legislation to create a current school vision/mission.
   C. Documentation will include copies of the newly created vision and mission statements. Other documentation to include would be the data researched to create the new mission and vision statements.

❑ 4. **Generate a Weekly Bulletin/Staff Newsletter**

   A. The purpose of this activity is to investigate and identify the current school and community activities, faculty and student news, and updates within a school and use a computer program to design and distribute a weekly bulletin/staff newsletter.

   B. The intern will need to interview and speak with various faculty members and students, highlight positive faculty and student information, investigate the various school/community activities for the week, keep abreast and include current educational policy and news, and provide Staff Development opportunities.

   C. Documentation will include interview notes and a school calendar with dates, events, and activities. The intern would also include the bulletin or newsletter. Any news or information that will assist in generating the bulletin/newsletter needs to be included, including research.

❑ 5. **Analyze Data and Address Student Issues and Needs**

   A. The intern will analyze data and identify the needs and concerns of various students throughout the school while assisting in the school's total vision and mission development.

   B. The intern will use the following types of data to investigate student issues and needs: State Standard Scores, 9 Weeks Exam Scores, Attendance, Discipline Referral Numbers, SAT Scores, and Final Course Grades. The intern will assess the data, find areas needing improvement, and plan a course of action to address the needs and issues of the students.

   C. Documentation will include summaries of State Standard Scores, 9 Weeks Exam Scores, Attendance Numbers, Discipline Referral Number, SAT Scores, and Final Course Grades from courses and classes from the current year. The intern will, based on the data, include a course of action that addresses the needs and issues of the student body.

❑ 6. **Organize and Facilitate Data Analysis and Plan with the Staff**

   A. The purpose of this activity is for the intern to become familiar and comfortable with analyzing data, plotting a course of action to improve areas of weakness, and to share and include staff in adequately using the data for the school and instructional improvement.

   B. The intern will use the data from Activity 5 under ISLLC Standard I; however, the intern will then share the results with the staff and allow staff members to take ownership of data analysis and the school improvement plan by soliciting their solutions to the designated areas needing improvement.

   C. Documentation will include all of the data and scores from activity 5 under ISLLC Standard I and the ideas and suggestions given by the faculty and staff. In addition, the intern should then review the suggestions and prepare a list of feasible solutions from the staff recommendations.

Other:

____ A. Lead a textbook adoption process

____ B. Conduct a projected building utilization study

____ C. Marshall resources to attain the vision

____ D. Identify and address barriers to accomplishing the vision

____ E. Assess programs and activities to ensure alignment with the vision

____ F. Serve on a strategic development and planning team

____ G. Review discipline referrals for needed school improvements

____ H. Review policies for student transportation

____ I. Chair the school improvement team

____ **J.** Address the school board on a key issue
____ **K.** Chair a team that is writing a grant
____ **L.** Conduct a needs assessment
____ **M.** Serve on the district technology planning committee
____ **N.** _____
____ **O** _____
____ **P.** _____

ISLLC Standard II: The Culture of Teaching and Learning

❑ **7. Professional Development Preparation**

A. The intern will assess the school climate and needs, to identify appropriate professional staff development programs. The intern will plan and schedule the Professional Development program, and obtain all necessary materials.

B. The intern will consult with in-house administrators and present possible ideas for staff development based on needs of the staff, the school climate, and current educational policy. The group will decide on one meaningful topic and the intern will arrange the necessary speaker(s) and materials for the program, including handouts, documents, refreshments, and exit comment slips.

C. Documentation will include brainstorming ideas, research materials, generated handouts and paperwork, and exit comment slips.

❑ **8. Create a New Program for Teachers, Staff, or Students**

A. The intern will assess the school climate, faculty morale, and student needs in order to design needed support for an improved school climate, including faculty/staff and/or student body in a way that positively affects the overall school success. With this activity, interns will also learn to adequately assess the worth and success of the present school ethos in supporting new programs.

B. The intern will assess the organization and its stakeholders to determine the need for a new program implementation. The intern will work with administrators, lead teachers, and faculty members to assess what would be a beneficial program for the success of the entire school, based on need. At this point, the intern will work with other members in the school to design a program and implement it within the school.

C. Documentation will include the list of brainstormed ideas, data and reasons to support the implementation of the new program, and all documentation involving the new program, including documents, paperwork, and resources produced.

❑ **9. Plan a School-Sanctioned Event**

A. The intern will work with school organizations, faculty, students, the Activities Director, and the bookkeeper to develop, promote, and coordinate a school-wide activity.

B. Based on recommendations of staff, students, and school organizations and clubs, the intern will prepare an event (movie night, dance, talent show, athletic night) from start to finish; from planning to follow through. The intern will need to have a brainstormed list of ideas, submit them to the administration, and then choose a final event to prepare. Working with school organizations, students, faculty, parents, administration, custodial staff, security, the bookkeeper, and other people (possible businesses), the intern will advertise, plan in detail, and implement a school-sanctioned event, providing proper security, refreshments, custodial staff, and appropriate entertainment.

C. As far as documentation is concerned, the student will submit the brainstormed ideas list, financial paperwork, list of necessary materials, appropriate chaperone/staff lists, advertisements, and any other documentation prepared for the school event.

☐ **10. Analyze Attendance Rate and Create an Improvement Plan**

A. Benefits of this activity include reviewing and analyzing attendance data and making appropriate goals for improvement based on the data analysis and areas needing improvement.

B. Working with administrators, teachers, and parents, the intern will analyze the data, assess weak areas with attendance/attendance policy, and will then, based on the results and suggestions, create a plan to improve attendance at the school level.

C. For documentation purposes, the intern will submit a summary of the current attendance data, the list of areas needing improvement in attendance, goals, and the improvement plan to be implemented.

☐ **11. Create Commendation Letters for Staff**

A. Benefits of this activity include designing various types of letters for different celebratory events for faculty and staff members.

B. The intern will solicit "Hoorays" from every instructional and support department and generate a commendation letter for faculty and staff members for both big and small accomplishments.

C. Documentation for this activity will include sample letters to faculty and staff for numerous celebratory events.

☐ **12. Attend a Professional Conference**

A. Benefits of this activity include learning how to request professional leave and how to both share and use the information obtained at the conference.

B. The intern will consult with the administrator and suggest possible conference topics. The intern and administrator will decide on a conference for the intern to attend and collect information, share information back with the school, and discuss how it might affect current practice.

C. Documentation for this activity will include highlights for the faculty and staff from the conference and results of discussion of information shared.

☐ **13. Suggest Effective Teaching Strategies**

A. Benefits of this activity include researching new best practice teaching strategies and being aware of current teaching strategies to assist and assess teachers.

B. Researching new best practice teaching strategies for three departments, the intern will make presentations to each group of teachers (Sciences, Social Studies, Math, English, Foreign Language, Health/PE, Career and Technical Education, and Electives) and provide strategies for each department to assist with student success and the school's mission and vision.

C. Documentation will include research for effective teaching strategies, minutes from group discussion, and any documents that are created for each group of teachers.

☐ **14. Train Teachers to Use a Computer Program**

A. Benefits of this activity include learning how to instruct other educators on a new or unfamiliar computer program and comprehending and working with various computer programs.

B. After meeting with the administrators, the intern will decide on a computer program that teachers need to use on a regular or daily basis to improve student learning/instruction or for daily functions, such as attendance and discipline. The intern will be responsible for teaching all elements of the program and its functions to the faculty and staff.

C. Documentation will include step-by-step instructions for teachers on use of the computer program.

❏ **15. Plan a Classroom Lesson with a New Teacher**

A. Benefits of this activity include becoming familiar with the various curricula in the school, working with teachers one-on-one, and becoming familiar with the schedules and planning methods of various teachers and what can help the most in improving lesson planning.

B. The intern will consult with administrators to find an appropriate new teacher with whom they can work to write out and plan a classroom lesson. In this event, the intern will collaborate and share ideas with the teacher, write out a classroom lesson with state standard objectives, activities, and material needed, and discuss ways in which to present the lesson to students.

C. Documentation will include a copy of the collaborative lesson plan generated by the intern and the new teacher and any comments from the new teacher regarding benefits.

❏ **16. Implement State Learning Standards into Non-State-Standard-Based Courses**

A. Benefits of this activity include becoming more familiar with state learning objectives (SLO) and various ways to implement those in non-SLO-based courses. In addition, it provides the intern with practice of offering creative alternatives for instruction for those teaching non-SLO-based courses.

B. The intern will work with teachers to develop creative instructional methods and practices for teachers of non-SLO courses, which are based on the State Standard of Learning Objectives. For this activity, the intern will be responsible for accumulating a list of ideas to present to those teachers of non-SLO-based courses and provide guidelines and suggestions on how to implement those in the classroom.

C. Documentation for this activity would be a list of ways to implement SLO objectives in the non-SLO-based courses.

❏ **17. Supervise a Curriculum Revision**

A. Benefits of this activity include becoming familiar with the process of curriculum revision and the alignment of the curriculum to the needs of the students in the school and the state standards. In addition, the intern will work with the supervisors at the central administrative level for district alignment.

B. The intern will distribute copies of the current curricula and the staff members will then suggest corrections and new strategies and additions to the curriculum. Then, all members of the department and the intern will come together in a meeting and piece together an updated curriculum that is most beneficial to the students. Once the new draft is approved, it will be sent to the central administration building supervisor for approval and then typed up, formally, and distributed to the staff members in the various subject areas.

C. Documentation will include the drafts and the final formal copies of each newly revised curriculum.

❏ **18. Plan Educational Programs for Exceptional and Diverse Students**

A. Benefits of this activity include working with students, teachers, and parents designing programs for various academic abilities, age levels, and handicapping conditions; working with different facets of educational law; assessing student needs within the building; and designing programs based on those assessments.

   B. The intern will identify the various types of exceptionalities of students in the school and analyze the current programs, or lack thereof, for the exceptional and diverse students in the school. After analysis, the intern will then work with teachers to design or update an educational program for exceptional and diverse students, keeping laws and student interests in mind. The intern will generate a written plan, curriculum, and/or a proposal for a new special education program. Once this is complete, the intern will submit the written proposal to the administrators and the administration in the district for approval.

   C. Documentation for this activity will include the current program list for the students, the assessment of student needs, and the proposal for new educational program(s).

19. **Study District Policies and Analyze School's Implementation**

   A. Benefits of this activity include becoming familiar with the district policies, practice in assessing implementation of district policies within a single school, and altering those school policies not aligned with the district.

   B. The intern will obtain a copy of district policies and will look at the individual school policy and see what is not in alignment with the district policies, make note of that, and suggest methods to improve alignment.

   C. Documentation will include a list of school-based policies not aligned with those of the district. In addition, the intern will submit suggestions on how to align the school policies with those of the district.

20. **Colleague Sharing Session of Best Practices**

   A. Benefits of this activity include learning to facilitate a collegial sharing session and compiling a list of teachers' best practices.

   B. The intern will generate interest and send a memo, announcing the time, place, and purpose of the collegial meeting. Once the meeting begins, the intern will act as facilitator, scribe, and mediator and develop a means to compile a list of best practices for various subject areas.

   C. Documentation will include the generated memo for the appropriate faculty members and the list of best practices facilitated in the colleague sharing session.

21. **Collaborate with Instructional Staff to Identify and Assess At-Risk Students' Needs**

   A. Benefits of this activity include practicing and learning how to assess students labeled at risk, working with and discussing confidential matters and information, becoming familiar with identifying types of at-risk students, and planning appropriate interventions and strategies for their success.

   B. The intern will ask teachers to reflect and give a list with explanation of students who are at risk and in what way those students are at risk. The intern will take those names, study the various profiles of students given by teachers, determine an effective strategy/intervention for each student, and develop intervention strategies. Compare intervention strategies with student IEPs.

   C. Documentation will include the list of student exceptionalities and the types of intervention/strategies the intern has proposed for individual students.

22 **Attend a Superintendent's Administrative Meeting**

   A. Benefits of this activity include learning the focus points, goals, mission, and concerns from the top administrative level, how the administrative meetings are governed, how to work with other administrative staff and school administrators, and the pressing issues of the district.

    B. The intern will attend and take notes during the meeting, then reflect on those notes at another time and see how they relate to current school issues. The intern will comment on areas of discussion.

    C. Documentation will include an agenda from the superintendent's meetings and the notes taken by the intern and how they relate to current school issues.

☐ **23. Prepare Standard School Reports for School Board, Central Office, and/or State Department of Education**

    A. Benefits of this activity include becoming familiar with reports that need to be submitted, the process for submitting reports, and working with deadlines and various report formats.

    B. The intern will consult with the school-based administrators and take on responsibility for reports that need to be completed, processed, and submitted to the various educational units. The intern will be guided and instructed on which reports to complete, the information needed, the process of filling out the forms, and the process of submitting the forms on the appropriate deadlines. The intern will be responsible for any needed followup.

    C. Documentation will include copies of the forms filled out, processed, and submitted to the various educational organizations.

☐ **24. Create Inclusive Learning Communities**

    A. Benefits of this activity include learning how to assess the school climate and student needs to create an inclusive learning community and working with special education laws and various types of students to create a working inclusive climate.

    B. The intern will assess the school climate and student needs and brainstorm some strategies and a plan to create inclusive learning communities within a single school building. In this activity, the intern will collaborate with the special education department, the administrators, and the lead teachers. There will be a group meeting among all of the above stakeholders, professional dialogue will occur, and the intern will chair the group as it generates ideas and strategies to design inclusive learning communities. The intern will make a list, submit it to the above stakeholders, brainstorm with administrators, and come up with a process for creating a more inclusive learning community within the school.

    C. Documentation will include all the notes the intern takes from the meeting, meeting agenda, minutes, and the final proposed strategy to design an inclusive learning community for the school.

Other:

____ A. Investigate root causes affecting student achievement level

____ B. Conduct an instructional needs assessment

____ C. Write a grant proposal for external funding for new pedagogical approaches

____ D. Improve student extracurricular activities

____ E. Participate in an accreditation visitation

____ F. Orient new staff members

____ G. Develop a plan of supervision for regular and special school situations

____ H. Arrange the opening and/or closing of school

____ I. Serve as a summer school principal

____ J. Design and implement study groups

____ K. Coach beginning teachers

____ L. Conduct walk-through and informal visitations

____ M. Plan and develop enrichment activities

____ N. Utilize multiple assessment to evaluate student learning

____ **O.** Review distribution of grades

____ **P.** Audit the effectiveness of professional development

____ **Q.** Chair the school professional development committee

____ **R.** Develop an instructional improvement plan

____ **S.** _____

____ **T.** _____

____ **U.** _____

ISLLC Standard III: The Management of Learning

❑ **25. Prepare Accountability Reports for Local, State, and Federal Compliance**

    A. Benefits of this activity include working with and identifying various accountability reports, how to fill those out, and the proper format and deadline for submitting those reports.

    B. Consulting with the school based administration, the intern will be briefed and shown past accountability reports and then given various reports to complete. The intern will be responsible for properly formatting the reports, obtaining needed information, completing needed analysis and reports, and meeting appropriate deadlines.

    C. Documentation will include current reports prepared and submitted by the intern and approved by the school-based administration team.

❑ **26. Be Accountable for and Distribute Standardized Testing Materials**

    A. The purpose of this activity is to familiarize the intern with rules, regulations, and policies surrounding standardized testing.

    B. For this activity, the intern will meet with the school's testing coordinator, seek and publish dates and times when standardized testing will be done in the school, and talk with the testing coordinator about steps that need to be taken for distribution, collection, and special cases with testing. The intern will be responsible for school-wide testing, including the sorting of testing material for all teachers, providing a meeting to distribute information on testing, collecting all testing materials, sending them off, and ordering more if necessary.

    C. Documentation for this activity will include standardized testing ordering forms, teacher signature sheets, notes from the meeting with the testing coordinator, and any other critical documentation included in the standardized testing process.

❑ **27. Prepare a BIP and/or FBA for a Chronic Disciplined Student**

    A. The benefits include becoming familiar and confident in the laws and regulations of Special Education students, learning and comprehending the forms used in Special Education meetings and proceedings, and developing behavior modification strategies to assist teachers of those chronic disciplined students.

    B. The intern will consult with the Special Education teachers and obtain a list of students who have chronic behavior issues. The intern will coordinate the development of functional behavior assessments (FBAs). Meeting with the students, parents, teachers, and the special education coordinator, the intern will prepare the appropriate documentation for behavior intervention that follows the special education guidelines for individual students. A Behavior Improvement Plan (BIP) will be developed for each student.

    C. Documentation for this activity will include the BIP/FBA, the student's IEP/504, and any other document pertinent to the meeting and intervention plan.

❑ **28. Decide the Fate of an Appeal for a Student**

    A. Benefits of this activity include using ethics, fairness, and integrity in decision making and using investigative and communication skills when deciding the fate of an appeal.

    B. The intern will work with the principal or assistant principals and discuss all appeals that need to be addressed. The intern will learn the proper procedures for handling appeals from an administrator and will take on this responsibility and read through appeals, investigate further, if necessary, and work with others to make final judgments on the appeals.

    C. Documentation for this activity will include various written appeals by parents/guardians, any disciplinary paperwork from the disciplinary infraction, and the decisions made and reasoning on the appeals.

❑ **29. Conduct a Faculty Meeting**

    A. Benefits of this activity for the intern include generating an agenda, deciding on appropriate meeting topics, communicating and coordinating with staff, and utilizing and facilitating time appropriately.

    B. The intern will meet with all administrators, lead teachers, coaches, guidance director, and faculty to discuss the meeting. The intern will take notes, develop an agenda for, and coordinate the faculty meeting. The intern will be responsible for arranging for speakers, refreshments, equipment, and any needed followup from the meeting.

    C. Documentation will include the agenda and minutes for the faculty meeting and any needed followup.

❑ **30. Conduct a Parent–Student–Teacher Meeting**

    A. Benefits of this activity include learning how to facilitate potentially hostile meetings, learning how to mediate and provide appropriate commentary, when necessary, and taking notes on important talking points from the meeting.

    B. The intern will meet with the principal and assistant principal and discuss the logistics of the meeting and progress to take place. Once the intern has spoken with the administrators, the intern will meet with the teacher to understand the context in which the meeting was called. The intern will call a meeting with teacher, student, and parents and will act as the facilitator of the meeting and interject, when and if necessary. The intern will document the results of the meeting and follow up on any needed planning.

    C. Documentation will include notes from the meeting and any other documentation gathered from the activity (i.e., discipline referral, parent note, written evidence, teacher statement) and any followup action taken.

❑ **31. Manage Textbook Ordering/Inventory**

    A. Benefits of this activity include working with budget, lead teachers, and administrators, ordering texts based on need, creating and meeting deadlines, and storing and counting textbook inventory.

    B. The intern will be responsible for ordering new textbooks and creating/working with a system in which textbook inventory will be kept. The intern will work with the building-level person who orders textbooks, get the proper forms, obtain the numbers and types of textbooks needed, fill out appropriate paperwork, send it off, handle the textbook shipment when it arrives, inventory shipments, and distribute them to the appropriate departments. The intern will record textbook inventory and develop a "master list" for textbook inventory in Microsoft Excel or other appropriate software and update and change as necessary.

C. Documentation for this activity will include completed order forms for textbooks, textbook inventories for individual teachers, and the master list of textbook inventory for the school, by department.

☐ **32. Assist in Budget Preparation**
   A. Benefits of this activity include learning about various accounts, vendors, and financial information and how funds are allocated for various expenses throughout the school year.
   B. The intern will work with the principal and the bookkeeper to learn about funding for the various accounts in the school, decisions on how money is allocated, the origin of the funds, what not to do financially, what can be done financially, and what is important to know in budget preparation and accountability. The intern will assess upcoming expenses and needs for the new school year and generate a draft of materials and requests and the money allocated for each, in addition to basic school-year needs. The intern will prepare the final budget.
   C. Documentation for this activity will include financial printouts from the bookkeeper, a list of accounts and vendors, a list of needs for the upcoming school year, the money available to work with, and the draft of how the money should be spent, based on need and analysis.

☐ **33. Control Inventory/Receiving of Supplies**
   A. Benefits of this activity include budgeting money and spending according to plan, controlling inventory, and allotting resources appropriately based on need and prior orders.
   B. The intern will work with the bookkeeper to order the appropriate quantity of supplies. Being cognizant of deadlines, funding, and past orders, the intern will order supplies for two months, focusing on the money that is allotted for the products needed, taking care of the shipment when it arrives, and tending to financial details of the order.
   C. Documentation for this activity includes the completed order forms, the invoices from the order, and the payment generated for the orders. The intern will provide a dollar figure for funds allotted and how that money was spent.

☐ **34. Input Financial Data/Balance Books with Bookkeeper**
   A. Benefits of this activity include working with the budget and finances, learning the relationship between principal and bookkeeper, becoming aware of how to use a computerized bookkeeping and check register program, and learning the process of balancing books.
   B. Before the intern begins to perform these tasks, the intern needs to meet with the bookkeeper and go over the procedures for using a computerized bookkeeping program as well as the process for balancing receipt books and inputting that information into the computer. Once this is done, the bookkeeper will give the intern receipt books that need to be checked, balanced, and money that needs to be put toward the daily deposit. The intern will balance those books, put the money toward the deposit, and input the appropriate information into the computerized financial program.
   C. Documentation for this activity will include copies of purchase orders and printouts of the balanced accounts.

☐ **35. Conduct a Safety Audit**
   A. Benefits of this activity include becoming familiar with the process of a safety audit and working with local police, fire stations, administrative personnel, and other designated personnel to conduct and plan for a proper safety audit.
   B. The intern will walk through the school and develop the safety plan and/or complete a safety audit with the principal or the Assistant Principal of

Operations to understand the "look-fors" during the safety audit visit. Once this is done, the intern will then use the designated checklist and complete a walk through, independently, make notes and assess the various captions on the designated checklist, and report back to the principal or the Assistant Principal of Operations. The intern will suggest changes that need to be made to repair those areas needing improvement.

C. Documentation for this activity will include the completed safety audit checklist, any suggestions for repair and strategies to implement those necessary changes, and planned followups.

❏ **36. Oversee Building Maintenance**

A. Benefits of this activity include working with the daily and special operations of the school building, assessing repair needs, working with teachers in need of assistance, and communicating with the essential personnel to handle maintenance and repair within the school.

B. The intern will survey the school building, going into individual classrooms to see where and if repair is necessary in various parts of the building. Using the generated check-off list, the intern will identify areas in the building that need attention and maintenance. The intern will then take the sheet to the appropriate in-house administrator or personnel for implementation, appropriate repair, and followup.

C. Documentation for this activity will include the check-off lists for rooms throughout the school and the written requests for maintenance and repair.

❏ **37. Arrange Bus Transportation for a Special School Event**

A. Benefits of this activity include working with the school-based transportation personnel and program, arranging and securing proper adequate transportation for the event, and consulting with the event sponsor for arrival and departure times for students.

B. The intern will work with the sponsor of the school event to decide how much transportation is necessary, various arrival and departure times for students, and routes for picking up students, and will complete and turn in all of the necessary paperwork for transportation for this event.

C. Documentation for this activity will include the completed bus requests, a list of bus numbers and routes, the numbers of students and necessary transportation, and all documents needed to arrange transportation.

❏ **38. Master Schedule Preparation**

A. Benefits of this activity include working with student schedules, working through conflicts, using a computerized scheduling program, being cognizant of teacher class load and scheduling, and working with staff members, building space, and the guidance department to properly schedule students.

B. The intern will work with the assistant principal or the coordinator of master scheduling and be trained on master schedule preparation. Once this has been completed, the intern will receive a list of students and their desired courses and will schedule students for classes for the school year, keeping in mind staffing, class size, and building accommodations.

C. Documentation for this activity will include rough and final copies of the master schedule, documentation on conflicts resolved, a list of class offerings, and a list of the school staff members.

❏ **39. Input Discipline Information into a Computer Program**

A. Benefits of this activity include mastery of a computerized discipline program and properly recording accurate disciplinary information for a variety of students.

B. The intern will go through training on the computerized discipline system and become competent. Once this has been accomplished, the intern will obtain referrals from various grade levels, teachers, and incident areas. Adhering to the rules and regulations of the school, the intern will determine appropriate action for the disciplinary incident, input that into the computer, and print out the disciplinary action information for the student and the teacher and deliver it appropriately.

C. Documentation for this activity will include referrals and disciplinary action paperwork from various inputs into the computerized discipline program.

☐ **40. Complete a New Teacher Observation**

A. Benefits of this activity include becoming familiar with the teacher performance appraisal/observation program, being aware of common "look-fors" in teacher observations, properly and appropriately documenting the observation notes, and relaying the outcome of the observation to the teacher in order to develop a plan of action for teacher improvement.

B. The intern will become accustomed with the process of teacher observation and the various forms and documents that accompany that process. Meeting with an administrator and teachers, a joint decision will be made on which teachers are to be observed. Once this is established, the intern will complete the appropriate documents, observe the teacher, and finalize the paperwork from the observation. After the observation, the intern will complete a post-observation planning conference with the teacher using notes and type up a post-conference observation form outlining plans for teacher improvement.

C. Documentation for this activity will include the typed notes to present to the teacher during the post-observation conference and the finalized teacher improvement plans that will be implemented by the teacher. Any plan for followup should be included by date.

☐ **41. Prepare a Specialized School-Based Report**

A. Benefits of this activity include becoming accustomed with the proper way to develop and prepare a school-based report, meeting appropriate deadlines, and ensuring the documentation arrives to the correct location.

B. The intern will consult with the school administrators to identify special school-based reports that need to be prepared and dispatched to the appropriate location and person. The intern will seek and find all necessary information and persons to complete the report as requested.

C. Documentation for this activity will include the final prepared school-based report.

☐ **42. Find Funding Sources for Individual Student Needs**

A. Benefits for this activity include working with budgets and school funds, analyze and meeting the needs of individual students, and researching possibilities for various interventions and equipment to reach the individual needs of students.

B. The intern will investigate various students with individualized needs and discover and assess what those students need to be more successful. Once this is done, the intern will meet with the administration and the bookkeeper to investigate the funding available to meet the individualized needs of these students and submit a "list of needs" to the administration, have it approved, and purchase the equipment or intervention necessary for these students to be successful. After purchasing the proper materials, the intern will ensure that they are distributed and used appropriately and in a timely fashion.

C. Documentation for this activity will include the number of students with individual needs, the necessary equipment and materials for these students, funding possibilities and a price list, financial documents from the bookkeeper (including approved purchase order forms), and the distribution list for purchased materials.

☐ **43. Support High Expectations for Student Behavior**

A. Benefits of this activity include working with the vision and mission of the school to develop, promote, and advertise high expectations for student behavior and enforcing and modeling those desired behaviors.

B. The intern will analyze and read the school's current mission and vision. From there, the intern will develop a list of expectations for student behavior and/or academic performance and discover various outlets in which to promote and advertise using school-based broadcast, print media, and so on. In addition, the intern can access athletics, school clubs, and organizations to assist in the promotion of expectations (flyers, posters, announcements, and booths).

C. Documentation for this activity will include the list of behavioral expectations and the various programs and promotions for the expected behaviors/academic performance within the school.

☐ **44. Develop Proactive Strategies for Intense Student Academic Support**

A. Benefits of this activity include preparing interns to work with students with specialized academic needs, preparing teachers for working with students needing special support, and discovering a variety of strategies to assist the diverse academic needs of students.

B. The intern will identify those students in the school that would benefit from greater academic support and plan a list of strategies, coordinated staff efforts, and staff development based on student needs.

C. Documentation for this activity will include the number of students needing support, the names of the staff working with those students with special academic needs, and the list of strategies, programs, staff involved, and staff development for teachers.

☐ **45. Order Material to Support Instructional Needs**

A. Benefits of this activity include working with lead teachers to obtain the materials order, working with a designated company and the bookkeeper to purchase materials, and working with a budget to obtain resources to meet the needs of the students based on the recommendations of the lead teachers and their department members.

B. For this activity, the intern will work with the lead teachers, the principal, and the bookkeeper to assess and provide for the instructional needs by purchasing instructional materials.

C. Documentation for this activity will include the list of materials from the different departments, the amount of money budgeted for these materials, the breakdown of money distribution by department, and the purchase orders and invoices from the material ordered.

Other:

_____ A. Monitor attendance and truancy

_____ B. Use a computer administrative system and utilize computer software

_____ C. Design, develop, and implement a staff development program

_____ D. Coordinate and monitor a comprehensive building program

_____ E. Terminate a staff member

_____ F. Participate in the hiring/selection process

_____ G. Monitor cleanliness and operations of school plant

_____ H. Monitor student health and special needs

_____ I. Develop and present study of incidence and source of discipline problems

_____ J. Develop/update job descriptions

____ **K.** Study the effectiveness of a computerized system for instruction and/or administration

____ **L.** Develop a personal time management system

____ **M.** Administer student recognition, graduation, or some other program

____ **N.** Evaluate technology support

____ **O.** Review and revise school handbook

____ **P.** Evaluate the school nurse, counselors, or office personnel or some other non-teaching position

____ **Q.** Inventory technology in use

____ **R.** Investigate a filed grievance

____ **S.** Work with teachers needing improvement

____ **T.** Disaggregate student assessment data

____ **U.** Discuss unwritten rules, procedures, and expectations

____ **V.** _____

____ **W.** _____

____ **X.** _____

ISLLC Standard IV: Relations with the Broader Community

❑ **46. Develop a Program for School–Community Relations**

  A. Benefits of this activity include working with parents, students, community organizations, and local businesses in developing a program for fostering relations between the school and the community.

  B. The intern will meet with the appropriate individuals and brainstorm a list of ideas and suggestions on the type of school–community program needed for the school. Once this is complete, the intern will work with a representative group to design a program that meets the needs of the school, its stakeholders, and the surrounding community.

  C. Documentation for this activity will include a list of the representative groups, memos, letters, agendas, list of brainstormed ideas, and the final proposal for a school–community program.

❑ **47. Work with PTSA for "Activity-a-Month" Event**

  A. Benefits of this activity include working with school-based organizations, parents, community members, members of the student body, and various local businesses. The intern will also gain insight into how to plan, organize, and follow through on an event.

  B. The intern will collaborate with the PTSA to plan an activity for each month. The intern will come up with a proposed budget to carry out the various planned activities throughout the school year. The intern will submit a plan to an administrator, have the activities approved, and inform the PTSA. Once the ideas have been approved, the intern will get these activities on the school-wide calendar and will plan, coordinate, monitor, and evaluate activity working with the PTSA. In this capacity, the intern will carry out the planned events, obtaining school building space and materials, and will follow through on all events.

  C. Documentation for this activity will include the proposed and signed budgets, documentation of the planned events, the school calendar, and correspondence related to the implementation of the events.

❑ **48. Involve Family, Business, and/or Community Members in a School-Wide Project**

  A. Benefits of this activity include working and communicating with a diverse group of people and handling and being responsible for a large-scale project.

  B. The intern will consult with administration, staff, and the community and together, this group will decide on a school-wide project that would be beneficial and feasible for the school. The intern will be responsible for planning and presiding over various meetings; creating, obtaining, and handling documentation; and any other facets of the school-wide project necessary for implementation and success.

C. Documentation for this activity will include the project itself; lists and examples of the various strategies for advertising this project; memos, documents, agendas, and other pertinent documents; and paperwork for this school-wide project.

☐ **49. Prepare a News Release**

A. Benefits of this activity include working with the local (and other types of) media and becoming familiar with the proper protocol in preparing a news release.

B. The intern will investigate and adhere to the proper district protocol for submitting a news release for a newsworthy activity or event in the school. The intern will compose a news release, provide a photo, and send this information to the appropriate contact person.

C. Documentation for this activity includes the final draft of the news release, a photo, if applicable, and the finalized article as is appeared in the media or on TV (VT, DVD, or CD), as available.

☐ **50. Oversee Volunteer Hours/Placements**

A. Benefits of this activity include working with stakeholders outside of the school, creating a solid tracking system for volunteers, properly placing volunteers based on ability and staff needs, and accessing program success.

B. The intern will be responsible for handling volunteer applications, directing them to the proper location for fingerprinting/background checks, submitting paperwork to the administration regarding volunteers and their hours, preparing a tracking and recording system for the volunteers, productivity training, and evaluating the effectiveness and success of volunteer programs. The intern will also be responsible for establishing a method of recognition and appreciation for the volunteers.

C. Documentation for this activity will include a copy of the volunteer application, a copy of the tracking system for volunteers and their hours, assessment of volunteer program success, and the different types of recognition for the school-based volunteers.

☐ **51. Demonstration and Articulation of School Context**

A. Benefits of this activity include articulating the goals, mission, and programs of the school to the community and receiving input. Within this activity, the intern will learn how to read the sentiment of the community regarding school programs and activities.

B. The intern will be responsible for examining the goals, mission, and programs of the school and discussing them with the community. The intern will analyze the school mission, goals, and the various practices and implementations and evaluate them in terms of the mission and goals of the district and the community to discover alignment or lack thereof. The intern will make a list of suggested approaches in which the school mission and goals can become more clearly aligned with the mission and goals of the community.

C. Documentation for this activity will include a copy of the mission and goals for the school and the school district, a sense of community beliefs about the school, the list of items that are not aligned, and the suggested actions necessary for proper and substantial alignment.

☐ **52. Contact or Assess Community Resources to Provide Student/Family Enrichment**

A. Benefits of this activity include identifying and communicating with the proper community resources to articulate goals and student/family needs and designing a method to deliver various types of service for students and their families.

B. The intern will be responsible for contacting service providing agencies and groups and identifying service organizations in the community that can assist with identified needs of the students and their families. The intern will generate a list of community resources and organizations that assist students and families within that school/school district and submit that to the administration along with a plan on how more formal relationships might be developed/implemented or assessed.

C. Documentation for this activity will include a list of the community resources designated by each organization or community group and a plan/assessment for their involvement.

Other:

_____ A. Assess academic/career guidance and decision making

_____ B. Plan and conduct a school fund-raising event

_____ C. Present school improvement initiatives to the community

_____ D. Establish community, business, institutional, and/or civic partnerships

_____ E. Facilitate constructive conversations on student learning and achievement

_____ F. Write a bulletin and/or newsletter for parents and community

_____ G. Plan and conduct parent information meetings

_____ H. Survey community to elicit recommendations

_____ I. Answer telephones and meet guests in the front office

_____ J. Develop a proposal for improving parent involvement

_____ K. Develop an orientation videotape/streaming video and/or typed brochure for parents and visitors

_____ L. Develop parenting skills courses

_____ M. Present the school program to a community service organization

_____ N. _____

_____ O. _____

_____ P. _____

ISLLC Standard V: Integrity, Fairness, and Ethics

❑ **53. Analyze School in Terms of Ethics, Fairness, and Diversity**

A. Benefits of this activity include becoming knowledgeable about the definitions and practices of ethics, fairness, and diversity. The intern will be able to identify those school practices that violate the standard ethical and fair school practices and regulations.

B. The intern will examine various educational legislation, laws, and community/national values and extract critical portions of current legislation and laws and generally promoted values, then analyze the practices of the school versus what the laws, legislation, and value demand and submit the findings in an appropriate document.

C. Documentation for this activity will include an analysis of the school's adherence (or lack thereof) to designated ethical and legal practices. There also needs to be a list of suggested strategies to improve the correlation with ethics practiced in the school.

❑ **54. Mobilize Staff to Create Positive Culture**

A. Benefits of this activity include assessing staff morale, working with an assortment of personalities and people, constructing ways to create a positive school climate, modeling expectations, and articulating goals and outcomes.

B. The intern will assess the overall culture of the school, identify areas needing improvement, and propose a strategy to involve all stakeholders in the process of creating a positive school climate. The intern will list ways in which all stakeholders can be involved and prepare a list of strategies to create a lively, positive school culture.

C. Documentation for this activity will include lists of potential obstacles and descriptions that identify and explain the culture of the school and its needs. The intern will submit ways in which the stakeholders can be involved in the process, as well as strategies to achieve, promote, and maintain a positive school culture.

❑ **55. Approve Faculty/Staff Leave**

A. Benefits of this activity include assessing staff and school needs, applying the rules and regulations for staff leave, and adhering to the district guidelines for faculty/staff leave.

B. The intern will approve faculty/staff leave for a period of time. During this process, teachers and staff will submit leave forms and the intern will analyze the reason for each absence, make sure that the staff member filled out the proper paperwork completely and correctly, and (depending upon appropriateness and substitute availability) approve leave for faculty and staff members. The intern will make all needed arrangements and follow policy.

C. Documentation for this activity will include a sample of the completed and approved faculty and staff forms and a form to arrange for substitutes for each of those staff members on the designated days.

❑ **56. Conduct a Seminar in Sensitivity Training**

A. Benefits of this activity include being aware and recognizing the need for sensitivity training, researching and presenting the information, and modeling desired behavior and expectations.

B. The intern will complete research on the topic, utilizing conference material, various reputable websites, texts, research, and other sources to create and generate adequate information for a staff seminar in sensitivity training. The intern will be responsible for advertising this event to staff members, verifying attendance, preparing all necessary documentation for the training (handouts, information packets, PowerPoint presentation, evaluation forms), arranging speakers, and handling logistical matters.

C. Documentation for this activity will include research obtained on the topic and any handouts, packets, PowerPoint presentations, or forms used in the seminar and evaluations.

❑ **57. Oversee IEP/Causality Meeting**

A. Benefits of this activity include working with the Special Education Department and laws, assuming the role of mediator/facilitator, upholding the Special Education laws, and being aware of the structure and purpose of these meetings.

B. The intern will coordinate with the Special Education Lead Teacher and schedule the IEP and Causality meetings. The intern will obtain the files on the various students, become informed about the students and the purpose for these meetings, and coordinate these meetings, acting as a facilitator, scribe, and mediator, if necessary.

C. Documentation for this activity will include IEP copies, causality information, notes generated from the meeting, and outcomes/concerns from those meetings.

❑ **58. Oversee Staff Dismissal Procedures**

A. Benefits of this activity include becoming knowledgeable about staff dismissal procedures, proper protocol and law surrounding staff dismissal, and appropriate law, fairness, and ethics.

B. The intern will be involved in the process of staff dismissal, including approach of the principal; documents and paperwork produced and utilized; relevant laws, policies, procedures, and best practices; fair and ethical behavior; and the manner and professionalism of the principal and other administrators in the staff dismissal.

C. Documentation for this activity will include the notes taken by the intern during the staff dismissal process.

❑ 59. **Revisit Leadership Platform for Administrative Action**

A. Benefits of this activity include developing, updating, and revising the administrative platform based on current educational trends, laws, experiences, and appropriate integrity and ethics.

B. The intern will reflect on the current leadership platform based on ethical standards and integrity and update and revise the leadership platform based on these standards as well as insights gained during the process.

C. Documentation for this activity will include a copy of the former leadership platform of the intern and a new, revised copy with ethical improvements.

❑ 60. **Assess Ethics for a School Leader**

A. Benefits of this activity include assessing the necessary and essential ethics of school leadership.

B. The intern will reflect on leadership behavior and appropriate ethics to identify any potential conflicts. Using the internship experiences, the intern will generate a list of possible ethical conflicts or conflicts of interest that might jeopardize the integrity of the administrator, school, and/or district.

C. Documentation will include the list of important ethical standards for each administrator, school, and/or district and actual or potential conflicts that develop related to each ethical standard.

❑ 61. **Promote Equity, Fairness, and Respect for School/Community Members**

A. Benefits of this activity include becoming aware of means in which equity, fairness, and respect can be promoted among school and community members and the role of the administrator in establishing these qualities.

B. The intern will ascertain whether and how equity, fairness, and respect are being promoted inside and outside of the school. If they are not present or encouraged, the intern will develop a list of strategies on how these traits or values can be promoted within the school and the community. If the characteristics are not apparent in the school and the community, the intern will provide a list of strategies to uphold, improve, and strengthen those behaviors.

C. Documentation for this activity will include a list of strategies to apply to maintain the characteristics of equity, fairness, and respect in the school. If these characteristics are visible, the intern will submit a list of strategies to uphold, improve, and strengthen the characteristics in the school and the community.

❑ 62. **Clarify Principal's Role in Staff Rights and Confidentiality (recommended as the first activity)**

A. Benefits of this activity include working with and comprehending laws regarding confidentiality in human resource, personnel matters, and staff information. The intern will become skilled at using appropriate language, communication skills, and professionalism regarding staff rights and confidentiality.

B. The intern will hold a meeting with the principal and discuss the numerous events, documentation, information, and paperwork that are deemed to be confidential. The intern will learn what information is "public knowledge" and what information cannot be shared with other organizations or people in the district. An individual's rights will be reviewed in relation to staff issues. The intern will discuss "unwritten" rules, procedures, and expectations.

C. Documentation for this activity will include notes from the meeting about how to handle confidential staff information. In addition, the intern will define what is appropriate and inappropriate information to divulge to district organizations and necessary administrative personnel about staff members. Staff rights regarding an issue will be documented, and the relevant written policy and procedures attached.

Other:

____ A. Conduct appeals/expulsion hearing

____ B. Validate legal and ethical use of technology

____ C. Evaluate a planned holiday program for offensiveness and/or constitutionality

____ D. Assess decisions being made on the basis of ethical standards

____ E. Promote equity, fairness, and respect

____ F. Defend the ethical basis and integrity of a difficult decision you made as an intern

____ G. Examine the fairness of methods used to gain consensus

____ H. Address the heritage and values of diversity in school programs

____ I. Assess the ethical practices of students within the school

____ J. Audit the ethical standards in your administrative platform, school handbook, and/or board policy manual

____ K. _____

____ L. _____

____ M. _____

ISLLC Standard VI: The Political, Economic, Legal, and Cultural Context

❑ **63. Plan a School-Wide Cultural/Educational Celebration**

A. Benefits of this activity include recognizing diverse cultures and populations within the school community; working with a variety of staff and community members; and preparing, planning, and carrying out an event.

B. The intern will work with the administrators, teachers, and community to brainstorm a list of possible cultural and educational celebrations that could be observed during the year. The intern will choose an assortment of school-wide observances to have throughout the year that are both cultural and educational. The intern will be responsible for making all arrangement for the event, including securing dates, locations, staff, supplies, and materials, and any other facet of the plan that is necessary for its implementation.

C. Documentation for this activity will include the list of celebrations, the calendar showing when the various celebrations will be held during the year, the plan for each celebration, a list of materials needed, staff required, location, and any other documents of paperwork pertinent to the school-wide celebration.

❑ **64. Identify, Assess, and Address Social Factors Affecting the School**

A. Benefits of this activity include working with economic, cultural, and political factors in the surrounding area; being sensitive to the student body and their needs; targeting issues; and finding strategies to address, conquer, and alleviate the possibility of negative factors impacting the school.

B. The intern will compile data, present the data to administrators and/or faculty and staff and community, and discuss possible issues that need to be addressed. The intern will come up with possible solutions of how to address these issues as a school unit. The intern will work with teachers on how they might address these issues within their classrooms.

C. Documentation for this activity will include the data analysis on parents, students, and frequent school visitors; a document that compiles the data; and a document for faculty and staff on ways in which they can address these same issues within the smaller context of a classroom.

☐ **65. Evaluate School Programs for Political, Cultural, Economic, and Legal Correctness**

A. Benefits of this activity include learning about and being sensitive to correctness; appropriately determining the value of the school programs; and suggesting changes based on political, cultural, economic, and legal issues.

B. The intern will obtain a list of school programs and enrollment numbers from the current year and the previous year. The intern will examine the various programs for correctness and the community demographics and beliefs. The intern will compile a list of suggestions for courses needing to be modified or added or deleted. The rationale behind the changes and adjustments suggested by the intern needs to accompany the list of suggestions and be based on a political, cultural, economic, and/or legal basis.

C. Documentation for this activity will include the list of school programs or activities needing adjustment and the list of suggestions for adjustment, accompanied by the rationale for changes or additions/deletions of the school-based programs.

☐ **66. Influence Public Policy to Support Student Success**

A. Benefits of this activity include being cognizant of what students need to be successful and how that can be achieved through influencing public policy.

B. The intern will attend local school board meetings and other educational regional and state meetings. The intern will work through the identified power structure to serve as an advocate for a needed educational policy. The intern will speak on behalf of the policy, articulating in a professional manner the needs of the school and its stakeholders to the appropriate power structure/political body.

C. Documentation for this activity will include a list of times, topics, presentations, and dates of meetings attended; a list of policy and finances that the school needs for student success; and a presentation of lobbying completed to gain approval for policy and/or funding.

☐ **67. Develop/Apply Anti-Harassment Policy and Strategies**

A. Benefits of this activity include acknowledging, understanding, and enforcing the laws regarding harassment, and developing strategies to prevent those situations in the workplace. The intern will learn how to avoid, address, and deal with harassment in the workplace.

B. The intern will study and research the laws regarding harassment and bullying. The intern will complete/revise a school-based harassment policy, a preventive program, or an investigation of harassment.

C. Documentation for this activity will include the research obtained on harassment, the generated school-based harassment policy, documentation of programs, results of investigations, and/or strategies to discourage harassment in the workplace.

☐ **68. Study and Implement District-Wide Policies on a School Issue**

A. Benefits of this activity include becoming aware of district policies and the appropriate implementation of those policies.

B. The intern will choose a school issue on which to focus. The intern will research and study the district policy with regards to the school issue and will then implement the appropriate strategies based on the regulations.

C. Documentation for this activity will include the list of district policies on the chosen issue, a record of strategies to address that issue based on district policy, and what was finally done.

❑ **69. Work to Influence the Policy for Student Achievement (District and Local)**

A. Benefits of this activity include being aware of the policy for student achievement and how it is developed.

B. The intern will work with the school-based administration team and identify areas of student achievement that need to be amended and addressed. The intern will obtain a list of state, district, and local meetings related to policy affecting the issue. The intern will present to the officials and organizations that influence policy. The intern will work within the power structure to influence policy.

C. Documentation for this activity will include a list of the student achievement areas needing attention, the list of district and local meetings, and the script/speech to be presented to the educational officials or at the meetings.

Other:

____ **A.** Actively participate in professional, political, or cultural organizations
____ **B.** Submit an article for publication
____ **C.** Actively participate in professional contract negotiations
____ **D.** Support a defense team involved in a legal conflict
____ **E.** Lead a student due process hearing
____ **F.** Work with judicial system in the resolution of a Juvenile Court case
____ **G.** Review recent court cases and determine impact on programs and supervision
____ **H.** Develop and/or manage a legal and contractual agreement
____ **I.** Influence the legislation on policies that benefit students
____ **J.** Shape a culture of high expectations
____ **K.** _____
____ **L.** _____
____ **M.** _____

It is important that you work with your external mentor and university advisor to select the activities that will be best for your internship experience. Hopefully, you will select the types of activities from which you will gain the greatest benefit. Each educational leadership program will also have its own unique requirements and expectations regarding types of activities that best prepare you for an educational leadership role. The overall objective is to be involved in activities that will help you the most to prepare for educational leadership and that provide experiences that closely replicate daily administrative life (Hackmann, Schmitt-Oliver, & Tracy, 2002; Martin, Wright, & Danzig, 2003; McCreight, 2004; Morgan, Gibbs, Hertzog, & Wylie, 1997).

OTHER CONSIDERATIONS

Certainly, there are many practical considerations or realities that come into play on the selection of activities in which you will be involved. High on the list of practical considerations might be trying to fit the internship around full-time employment. Other considerations relate to special activities that may be occurring at the sponsoring site, the openness of mentors and/or sponsoring school systems to allow the intern to participation in all types of activities, and, certainly, how well prepared interns are to take on these challenging tasks. You also must have the necessary time to see an activity through to completion and not leave a project partially completed for the staff to end up trying to pick up the pieces after you leave.

Problems can occur when planned internship activities are cancelled or scheduled earlier or later than expected. Also, there are some activities that would be great experiences but they will not occur at any time during the internship's scheduled time frame. Thus, there are a number of extenuating circumstances that may not allow interns to gain all the experiences that they had hoped to schedule. This is a normal part of the internship. The key quality here is flexibility.

Activities and Controversies

Always discuss any selected or assigned activity that seems inappropriate, awkward, or questionable with your university instructor and advisor. There are also legal implications that are connected with any activity in which you are involved. First, there are issues of confidentiality and ethics (see Activity 62) that must be observed. You may be placed in sensitive job functions involving student discipline actions, professional and classified job actions, and parent issues, to name a few. Revealing confidential information can damage the school image and your reputation as a trustworthy and reliable leader, resulting in defamation charges opening you and the school district to damages. Freedom of information requests may be made involving your timely and professional action. Failure to handle these requests properly may be a source of legal and public relations concern.

Additionally, issues arise from time to time that are controversial in nature, causing division in the community. It is important to know what issues are classified as matters of public concern. The Supreme Court has defined free speech more narrowly for public employees than for the public at large. If controversial issues arise, it is important to know that taking sides and speaking out against some proposed School Board action may undermine the effectiveness of the district and result in disciplinary action unless that speech involves matters of public concern.

It is important to remember that an administrative intern holds a quasi-administrative function. In some areas, acting in such an internship position may be viewed as acting as an agent for the school district or the school. As such, it is vital for the intern to know the school district's position on the role of the intern as an agent of the organization and to clearly delineate those parameters when dealing with clients.

· **Form 8.1** ·

Administrative Skills Assessment Instrument

Directions: For each of the following items, please darken the number (from 1 to 6) that represents your assessment of your strengths related to that particular skill. (For the purpose of this scale, please assume that 1 = very weak and 6 = very strong).

	very weak					very strong
Setting Instructional Direction: Implementing strategies for improving teaching and learning, including putting programs and improvement efforts into action. Developing a vision and establishing clear goals, providing direction in achieving stated goals, encouraging others to contribute to goal achievement, securing commitment to a course of action from individuals and groups.	①	②	③	④	⑤	⑥
Teamwork: Seeking and encouraging involvement of team members. Modeling and encouraging the behaviors that move the group to task completion. Supporting group accomplishment.	①	②	③	④	⑤	⑥
Sensitivity: Perceiving the needs and concerns of others, dealing tactfully with others in emotionally stressful situations or in conflict. Knowing what information to communicate and to whom. Relating to people of varying ethnic, cultural, and religious backgrounds.	①	②	③	④	⑤	⑥
Judgment: Reaching logical conclusions and making high quality decisions based on available information. Giving priority and caution to significant issues. Seeking out relevant data, facts, and impressions. Analyzing and interpreting complex information.	①	②	③	④	⑤	⑥
Result Orientation: Assuming responsibility. Recognizing when a decision is required. Taking prompt action as issues emerge. Resolving short-term issues while balancing them against long-term objectives.	①	②	③	④	⑤	⑥
Organizational Ability: Planning and scheduling one's own and the work of others so that resources are used appropriately. Scheduling flow of activities, establishing procedures to monitor projects. Practicing time and task management, knowing what to delegate and to whom.	①	②	③	④	⑤	⑥
Leadership: Getting others involved in solving problems, recognizing when a group requires direction, effectively interacting with a group to guide them to accomplish a task.	①	②	③	④	⑤	⑥
Educational Values: Possessing a well-reasoned educational philosophy, receptiveness to new ideas, use of an ethical framework, and demonstrating professionalism.	①	②	③	④	⑤	⑥
Stress Tolerance: Performing under pressure and during opposition, thinking on one's feet.	①	②	③	④	⑤	⑥
Oral Communication: Clearly communicating. Making oral presentations that are clear and easy to understand.	①	②	③	④	⑤	⑥
Written Communication: Expressing ideas clearly in writing, demonstrating technical proficiency. Writing appropriately for different audiences.	①	②	③	④	⑤	⑥
Development of Others: Teaching, coaching, and helping others. Providing specific feedback based on observations and data.	①	②	③	④	⑤	⑥
Understanding Own Strengths and Weaknesses: Identifying personal strengths and weaknesses. Taking responsibility for improvement by actively pursuing developmental activities. Striving for continuous learning.	①	②	③	④	⑤	⑥
Conflict Management: Intervening in conflict situations and developing solutions that are agreeable to all persons involved.	①	②	③	④	⑤	⑥
Political Astuteness: Perceiving critical features of the environment such as power structure, principal players, and special interest groups. Formulating alternatives that reflect realistic expectations.	①	②	③	④	⑤	⑥
Risk Taking: Calculating risks and taking action based on sound judgments.	①	②	③	④	⑤	⑥
Creativity: Generating ideas that provide new and different solutions to management problems or opportunities.	①	②	③	④	⑤	⑥

Source: Most of the above administrative skills and descriptions come from *Selecting and Developing the 21st Century Principal: Skills Dimensions.* Copyright © 2001, National Association of Secondary School Principals, www.principals.org. Reprinted with permission.

●   **Form 8.2**   ●

Intern Experiences Pre-Planning Worksheet

Select a specified number of activities for each ISLLC Standard by placing an X in the potential activities column. (Other parallel standards can be substituted for ISLLC standards.) All students must complete activity 62 prior to any other activity, because it covers basic ethical parameters within which all interns must conduct themselves.

Internship Activity	Potential Activities	Knowledge and Support Needed	Needed Mentor Assistance	Estimated Hours to Complete
ISLLC Standard I: The Vision of Learning				
1. Principal for a Day				
2. Analyze Testing Data to Improve Instruction				
3. Redefine the Mission/Vision of the School				
4. Generate a Weekly Bulletin/Staff Newsletter				
5. Analyze Data and Address Student Issues and Needs				
6. Organize and Facilitate Data Analysis and Plan with the Staff				
Other:				
A. Lead a textbook adoption process				
B. Conduct a projected building utilization study				
C. Marshall resources to obtain the vision				
D. Identify and address barriers to accomplishing the vision				
E. Assess programs and activities to asses alignment with the vision				
F. Serve on a strategic development and planning team				
G. Review discipline referrals for needed school improvements				
H. Review policies for student transportation				
I. Chair the school improvement team				
J. Address the school board on a key issue				
K. Chair a team that is writing a grant				
L. Conduct a needs assessment				
M. Serve on the district technology planning committee				
N.				
O.				
P.				

Internship Activity	Potential Activities	Knowledge and Support Needed	Needed Mentor Assistance	Estimated Hours to Complete
ISLLC Standard II: The Culture of Teaching and Learning				
7. Professional Development Preparation				
8. Create a New Program for Teachers, Staff, or Students				
9. Plan a School-Sanctioned Event				
10. Analyze Attendance Rate and Create an Improvement Plan				
11. Create Commendation Letters for Staff				
12. Attend a Professional Conference				
13. Suggest Effective Teaching Strategies				
14. Train Teachers to Use a Computer Program				
15. Plan a Classroom Lesson with a New Teacher				
16. Implement State Learning Standards in Non-State-Standard-Based Courses				
17. Supervise a Curriculum Revision				
18. Plan Educational Programs for Exceptional and Diverse Students				
19. Study District Policies and School's Implementation				
20. Colleague Sharing Session of Best Practices				
21. Collaborate to Identify and Assess "At-Risk" Students' Needs				
22. Attend a Superintendent's Administrative Meeting				
23. Prepare School Reports for School Board/ Central Office/State DOE				
24. Create Inclusive Learning Communities				
Other:				
A. Investigate root causes affecting student achievement level				
B. Construct an instructional needs assessment				
C. Write a grant proposal for external funding for new pedagogical approaches				
D. Improve student extracurricular activities				
E. Participate in an accreditation visitation				
F. Orient new staff members				
G. Develop a plan of supervision for regular and special school situations				
H. Arrange the opening and/or closing of school				
I. Serve as a summer school principal				

Internship Activity	Potential Activities	Knowledge and Support Needed	Needed Mentor Assistance	Estimated Hours to Complete
J. Design and implement study groups				
K. Coach beginning teachers				
L. Conduct walk-through and informal visitations				
M. Plan and develop enrichment activities				
N. Utilize multiple assessment to evaluate student learning				
O. Review distribution of grades				
P. Audit the effectiveness of professional development				
Q. Chair the school professional development committee				
R. Develop an instructional improvement plan				
S.				
T.				
U.				
ISLLC Standard III: The Management of Learning				
25. Prepare Accountability Reports for Local, State, and Federal Compliance				
26. Be Accountable for and Distribute Standardized Testing Materials				
27. Prepare a BIP and/or FBA for a Chronic Disciplined Student				
28. Decide the Fate of an Appeal for a Student				
29. Conduct a Faculty Meeting				
30. Conduct a Parent–Teacher Student Meeting				
31. Manage Textbook Ordering/Inventory				
32. Assist in Budget Preparation				
33. Control Inventory/Receiving of Supplies				
34. Input Financial Data/Balance Books				
35. Conduct a Safety Audit				
36. Oversee Building Maintenance				
37. Arrange Bus Transportation for Special School Event				
38. Master Schedule Preparation				
39. Input Discipline Information into Computer Program				
40. Complete a New Teacher Observation				
41. Prepare a Specialized School-Based Report				
42. Find Funding Sources for Individual Student Needs				

Internship Activity	Potential Activities	Knowledge and Support Needed	Needed Mentor Assistance	Estimated Hours to Complete
43. Support High Expectations for Student Behavior				
44. Develop Proactive Strategies for Intense Student Academic Support				
45. Order Material to Support Instructional Needs				
Other:				
A. Monitor attendance and truancy				
B. Use a computer administrative system and utilize computer software				
C. Design, develop, and implement a staff development program				
D. Coordinate and monitor a comprehensive building program				
E. Terminate a staff member				
F. Participate in the hiring/selection process				
G. Monitor cleanliness and operation of school plant				
H. Monitor student health and special needs				
I. Develop and present study of incidence and source of discipline problems				
J. Develop/update job descriptions				
K. Study the effectiveness of a computerized system for instruction and/or administration				
L. Develop a personal time management system				
M. Administer student recognition, graduation, or some other program				
N. Evaluate technology support				
O. Review and revise school handbook				
P. Evaluate the school nurse, counselors, or office personnel or some other non-teaching position				
Q. Inventory technology in use				
R. Investigate a filed grievance				
S. Work with teachers needing improvement				
T. Disaggregate student assessment data				
U. Discuss unwritten rules, procedures, and expectations				
V.				
W.				
X.				

Internship Activity	Potential Activities	Knowledge and Support Needed	Needed Mentor Assistance	Estimated Hours to Complete
ISLLC Standard IV: Relations with the Broader Community				
46. Develop a Program for School–Community Relations				
47. Work with PTSA for "Activity-a-Month" Event				
48. Involve Family, Business, and/or Community in School-Wide Project				
49. Prepare a News Release				
50. Oversee Volunteer Hours/Placements				
51. Demonstration and Articulation of School Context				
52. Contact or Assess Community Resources to Provide Family/Student Enrichment				
Other:				
A. Assess academic/career guidance and decision making				
B. Plan and conduct a school fund-raising event				
C. Present school improvement initiatives to the community				
D. Establish community, business, institutional, and/or civic partnerships				
E. Facilitate constructive conversations on student learning and achievement				
F. Write a bulletin and/or newsletter for parents and community				
G. Plan and conduct parent information meetings				
H. Survey community to elicit recommendations				
I. Answer telephones and meet guests in the front office				
J. Develop a proposal for improving parent involvement				
K. Develop a orientation videotape/ streaming video and/or typed brochure for parents and visitors				
L. Develop parenting skills course				
M. Present the school program to a community service organization				
N.				
O.				
P.				

Internship Activity	Potential Activities	Knowledge and Support Needed	Needed Mentor Assistance	Estimated Hours to Complete
ISLLC Standard V: Integrity, Fairness, and Ethics				
53. Analyze School in Terms of Ethics, Fairness, and Diversity				
54. Mobilize Staff to Create Positive Culture				
55. Approve Faculty/Staff Leave				
56. Conduct a Seminar in Sensitivity Training				
57. Oversee IEP/Causality Meeting				
58. Observe Staff Dismissal Procedures				
59. Revisit Leadership Platform for Administrative Action				
60. Assess Ethics for a School Leader				
61. Promote Equity, Fairness, and Respect for School/Community Members				
62. Clarify Principal's Role in Staff Rights and Confidentiality (recommended first)				
Other:				
A. Conduct appeals/expulsion hearing				
B. Validate legal and ethical use of technology				
C. Evaluate a planned holiday program for offensiveness and/or constitutionality				
D. Assess decisions being made on the basis of ethical standards				
E. Promote equality, fairness, and respect				
F. Defend the ethical basis and integrity of a difficult decision you made				
G. Examine the fairness of methods used to gain consensus				
H. Address the heritage and values of diversity in school programs				
I. Assess the ethical practices of students within the school				
J. Audit the ethical standards in your administrative platform, school handbook, or board policy manual				
K.				
L.				
M.				
ISLLC Standard VI: The Political, Economic, Legal, and Cultural Context				
63. Plan School-Wide Cultural/Educational Celebration				
64. Identify, Assess, and Address School Social Factors Affecting the School				

Internship Activity	Potential Activities	Knowledge and Support Needed	Needed Mentor Assistance	Estimated Hours to Complete
65. Evaluate School Programs for Political, Cultural, Economic, and Legal Correctness				
66. Influence Public Policy to Support Student Success				
67. Develop/Apply Anti-Harassment Policy and Strategies				
68. Study and Implement District-Wide Policies on School Issue				
69. Work to Influence Policy for Student Achievement				
Other:				
A. Actively participate in professional, political, or cultural organizations				
B. Submit an article for publication				
C. Actively participate in professional contract negotiations				
D. Support a defense team involved in a legal conflict				
E. Lead a student due process hearing				
F. Work with the judicial system in the resolution of a Juvenile Court case				
G. Review recent court cases and determine impact on programs and supervision				
H. Develop and/or manage a legal and contractual agreement				
I. Influence the legislation on policies that benefit students				
J. Shape a culture of high expectations				
K.				
L.				
M.				

chapter 9

Confusion, Conclusion, and Assessment

The internship is often loaded with unknown and/or unexpected situations and teaches the important quality of working through ambiguities—making connections, relating the unknown to the known, seeing patterns, perceiving commonalities, working through uncertainty and sometimes chaos, and understanding consequences. Rexford Brown of the Education Commission of the State tells us that the primary conditions of thoughtfulness are mystery, uncertainty, disagreement, questions, ambiguity, and curiosity. Margaret Wheatly (1992) suggests that chaos is a natural life-enhancing process. This chaos is often created when an individual feels overwhelmed by a situation. Chaos tends to be exactly what we fear in our professional lives. It is very uncomfortable when you are in a leadership role and you don't know or understand something. As a result, there is a natural tendency to retreat (flee), fight, or create some artificial sense of understanding and tighten control.

Leaders have a great fear of such situations that are confusing and complex. They don't want to be uncomfortable and uncertain, particularly when they are in a leadership role, so they try to make sense out of their confusion and falsely present the sense that they have the appropriate answers—they are very decisive. We see confusion as a sign of failure. Yet, we know that one person seldom has all the information, understanding, and knowledge to be able to develop the best solutions for the complex situations that we face as educational leaders.

Gentz and Murphy (2005) suggest that confusion is an asset for leaders (and interns) who are open to improving communication, challenging old assumptions and values, and developing more creative approaches to problem solving. But, this means giving up the controlling, decisive, take-charge demeanor. They state,

> No matter how capable or well prepared, managers regularly find themselves confronting bewildering events, perplexing information, or baffling situations that steal their time and hijack their carefully planned agendas. Disoriented by developments that just don't make sense and by challenges that don't yield to easy solutions, these managers become confused—sometimes even lost—and don't know what to do. (p. 359)

This is a particular challenge for interns, who are often confronted with new situations, with minimal information to go on and in an unfamiliar environment. The response is typically to deny a sense of confusion, keeping quiet about it, and to hide or cover it up. This often results in opting for action even when totally confused—not a good leadership practice. The belief of some interns is that "anything less than take-charge decision making shows abject weakness."

INTERN REPORT

My principal/mentor wanted to conduct a whole-staff orientation/development session and had a very tight and aggressive timetable in order to get it done. The planned date was less than two months away and the principal/mentor told me "I haven't much time to discuss the orientation/development program but I'm really not concerned because the program is pretty straightforward. You need to have the plans completed in the next two weeks." I did not see the program as straightforward and, in fact, was confused and thought to myself "'Not much time,' what an understatement!" I really needed much more clarification but did not want to appear stupid so I did not ask additional questions for clarification. Deciding to withhold my confusion in a followup discussion with the assistant principal, I stated, "It's too bad we didn't have more time with the principal, but I think we've got enough to begin planning." I later learned that the assistant principal was thinking, "It's good the intern is in charge and can make sense of this. It seems the intern is clear even though I am not."

When the principal saw my plan, she was very disappointed. The plan was far off the mark from what she wanted. I'm sure she was thinking, "Wow! I had more confidence in the intern than deserved. I won't make that mistake again." She really was confused on how the plan could be so off the mark and admonished me *and* the assistant principal, creating further strained relations between all of us. I realized that concealing my confusion had not resulted in greater respect, as I had hoped, but instead, with strained relationships and loss of respect from both my mentor and the assistant principal. Crucial weeks and many staff hours had been wasted and I was treated differently. In the future I will never try to conceal my confusion when I am responsible for a task. That is not good leadership.

Gentz and Murphy (2005) created the five-step Reflective Inquiry and Action (RIA) model to address situations where there is confusion, chaos, and/or complexity. This model provides an orderly way to move forward even when you are confused. The five steps are:

1. *Embrace your confusion.* Confusion is not weakness. In fact, it takes courage to acknowledge that you are confused and will have to search with others to discover solutions.
2. *Assert your need to make sense.* Unambiguously assert, with conviction and without apology, your sense of being confused and your need to engage in a process of shared learning to understand the situation and options prior to beginning planning and decision making.
3. *Structure the interaction.* You must quickly provide a structure to search for new bearings, conditions for others to enter into a joint inquiry, a timetable, and identification of the information the team will need to clarify and resolve the issues. It is very important in this stage to take control and make it clear you are in charge—and in charge of a process that will produce a clear outcome.
4. *Listen reflectively and learn.* It is essential that you listen reflectively to understand what was said with an open mind, allowing your basic assumptions to be challenged as you check the depth and accuracy of your thinking under conditions of joint inquiry.
5. *Openly process your effort to make sense.* Externalize your thinking process regarding the issues at hand by discussing what your understanding is out loud so others can understand how you are now thinking, thus avoiding premature closure. (Gentz & Murphy, 2005, pp. 362–365)

The RIA process asks us to think outside the box so we can better understand our confusion. This model is particularly helpful for interns who are thrown into situations for which they have had limited experience or historical knowledge and no network of reliable sources beyond their mentor and university supervisor (who undoubtedly have limited time available).

BENEFITS OF THE INTERNSHIP

The experience of learning how to handle the knowns and the unknowns in educational administration is the major benefit to completing the internship. You will learn more about leadership and how it works in action. You will gain much-needed experience and you will learn to handle all types of situations, even those that seem ambiguous and chaotic. Perhaps most important, the experience is a confidence builder, helping interns to develop supportive beliefs in their own capabilities to handle the job, even with a relatively heavy workload. As one student states, "It's a good chance to get your hands dirty and learn what you're made of." It also helps to recognize that there is still much to learn and wisdom to gain, before being able to best fulfill the duties of an administrator. However, there is the recognition that the foundation has been laid, and the wisdom will come through continued education and experience. The internship should give the intern the confidence to walk into an educational leadership position feeling prepared, regardless of what challenges may occur.

A major benefit of the internship is building the confidence needed to pursue a position in educational leadership. Browne-Ferrigno and Muth (2004, p. 475) found that:

> The students who assumed positions as quasi-administrators or interns appeared to be more confident and goal oriented toward assuming the principalship than their cohort peers who continued to work as teachers. Those engaged in administrative work linked content topics being studied in their coursework to real-world applications, and they often discussed how their mentors addressed problems of practice. They were able to contextualize what was being discussed and to link textbook learning to authentic practice.

There is no foolproof way to adequately prepare for an educational leadership position. In a 2001 study, these authors suggested, "that readiness to assume a principalship following completion of an administrator preparation program depends upon: (1) an individual's prior leadership opportunities and experiences within K–12 education; (2) encouragement from and mentoring by practicing principals; and (3) personal issues such as family responsibilities and career goals." Interns are much more likely to take state licensure exams, obtain state administrative and supervision certification (endorsement), and interview for positions in educational administration than are those who focused mainly on teaching during their administrative preparation programs (Browne-Ferrigno & Muth, 2001).

CONCLUDING THE INTERNSHIP

It is important that you complete any unfinished business and debrief existing administrators regarding the status and outcome of your work (especially unfinished work) and anything that needs to be solved, discussed, and/or dealt with prior to concluding your internship experience. This provides an excellent time to reflect on what you have learned, the ways you have grown, the skills you have developed, and what you have achieved. You might ask yourself questions like:

1. What important instructional improvement goals did I complete as part of my internship? What was my level of success in these efforts?
2. What hindered the implementation of goals?
3. What facilitated the accomplishment of goals?
4. What are the things I liked (a) most about my leadership? (b) least about my leadership?

The end of your internship presents an excellent opportunity to critically examine your leadership behavior. Brown and Irby (2001) proposed a four-stage structure for approaching this retrospection process. Their questions for the self-assessment process are excellent for completing a review of your internship experience and what was learned.

1. Did the action(s) taken result in the intended outcomes?
2. Were the actions effective and appropriate for the situation?
3. Were the actions consistent with the espoused Leadership Framework?
4. What impact did decisions or actions have on students, teachers, and/or the community?
5. Is this leadership behavior representative of district expectations?
6. Were options that were derived from multiple perspectives considered?
7. Were a variety of alternatives considered?
8. How might this situation have been approached in a different manner? And what types of results might be expected?
9. What action(s) might have resulted in a more positive impact?
10. How does this experience promote growth? (Brown & Irby, 2001, p. 32)

You will want to assess your personal level of proficiency in relation to the standards on which you based your internship experience (i.e., ISSLC, ELCC, state, or others). The entire process of retrospection serves as a catalyst for self-development, self-confidence, and ultimately, improved performance.

Retrospective Assessment

The conclusion of your internship provides an ideal opportunity to discuss your strengths and skills with your mentor and others as well as the areas in which you need to increase your abilities, and how best to achieve those improvements. You might begin by providing a brief overview of the experience and summarizing what you have learned and taken from the experience. You might integrate important learning experiences with theory, research, knowledge, and best practice. There might be discussion of how to apply what was learned to future leadership situations, with a focus on areas needing improvement.

You and your mentor may wish to include an assessment of successes and less than expected results in regards to your activities and experience. The Performance Standards for Prospective Principals form provided in Form 2.4, which is discussed under "Mentor's Assessment" on page 27, might be useful in this process. The qualities to be addressed are typically leadership behaviors; strategic planning; facilitating student learning; developing, implementing, and evaluating curriculum and instruction; supervising and evaluating faculty and support staff; relations with faculty and support staff; professional development; community relations; management; maintaining physical security of students, faculty, and support staff; and operations (see Chapter 2 section Supervisor Visits and Triad Meetings). This meeting should end on a very positive note, with a good sense of closure for all involved.

You are to be congratulated on your work efforts that meet or exceed performance standards and should be thanked for your achievements. But, equally important are the specific areas where you need to improve performance. This does not detract from your strong points; in fact, everyone has areas in need of improvement. You need to actively listen to comments relating to areas in which you failed to meet expectations, discuss why, and explore how you might improve in future situations. Actively participate in this discussion and agree to specific actions that might be taken to improve your leadership ability. See how you can build on your strengths and set methods and dates for achieving improvements and possibly a followup with your mentor and/or your university instructor. Let "Continuous Improvement" be a motto for yourself and your organization.

This is a good time for some introspective analysis. You might use this time to redefine yourself as a leader. Some questions you might ask include:

- Who am I as a leader and what do I stand for?
- What provides me the greatest/least satisfaction?
- What are my strengths/areas needing improvement as a leader?
- What have I accomplished and what still needs to be done?
- What do I now want to do differently in my professional life?
- What are some areas of professional growth on which I will concentrate?

As a side point, these are examples of the types of questions you may receive during your job interview (see Chapter 15). Make time to process your experience and refine your thinking about your future role in educational leadership. Think through how the social web of your relationships has changed and how it might change again. How have these relationships redefined you? How will this change? Have you met your goals? Do you now have more confidence as a leader? The questions are almost endless and only you can know what questions are important to you.

Ending on a Positive Note

Terminating the intern/mentor relationship is rewarding in knowing what you have achieved. However, it is also a little sad because your duties and relationships will change, at least until you are promoted to an administrative position. You will certainly want to discuss appropriate ways to make yourself visible for future promotion (see Chapter 15), how to be in line for career opportunities that may develop in educational administration, and if your mentor would be open to providing recommendations and if you can seek advice and council from him or her in the future. Because of your mentor's commitment, it is important that you recognize her or his willingness to have taken on these responsibilities and spend time with you. You will want to end by providing a thank you card or note and a small gift to your mentor, to express appreciation for the time and energy he or she has given to you.

A FINAL THOUGHT

Assessment can help in determining the effect and results of your efforts and help you to understand your progress toward becoming an effective leader.

However, if you can say that you received important insights from the internship that you can bring to the job, insight which will allow you to be much more effective, then the internship was a success. An intern stated, "I was given the opportunity to prove [to] myself that I could do it. This alone has allowed me to feel competent. I tested out my skills and got a professional feel about them. Now I have the key in my hand. I feel ready to move on. I am still not quite sure which doors this key will open, but I am sure that whatever I face I will deal with it as best as I know how" (Sweitizer & King, 2004, p. 279). Perhaps the acid test for the success of the internship does not occur until the intern gets her or his first job in educational administration.

Remember, "The journey is the reward." Putting your whole self into a task; engaging yourself in organizational improvement; encouraging your curiosity; developing passion, confidence, commitment, and camaraderie—these are the rewards.

It is, of course, important to recognize that professional development does not end with completing the internship, graduating from a leadership preparation program, receiving administrative licensure, or even obtaining an administrative position. These are only the beginning of the development process of becoming an outstanding educational leader. Further development, lifelong learning, occurs on the job and through professional associations; continuing education; attending national, state, and local conferences and workshops; reading books and journals; applying for grants; completing research and writing articles; and serving as a mentor.

You have earned your "rite of passage." Your journey is well underway and, hopefully, will continue throughout your life. Remember that satisfaction and happiness are not a destination; they must be found along the way of a successful career.

section **II**

THE IMPORTANT INTERNSHIP TOOLS

The first section provided a plan and placed the process of the internship in perspective; this second section develops a few of the major tools and techniques for completing the work of the internship.

Interns have typically read books and completed coursework that provide a comprehensive background for the types of skills that are needed in order to have a successful internship experience. These might be considered the foundational tools that interns will need to take on increasing responsibility during their internship experience. The chapters in this section represent short reviews of key issues that encapsulate some of what has been learned in coursework, research, and readings. These are some of the important issues that you will want to review as part of your internship.

This section of the text/handbook provides a condensed review of some models, techniques, tools, and procedures that can help you carry out your internship activities. These are the types of skills that are typically required in order to confront real problems of practice. People who lack vision, human relation skills, or even good intentions tend to become technicians; and yet, those who lack the technical skills to accomplish the work of leadership become dreamers. Both types are likely to fail as educational leaders.

The tools and technical skills discussed in this section offer some of today's best answers to the technical challenges of carrying out the responsibilities of educational leadership and implementing education improvement. These are processes that can be immediately implemented during internship experiences. This section is a review of the processes which were given a more expansive treatment during your administrative and supervision preparation program and/or readings and experiences.

This section could not review all of the processes, tools, and techniques of effective leadership, but it does cover a few of the more basic and essential skills that are often cited as necessary for success. The tools for focusing on problems of practice discussed in this section include time management and handling an in-box (Chapter 10); running a meeting, brainstorming, and building a consensus (Chapter 11); effective communication, effective listening, and recognizing outstanding performance (Chapter 12); and conflict management and managing crisis (Chapter 13). You may read this section prior to beginning internship activities, or it may become a reference when you realize that you need a quick review of certain skills needed to carry out the internship activities.

chapter 10

Managing Your Time as an Intern

Time management is often a problem that plagues interns. There is never enough time in the day to do all that is expected. First of all, due to inexperience, it will usually take an intern longer to perform most administrative tasks than it would a seasoned administrator. Obviously, time in the position is the only remedy for inexperience and the only way to become accustomed to the responsibilities. There are, however, some general suggestions which will help interns to better use their time.

An intern's day, like that of a principal, often consists of many tasks and encounters of short duration. Thus, an intern might face as many as fifteen to twenty encounters per hour. To handle this type of workload, interns must learn to analyze problems and identify solutions quickly, to think on their feet, and to shift gears often. Obviously, organization, time management, and coping skills become quite important if you are to keep up with the pace and the fragmentation (bits and pieces of information that do not come in all at once). The constant interruptions and obstacles, if you are not careful, can consume too much of the day (see www. naesp.org for more information for aspiring principals.)

TIME SAVERS

Most everyone expects to put in extra hours sometime. However, are you working late or longer than expected almost every day of the week? If your working day is consistently too short, then time management skills may help. Of course, some of the big time-robbers are procrastination and preoccupation, which create a lack of focus. Also, there may be obvious improvements, such as increasing your reading and typing speed. Here are some suggestions from time management experts (Jones, 1993; Laken, 1973; Mackenzie, 1990; Whipp, Adams, & Sabelis, 2002) to help you to gain control of your life and time:

1. *The nature of time.* Is time your ally or enemy? Are you always wishing you had more time? Time is the stuff that life is made of. When you make time your friend and learn to relate to it properly, you will learn to master your life. Remember that time stays, we go. You cannot save time. Each of us has been given exactly twenty-four hours a day. Time cannot be expanded or banked for later use, only used more wisely. It is irreversible and irreplaceable. This is not to suggest that you be preoccupied with time, but you should want to use it wisely. For example, don't be a perfectionist on an insignificant task. Make time your friend.

2. *Organizing and setting priorities.* Do not allow the urgent to take priority over the important. Determine the importance of each of your tasks and schedule

work in terms of priorities. You will want to start with some kind of a daily planner that includes the most current list of your work tasks. There is a fine line between over and under planning, which you must find for yourself. However, you will be much less efficient, or effective, for that matter, without a plan. You often cannot do everything there is to do; therefore, you need to establish priorities.

There is a simple system in which you make a list of things that require your attention and assign A, B, and C priorities along with estimated time to complete the A and B tasks. In this system, A = high importance (value), B = medium importance, and C = low importance or priority. Make a daily To Do list. Schedule the A items first (prioritize the A items), the B items second, and put the C items off to the end of the month. If no one is looking for C items by the end of the month, eliminate C items and refocus on A items. Do your priority or A items early in the day or when you have the most energy.

3. *Dealing with time wasters.* A time waster is anything that interferes with you achieving your most important objectives, your A items. Time wasters can include meetings, ineffective delegation, ineffective communication, lack of planning, confusion, shifting priorities, unclear objectives, disorganization, and lack of courage. Some ways to avoid time wasters are:
   a. Set priorities for the day each morning (see No. 2, organizing and setting priorities, above).
   b. Save up trivial matters for only one day a month.
   c. Delegate work to others and follow up.
   d. Generate as little paper work as possible.
   e. After initial grouping and prioritizing, handle paper only once (if you pick it up, don't put it down until it has been completed. See No. 4, below).
   f. Don't focus on things you have no control over.
   g. Avoid regret, guilt, second-guessing, and behaviors that sap energy.
   h. Don't do things that are very unimportant or unproductive.
   i. Set deadlines.
   j. Be organized and have a good filing system so you can find things quickly.

4. *Handling your in-box.* You will experience a hail of faxes, e-mails, voice mail, letters, memos, notes, reports, documents, cell phone messages, walkie-talkie messages, subpoenas, human interactions, and many, many more. You can end up as road kill on the information highway. Here is a process for handling the information overload:
   a. *Require written (not verbal) requests.* To enable your in-box processing to be effective and efficient, all messages must be written—e-mail or paper.
   b. *Process periodically.* Set aside one or two times a day to process all messages.
   c. *Group messages.* Go through your messages the first time very quickly to group (place in file) or paper clip messages that are related.
   d. *Prioritize messages.* Go through the groups (or files) to prioritize messages as to their importance (ABC priority).
   e. *Delegate.* Determine which messages you must respond to and assign all others to subordinates.
   f. *Record.* Record all major groups, who they were assigned to, a date by which the individual will get documentation back on how they were handled, and their present status.
   g. *Follow up.* Review records periodically to ensure that all grouped messages have been dealt with appropriately and they have come to a logical and hopefully positive conclusion. Determine if any followup is needed, docu-

ment it, and, if needed, go back to the delegate stage and loop through again.

   h. *Discard.* Throw away or place messages in a historical file once they have been dealt with.

5. *Replying to messages.* Set aside a specific time each day to get back to people. Make sure you protect this time. There is some danger in responding in writing; however, some messages may not be able to be handled in any other way, particularly e-mail. Just remember that whatever you write or e-mail back to a staff member or parent can very easily be made available to the rest of the world. Anything that is put in writing to a single person or group of persons, must be written as if it was going out to the world. This "publishing for the world" concern is nowhere near as great when you reply by phone or meet with the person. There is, of course, a trade-off of efficiency in all of this.

MANAGING INTERRUPTIONS

Interruptions often keep you from getting your own work done. They include telephone/e-mail interruptions, drop-in visitors, crises, and unexpected meetings or events. Voice mail, cell phones, and the internet have made this more complex, with 24-hour access. Remember, more people will want some of your time than you will have available. That means, whether you like it or not, you will be setting priorities on how you direct your time. You want to limit interruptions, but you don't want people to go away without a response. Some ways to reduce the length of time involved during an interruption include:

   a. Set a time limit and stick to it ("I have five minutes.")
   b. Stay standing with drop-ins, and have material on spare seats
   c. Meet in the other person's office ("I'll drop-by later.")
   d. Avoid small talk and explain that you are very busy
   e. Get people to the point, don't interrupt, don't bring up side points, and give undivided attention
   f. Tell them with whom they might discuss the issue and to get back to you on the status and when completed
   g. Ask them to put it all in writing and get back to you
   h. Encourage weekly or morning staff meetings (or newsletters) to keep everyone current
   i. Be less accessible and/or have a secretary screen calls/e-mails/visitors, control interruptions, prioritize and delegate inquiries
   j. Relinquish control and allow staff to be responsive
   k. Don't use voice machines; have a secretary write your messages from telephone conversations
   l. Have standard response forms that can be easily modified to reply to e-mails, letters, memos, and so on

Remember, greater control of your time means greater freedom. Find ideas that work best for you. Most of all, be an organization with a focus on vision and mission and not one that focuses on problem solving.

chapter 11

Conducting Effective Meetings

Most interns will be involved in chairing a meeting. Meetings help to define the group, determine needs, encourage reflection, develop collegiality, exchange information, and facilitate growth and effective decision making. Meetings help to build a solid base for a commitment to decisions made and the work that will need to be completed to implement those decisions. Committee members typically spread knowledge quickly and efficiently throughout the organization so plans can be implemented. This occurs through informal discussion with non-team members, training and information-sharing sessions, visits to observe relevant innovative practices, and written forms of followup.

The leaders of effective committee meetings begin by ensuring that all important groups related to the work are represented and the committee members are well prepared to take on the responsibility of committee membership. Committee members must have time for preparing, participating, reflecting, learning, thinking about the work, and deciding on needed actions. Members must understand their authority before being involved in discussion and decision making. Concerns like frequency, composition, motivation, decision process, authority, and acceptable areas of work responsibility should be addressed prior to committee formation. There should be a clear purpose for all meetings.

THE AGENDA

An agenda should always be set and distributed prior to the meeting. The agenda is very important and can speed and clarify the meeting. Papers that need to be discussed should be provided prior to the meeting. The agenda will help ensure that those attending the meeting will be well prepared when they come to the meeting.

The agenda should not include more items than the group can consider in the time allotted. The meeting should not cover items that are more easily and effectively communicated in a memo or e-mail. Items requiring urgent attention should be discussed before those that can be decided over a longer period of time. Sufficient information should be provided to consider all agenda items, especially the most important ones. It is a good idea to include the starting and finishing time on the agenda.

The purpose of the meeting helps to determine the agenda. It is useful to designate each agenda item as "for information," "for discussion," or "for decision" so that people at the meeting know what they are expected to accomplish during the meeting. To develop a good agenda, the chair must keep his or her finger on the pulse of the organization, including in the agenda only items that are important, and ones the group is prepared to discuss. This requires estimating the length of time needed for each item and allotting sufficient time. The agenda should focus on the most pressing concerns of the group and organization. The agenda items typically present themselves in relation to the work that is to be accomplished. What decisions need to be made and implemented? What information is needed by the group in order to conduct their work? What new programs or responsibilities have been assigned to the group? How has the vision for the group shifted? What information does the group feel that they need to discuss? What do you need help with in regard to the goals of the group? What authority does the group have?

MEETING FACILITATION

The chairperson should establish mutual trust, foster mutual respect and build a positive atmosphere, ensure that the group maintains direction and moves expediently toward goals, and provide opportunities for all members to participate and contribute. The chairperson should make it clear where the meeting should try to get to by the end. During the meeting the chairperson or facilitator fulfills *task* functions, which carry forward the purpose of the meeting, and *maintenance* functions, which help group members to participate and develop effective work relationships. The person in charge of the meeting stimulates discussion, maintains focus, and helps the group come to closure. The leader should keep his or her interventions and comments very brief.

The effectiveness of the team will be determined by the quality of information brought out and the judgments and decisions made based on this information. Success can best occur when the facilitator keeps meetings on track and eliminates unnecessary disruptions. Meetings should not last much longer than two hours. Give members an opportunity for listening, sharing, thinking, formulating ideas, analyzing information, and tying facts together. Close discussion when it becomes clear that more information is required, other people should be at the meeting, members need more time than is available, or, best of all, a decision has been reached.

HOW TO CONDUCT AN EFFECTIVE MEETING

The facilitator must have the ability to manage the meeting effectively. Some of these responsibilities are listed below. Check off those that you practice as a team leader.

1. ____ Start meeting on time
2. ____ Start with and stick to the agenda
3. ____ Relieve tensions and distractions
4. ____ Keep discussion relevant to the objectives of the meeting
5. ____ Draw out ideas and feelings related to purposes
6. ____ Reduce or eliminate wandering from the agenda and "hidden agenda" ploys
7. ____ Routinize problem scanning and solution generation
8 ____ Assure accurate understanding of each other's point of view
9. ____ Summarize progress toward objectives frequently
10. ____ Follow the energy. (If a person has strong feeling, knowledge, or background about the issue under discussion, allow him or her to help energize the committee.)

11. ____ Reach decisions by consensus
12. ____ Provide frequent, sincere reinforcement and unambiguous constructive feedback
13. ____ Don't allow the group to avoid decision making or to jump too quickly to a decision without adequate information
14. ____ Assign an alternating "process observer" to look at specific aspects of the meeting and report to the group at the end of each meeting (no discussion of process observer report allowed)
15. ____ Use audiovisuals and technology to complement oral communication
16. ____ Maintain control and ensure all attendees participate
17. ____ Recognize when agreement has been reached and terminate discussion on that issue
18. ____ Close on a note of achievement
19. ____ End meeting on time and summarize conclusions
20. ____ Follow up on action to be taken by you and others
21. ____ Periodically evaluate meetings

Following the meeting, concise minutes should be distributed, including the date, time, and place of the next meeting. In the minutes, identify persons who have made action commitments during the meeting. Follow up on all decisions and action commitments, ensuring that progress is reported and decisions are executed. Remove members who no longer provide relevance to the issues being discussed, and eliminate committees that have accomplished their intended purpose and are no longer needed.

Brainstorming Ideas

Brainstorming can provide a quick and easy way to gather ideas that exist among the members of a committee. Brainstorming provides a positive, nonthreatening way to generate a lot of creative ideas related to an important issue, question, problem, direction, and so forth. It usually develops a broad range of alternative solutions or ideas to be considered by the committee in relation to an actual area of responsibility. The committee is asked to allow a free flow of ideas related to an important need with the purpose of using the ideas to develop a vision, understanding, or possible solution related to work achievement.

An example of typical steps in brainstorming (/I/D/E/A/, 1991) are:

1. Committee chair explains purpose of brainstorming and its use.
2. Individual presents problem or question.
   a. Committee listens to a participant describe a problem, opportunity, or challenge related to an agenda item.
   b. The description of the opportunity should include the essential elements of the situation—those elements which would need to be considered in a solution.
   c. Close the discussion by writing and publishing the question. A more focused request will likely bring forth helpful ideas.
   d. After the question has been presented, members ask clarifying questions to ensure that everyone understands the situation and the problems. Avoid making any suggestions during this clarification period.
3. Revisit and perhaps rewrite the question, if the problem presenter or group has changed what he or she wants to know.
4. Facilitator announces that the committee will have time to generate as many potential ideas for the stated question as possible (they may be asked to post them in plain sight of all group members).

5. Facilitator reviews rules of brainstorming:
   a. No criticism allowed, no explanation needed
   b. Be free wheeling, anything goes
   c. Seek combinations and improvements
   d. Seek quantity over quality
   e. Rotate around each individual in the group in order
   f. On each rotation, the participants offer one (1) idea or says "pass"
   g. All ideas are accepted without judgment or comment
   h. Piggyback off other ideas
   i. Relax and have fun
6. Facilitator asks groups to select one or two recorders, depending on the activity.
   a. Recorders should make contributions.
   b. Individuals are responsible to see their own contributions get recorded in plain view of the participants.
   The group brainstorms many creative responses to the question. Either put a time limit on brainstorming or allow the problem presenter(s) to stop the brainstorming when they have enough suggestions by thanking the group.
7. Ask the problem presenter or the committee if any further explanation of any of the suggestions is needed. Go through each suggestion to make sure it is clear.
8. The recorded suggestions are used by the committee to finalize discussion and make a decision.
9. Those responsible report back to the group on the level of success achieved related to the brainstormed decision.

Building Consensus

Consensus, first of all, means a general agreement,"the judgment arrived at by most of those concerned," and "group solidarity in sentiment and belief." Research suggests that consensus is an effective way of arriving at group decisions and is an integral part of school improvement (Golary, 1992). There have been many benefits associated with consensus decision making (Golary & Golary, 1995; McEwan, 1997; Peterson-del Mar, 1994).

The original Latin stem *sentiere* means *feel* and its prefix *con-* means *together*. Consensus, then is an affirmation of community. Consensus cannot be forced, any more than fellowship can be. It is important, then, that a committee becomes a team or a fellowship or a community before they attempt to arrive at consensus.

How does a group arrive at consensus? The group is presented with a problem and asked to arrive at a solution to which each group member can agree; right from the start the group members assume that they will have differences of opinion. Disagreement is taken for granted but not emphasized.

According to the Institute for the Development of Educational Activities (1991), each person's point of view is sought and the meaning of each item they value is listened to, with an emphasis on finding commonly held beliefs and values. There is a sense that once the person's interests, meaning, and point of view are truly understood, differences in positions will diminish or even disappear. If the group does not rush into solutions, but allows time to bring out relevant issues, to analyze and discuss relevant issues with respect for each other's views, then a consensus can usually be arrived at that people understand and can commit to. This is best achieved when the individuals start by presenting their interests and values regarding the decision and steer clear of positions and solutions until each person's interests are well understood (Fisher & Ury, 1981).

The remaining ideas are considered, and arguments pro and con are given. During this process some group members may change their minds, bringing the group closer to consensus. Another possibility is that group members may suggest modifications of an idea that will satisfy those who did not approve of the idea in its original form.

The group works within itself to agree on the two or three best (most workable, under the circumstances) solutions.

It is not necessary or advisable to take a vote regarding consensus. Most often the group can sense when a consensus has been reached. When this has occurred, the committee chair can test to see if everyone appears in agreement that a consensus has formed and that the group can move on to the next agenda item.

Consensus is not always the appropriate process for decision making. There are some situations in which a group may be providing information to an individual who makes the decision because that individual is accountable for its consequences and/or because that individual has data which cannot be shared with the group.

Nonfunctional Group Behaviors

An important aspect of a meeting is ensuring that everyone has a voice in decisions made at the meeting. This means that no one dominates the meeting and that attendees listen attentively. There are a number of nonfunctional group behaviors that can occur during committee meetings. The following are a few nonfunctional behaviors and how they might be handled:

1. *Domination.* Explain that the committee has to move on, ask direct questions to others, do not call on the dominant person(s), have a private chat, assign a project, pick out a comment and redirect as a question to someone else, send dominant member on an errand, or add strong new person to the group.
2. *Argumentative.* Question the person to get his or her ideas, ask others questions, point out quibbling is impeding progress, do not allow any criticism or debate during a period of time (invoke brainstorming rules).
3. *Socializing.* Invite the person to share with everyone, stop talking and look at the individual, speak more loudly, or more rapidly. Talk to the individuals about this after the meeting.
4. *Silence.* Ask questions in an area the person can speak with conviction, call on those with relevant experience, clarify the objective, refer questions to the group, silence on your part, be prepared to offer facts and ideas for consideration, plan something active, and reward good contributions with positive comments.
5. *Hot-potato subjects.* Explain not pertinent to the meeting objectives, remain neutral, promise not to take action but report to management, insist on objective consideration. Ask group if they want to continue on controversial subject.
6. *Group think.* Encourage taking issue with statements, probe opinions, silently record ideas, use Delphi technique or nominal group process (Cunningham, 1982), keep all statements anonymous, periodically change membership, invite outside experts, don't allow people to support their own ideas.
7. *Confrontations.* Redirect the question to the group, present facts and reasons, generate reasonable alternatives, table issue and work out later, use humor, state opposing views, clarify objective. Ask members of the group for support.
8. *Misdirected topic.* Put the topic at the end of meeting or for next meeting, interrupt and bring back to agenda, reorient and elaborate on objectives.

Other common group dynamic problems are individuals' unwillingness to abandon their publicly expressed points of view; the persuasive power of articulate, loud, and emotional individuals; and the band-wagon effect of a majority opinion. Many of these behaviors can be reduced by using a process observer who reports on nonfunctional group behaviors. The process observer is asked by the group to watch for certain types of behaviors during the meeting and to report back to the group about these behaviors at the end of the meeting. No comments are allowed on the process observer's report; the group simply listens and reflects individually on the information presented.

The most significant factors that make meetings nonproductive are:

- Lack of control by leader
- Lack of preparation by leader
- Lack of preparation by participants
- Objectives, topics, and agenda not clearly communicated
- Poor attitude of participants
- The wrong participants
- Improper notice to participants
- Little interest or enthusiasm
- Committee recommendations are ignored
- Lack of follow through and/or no action taken
- Hidden agendas

Lots of important work is completed through committee action, so being able to run an effective meeting is quite important for an intern. Make sure you are an effective committee chairperson.

chapter 12

Achieving, Recognizing, and Presenting Work

There are many more abilities and skills required to be an effective intern and leader than can be presented in this text/handbook. Perhaps none, however, are more important than simply accomplishing the work, motivating staff (via recognition), and making formal presentations to others. There have been many books written on these topics, and they are also a part of many administrative preparation programs, but these topics are still considered worthy of a brief refresher for those involved in an internship. What follows is only the tip of the iceberg of some very important subjects. These key challenges, if not handled properly, can be significant problems for interns. The following suggestions are offered to stimulate thinking and discussion. Each of these topics will be refined and revised throughout a lifetime of practice, but one must begin with models or paradigms for effective practice.

GETTING WORK ACCOMPLISHED

As you carry out intern job responsibilities, people must come first and the innovation or improvement second. Improvement and implementation is a developmental process. For progress to occur, successful change must be planned and a critical mass of support must be developed. Individuals involved in the improvement go through stages and have different requirements, needs, purposes, and strategies at each stage.

The first step in any change process is to understand the nature, needs, strengths, and limitations of the staff members who will be responsible for developing the improvement or innovation and those who will be responsible for its implementation and operation. The important point is the readiness of the staff to be able to take on the responsibilities of the change or improvement effort. The second step is to ensure that the necessary resources (including time) and support are available to see the project through to fruition. Understand before you get started that reform and improvement are very difficult and most likely will meet resistance at a number of different points along the way. Therefore, they are very time consuming and will challenge your interpersonal skills.

The process of change requires that people go through various stages in the innovation and implementation process, requiring different activities and skills at each stage. Table 12.1 presents a continuous improvement model, which is a good starting point for approaching challenges related to improvements within your organization (Cunningham & Cordeiro, 2006). This is a timeline—from what needs to be done in early stages of the improvement and innovation process, through many stages in the middle, all the way to the innovation being widely implemented and successful.

TABLE 12.1 **Steps for Success in Approaching Needed Improvements**

Note: Gathering and dispersing information is an essential element for each of the steps discussed below.

ACTIONS REQUIRED	STEPS TO SUCCESSFUL INNOVATION AND PROBLEM SOLVING	TYPICAL BEHAVIOR
I. Staff need to recognize and develop a better understanding of needs.	Awareness	Build understanding of the challenges to be faced and open up new possibilities.
II. Concerned parties will want to increase knowledge about the situation and/or possibilities.	Gathering/seeking information	Develop the needed knowledge base to begin the planning/renewal process. (This step has to be revisited throughout the effort.)
III. Concerned parties are ready to begin looking at options, approaches, and innovations.	Orientation/deliberation	Seek out information and learn more about the possible innovations and reforms.
IV. Concerned parties need to begin pruning the options and developing a solution set.	Narrowing options/assessment	Develop criteria, assess options and directions to be taken and develop a universe of acceptable alternatives and approaches.
V. Appropriate parties need to gain political support for possible final approaches or solutions.	Political support	Assess and work within the power structure to build required support and political allies to help ensure the success of the innovation finally selected. (This step has to be revisited throughout the effort.)
VI. Decision team(s) needs to make a commitment to one of the options within the possible solution set.	Decision/ implementation planning	Narrow the options to the most desirable and supportable option through consensus. Initial development of an implementation plan.
VII. Provide the needed effort to ensure that all needed people are adequately aligned toward the renewal effort that was selected.	Building shared values and goals	Information is provided to a wide audience so that all involved understand the innovation and realize how it will affect them. The goals, values, and mission are internalized within the organizational culture.
VIII. Ensure that people have the needed skills to successfully complete the innovation.	Development	The organizational staff and others are readied and prepared for successful implementation of the innovation. This requires the development of staff and others.
IX. Ensure that the innovation becomes part of the organization as it is implemented.	Implementation and integration	The innovation and renewal effort is implemented and obstacles and problems begin to emerge. Efforts are made to make needed modifications and to begin integrating the innovation into the organizational culture and to ensure that it works effectively.
X. Work to ensure that the innovation becomes effective and is a systemic part of the organization because it has been fully embraced.	Refinement, coordination, and expanding support	Establish a widespread pattern of use and coordinate the efforts in using the innovation and in making and sharing information regarding performance and refinements. Groups are regularly discussing the innovation as it becomes a part of routine procedure.
XI. Collect needed data to determine the effectiveness of the newly implemented innovation.	Evaluation/reflection	Collect and analyze data to make needed adjustment and to ensure and increase the effectiveness of the innovation. Share and celebrate successes and quickly respond to, learn from, and make needed adjustments regarding failures. (This step occurs from Step IX through Step XII.)
XII. Address new needs that are not being considered in the present operation of the organization.	Refocusing and renewal	Users start to become aware of new problems, new needs, and new opportunities within the very dynamic context in which they operate. The process begins anew.

Source: Based on a model for adopting educational innovation from the Research and Development Department for Teacher Education at the University of Texas at Austin. From Cunningham and Cordeiro, *Educational Leadership: A Problem-Based Approach.* Published by Allyn and Bacon, Boston, MA. Copyright © 2006 by Pearson Education. Reprinted by permission of the publisher.

An element essential to the success of any innovation is to have political support through all phases of the project. You as an intern should not begin a project until you have the political support of those in power and, as you move along, the staff that will be needed to implement the program, as well as the students, parents, and community. You will need political support until you have generated the needed critical mass of supporters who will not allow the idea to die. Therefore, within the first two or three stages of planning you will need time to allow the political support for the initiatives to build. Supporters must understand why the innovation is important to the community, the students, the teachers, and to them personally. If you cannot get the needed political support, you probably should not continue with your efforts.

Recognizing the Work Effort

Staff will need to be recognized for their efforts, throughout the entire process. Recognition is a form of acknowledgment and reward for work well done. Recognition motivates or drives a person to want to excel in his or her work. Recognition is an extrinsic motivation because it is external to the individual.

By far, the most important form of motivation is intrinsic motivation, which comes from within a person. Individuals who direct their own lives gain personal satisfaction from achieving their goals, developing a sense of vital self-reliance. They have a strong sense of responsibility for themselves and they are satisfied with their own achievements. They are intrinsically motivated. However, extrinsic rewards and recognition still serve an important purpose.

Because we are social creatures, we want to be recognized and appreciated by others, especially when we make contributions to them. Recognition is a form of appropriate social and ethical behavior. Recognition is a way of expressing appreciation for something someone has done for you, your group, or the organization. Recognition can be as simple as a spontaneous gesture of sincere thanks or it can be as complex as a structured program of reward and recognition. It means the most to the individual in an organization when it is leader-initiated and based on the individual's performance. It can be as simple as, "I saw what you did, I appreciate it, it's important, and it results in . . . ."

One of the methods of providing immediate recognition for a job well done is by management-by-walking-around (MBWA). When you see good work being done, thank the individuals for their outstanding efforts and the quality of their work. Just take time to discuss the work with staff members. Involve employees in decisions and help them to feel a sense of ownership for their work. Share all positive reports and news about the success of the organization's or individual's achievement within the organization. Take the time to make others aware of significant achievements. Make work as fun as possible and not routine. Celebrate successes! Take time to talk and listen to employees.

Bob Nelson (2000) has come up with a list of no-cost recognitions. He suggests that leaders make time for the one employee incentive that will never break the company budget: timely, honest praise of workers who do well. Here are some examples of no-cost recognition (Nelson, 2000):

No-Cost Recognition
- Personal thanks
- Thank you notes
- E-mail praise
- Voice mail praise
- Public praise
- Pass around trophy

- Time with manager, president
- Employee parking space
- Read positive letters from customers at staff meetings
- Referenced in company newsletters
- Featured in community newspaper
- Wall of fame—photos of achievers
- Certificate of appreciation
- Balloons and computer banners
- Free lunch for employee
- Create an award (Golden star, excellence in achievement, meritorious contributions, etc.)
- Time off (extra break, long lunch, three-day weekend, etc.)
- Pass to get rid of least favorable work ("dump a dog" program)
- Victory celebration
- Featured in company ads

It is very important to be honestly appreciative of hard work and to let the employee know that his or her work is important and recognized and appreciated by you as an intern. The point is that great leaders recognize their staff in many ways and it is important that you as an intern give thought to how you will motivate and recognize staff.

MAKING FORMAL PRESENTATIONS

Another important part of recognizing is communicating the results of work achieved to various audiences. Everyone wants the light they have generated to shine. School leaders are expected to communicate successes to members of the school community and also with the community at large. Your communication and/or presentation should begin with an analysis of your audience in relation to their knowledge of the subject and their needs. You do not want to talk either above or beneath your audience and you want to focus on what they need to know. To be credible, you must be the master of your topic and know your stuff. You need to identify your presentation style so you have powerful presentation tactics. You might select a razzle-dazzler style (humorous, unconventional, surprising, very active); a good buddy style (include audience, develop rapport, identify with audience, use sentimentality); just-the-facts style (present statistics, research, experts, latest theory, best practice); high drama style (theatrical, dramatic, expressive, engaged); and so on. What style are you most comfortable with?

Think through how your particular body language and gestures influence your audience, whether by distracting or adding emphasis. Use your voice to punctuate your remarks. Make and use eye contact with your audience. Prepare and test all communication technology that you will use in your presentation. Practice your presentation prior to making an important speech. Finally, don't let yourself or your audience be distracted by external "noise" (bad chairs, noisy room, heat, bad acoustics) or internal noise (hunger, headache, daydreams, a family problem). Here are some suggestions for effective communication. Check the ones you typically practice.

1. _____ Gear your message to the audience's or individual's desire and need to know
2. _____ Be committed to your subject
3. _____ Have a clear sense of purpose
4. _____ Develop an appropriate structure and design for your presentation (specific purpose; attention grabbing introduction; body with main points, sub-points, and evidence; and conclusion)
5. _____ Check for ethical considerations (in good taste, be true to yourself)

6. _____ Bring your presentation to life through an energetic delivery
7. _____ Use media and visual aids
8. _____ Involve the audience
9. _____ Use skillful language
10. _____ Use vividness and emphasis to make a point
11. _____ Be precise (brief, clear, concise)
12. _____ Be credible (accurate, believable, realistic)
13. _____ Be fresh and interesting
14. _____ Use illustrations (examples, stories, testimonials)
15. _____ Sum up what you said
16. _____ Practice, practice, and do it
17. _____ Avoid habitual interjections such as (OK or ah).
18. _____ Look at people you are talking to
19. _____ Use good posture and facial expressions
20. _____ Get feedback on your presentation

Have a great story to tell and bring it to life. Hard stuff (numbers) get attention, but it is the soft stuff (emotion, passion, enthusiasm) that sells. Create the buzz and get the vibes going.

Form 12.1 presents an instrument that can be used to evaluate presentation skills. Of course, how we say things is very important to the mood created and the acceptance of our ideas.

Effective Listening

Part of an effective presentation is the ability to listen to and understand comments from your audience. Listening is an intellectual and emotional process that searches for meaning and understanding in a message. Here are some suggestions on how you might improve your listening skills. Check the ones you typically practice.

1. _____ Empathize with the other person
2. _____ Look at the other person
3. _____ Control your desire to mentally argue
4. _____ Avoid making assumptions
5. _____ Avoid hasty judgments
6. _____ Recognize your own prejudices
7. _____ Cut through distractions
8. _____ Stop talking
9. _____ Get the main points
10. _____ Discriminate between relevancies and irrelevancies
11. _____ Organize what was being said by main points
12. _____ Ask questions for clarification when confused
13. _____ Restate to test for understanding and interpretation
14. _____ Summarize key points mentally
15. _____ Follow up on what was said that is relevant to you

A good listener listens, reviews, and predicts—all of which means his or her mind is totally involved with the subject and the comments being made. The person thinks ahead, weighs verbal evidence, reviews periodically, and listens between the lines. The person has trained and disciplined him- or herself to concentrate and hear with understanding.

These important skills—planning, recognizing, and communicating—are essential to an effective internship experience. You will want to take this opportunity to practice these and other skills that are so important to effective administration. Take on a project that will require joint planning as part of your internship. Make a formal presentation to a group. Recognize staff for what they do. These are excellent habits to practice on a regular basis.

•   **Form 12.1**   •

Evaluating Intern Communication Skills

Please circle the choice that best describes your perceptions of the presentation.

Presenter's Name _____ Date _____

Title of Presentation _____ Time _____

	Rudimentary	Developing	Proficient	Accomplished
Content supporting the topic was original, unique.	1	2	3	4
Speaker seemed knowledgeable on the topic.	1	2	3	4
Speaker supported key ideas with good material.	1	2	3	4
Speaker used appropriate humor, philosophy, prose, theory, research, and/or practice to add interest and variety.	1	2	3	4
Speaker believed in the subject.	1	2	3	4
Introduction gained attention.	1	2	3	4
Thesis was stated in the introduction.	1	2	3	4
Main points were clearly stated.	1	2	3	4
Conclusion was a good summary and effective.	1	2	3	4
Wording was clear.	1	2	3	4
Transitions were used effectively.	1	2	3	4
Speaker maintained a spontaneous delivery.	1	2	3	4
Speaker maintained good eye contact.	1	2	3	4
Visual aids and media were used appropriately.	1	2	3	4
Speaker was involved/enthusiastic.	1	2	3	4
There was vocal variety and emphasis, projection and good tone, volume, and speed.	1	2	3	4
Nonverbal communication was effective/appropriate.	1	2	3	4
Posture and dress were appropriate.	1	2	3	4
Speaker appeared at ease and confident.	1	2	3	4
Handout was useful.	1	2	3	4

Major Strengths _____

_____

_____

Major Area Needing Work _____

_____

_____

_____

Mentor's Signature   **Date**

chapter 13

Conflict and Crisis Management

One of the areas that often gives interns problems is the ability to deal with conflict. They are very concerned about conflict and see it as a danger to their professional well being. Yet, conflict and disagreement are inevitably part of organizational life (see Chapter 9). The ability to openly recognize conflict and seek to resolve it through discussion and understanding is critical to your success as an intern. The approach is not to eliminate conflict, which probably is impossible, but to view it as essentially healthy—exciting, strengthening, stimulating, creative, and clarifying. Conflict can provide a chance for new ideas to occur if conditions are right. In this way, conflict is beneficial, developmental, communicative, and courageous. Perhaps the Chinese language best expresses the true nature of conflict. The written character for conflict in Chinese is made up of two equal symbols: one stands for danger and the other stands for opportunity. The ability to handle conflicts successfully is probably one of the most important skills of any leader, intern, or team facilitator. Interns often waste a lot of energy trying to eliminate conflict when it should be used for making the organization more productive.

Conflict occurs because different people have different viewpoints. The blending of viewpoints has proven to result in more effective decisions than those made by a single leader (Blake & Mouton, 1978; Collins, 2001; Halpin, 1966; Leithwood & Duke, 1999; Likert, 1967; and Peters and Waterman, 1982). The challenge is to figure out ways to effectively identify and resolve conflicting points of view without damaging the working relationships of those within the organization—without retaliation and in-fighting. The idea is to use all needed information and points of view in order to make optimal decisions. As Covey (1989) suggests, be sure you fully understand the other's interests and position before you try to explain your own. Participants are able to be heard and to hear those involved in the conflictual discussion.

Research shows that the best method for gaining the most from conflict is through using collaborative approaches to conflict (Deutsch, 1973; Kindler, 1995; Thomas, 1976; Thomas & Bennis, 1972; Thomas & Killman, 1979). People who are collaborating use disagreements to learn about each other's insights and to meet the needs of a much broader audience—creating greater inclusiveness. Before reading about the conflict management behaviors below, complete the Conflict Management Styles Instrument (Form 13.1) and then score it to determine which of the following styles you tend to favor. Remember, it is important to be reflective and accurately describe your behaviors when completing this instrument. This instrument will help you to identify the conflict-handling mode that you tend to favor when confronted with conflict, and can serve as a catalyst for reflection.

Five Approaches to Conflict Management

The Conflict Management Styles Instrument (Kindler, 1995; Thomas & Killman, 1979) identifies five specific ways of managing conflict.

Compete/Power

The individual pursues his or her own concerns at the other person's expense, using authority or position or other forms of power to make others obey. "The outcome is important to me in the situation and I owe it to myself and others who depend on me to prevail in conflicts. Therefore, I am willing to win at any cost." Conflict is suppressed in an authority–obedience approach—persuasive powers, hoarding information, threatening sanctions, and/or other power approaches. Competing and dominance results in a win/lose situation. This is an authority–compliance, my-way-or-the-highway style of leadership.

Accommodate/Support

The individual neglects his or her own concerns and those of the organization to satisfy the concerns, needs, and desires of others. "The relationship is more important than the issue, and conflict may damage the relationship, so it is best to acquiesce. Play down differences and obey others even when you believe it's not in your best interest or that of the organization." The individual gives in too easily in a lose/win situation. This is a comfortable, friendly, go-along-to-get-along, yes-person style of leadership.

Avoid/Do Nothing

The individual does not recognize the existence of the conflict and does not pursue his or her own concerns or those of the other person. The individual withdraws from or refuses to acknowledge the conflict—"Leave me alone and settle this any way you want. I'll expend as little energy as possible by being silent." Avoiding might take the form of double-talk, not caring, sidestepping, postponing, neutrality, or simply withdrawing from a conflict. The individual survives by not caring in a lose/lose situation. This is a do-nothing, wishy-washy style of leadership.

Compromise/Negotiate

The objective is to find some expedient, mutually acceptable solution in which everyone gives a little and gets a little. The focus of the solution is not on what is best but more on keeping those with power happy. Yet since no one gets exactly what they want and it is typically not the best decision, there is little real commitment. Compromising is achieved by splitting the differences, exchanging concessions, straddling the fence, testing the wind, or seeking quick, middle-ground positions. Politics and acceptability become the criteria for decision making rather then finding new ideas that might better meet the concerns and interests of all parties. The assumption is that it is never possible for everyone to be satisfied, therefore, it is best to be happy with a half-win/half-win situation. This is a negotiative, political, "I-got-mine-and-you-got-yours" style of leadership.

Collaborate/Participate

Collaboration involves an attempt to confront conflict, recognize the other person's expertise, and to find some solution that fully satisfies the concerns or interests of all involved. The focus is on the problem at hand and not on defending positions. Collaboration is distinguished by the appropriate information it reveals, the level of creativity that is fostered, the quality of the consideration given to an issue, the best of the group's thinking, and the appropriateness of the decision that emerges. It requires constructive identification of underlying concerns and interests, looking at data and facts, and involving important stakeholders in the decisions. "More heads are better than one," or "the whole of the group exceeds the sum of the individual members." Collaboration takes the form of involving others, exploring disagreements, resolving issues (or positions), or confronting and trying to find creative solutions. Collaborations often serve to strengthen the organization and relationships. Shared decisions are reached in a win/win situation. This is a participative, team-oriented, optimizing style of leadership.

Typically, collaborative approaches to decision making and conflict require those involved to be willing to assert their knowledge and interests in the discussion. Collaboration requires an ability to stand up for your rights, beliefs, and know-how and to respect the rights, beliefs, and abilities of others. Figure 13.1 presents the three possible behaviors that often influence how one approaches conflicts and relationships in general. Assertiveness requires standing up for yourself and letting others know what you are thinking and giving this same right to others. All people like to be dealt with honestly, directly, and openly, and that occurs through assertive behavior (Thomas, 1976; Thomas & Killman, 1979). Collaboration requires assertive behavior.

INTERESTS, NOT POSITIONS

Research on leadership (Blake & McCanse, 1991; Bolman & Deal, 2003; Collins, 2001; Cunningham & Gresso, 1993; Leithwood, 1992; Likert, 1967; Peters & Waterman, 1982; Senge, 1990; Stogdill, 1981; Wheatley, 1992) would suggest that the collaborating approach is the most effective within organizations and is compatible with participative team leadership. In this case, each individual's position is well understood, but the emphasis of the group is on trying to solve the problem or develop the best approach, rather than on defending or giving in on a particular position in an either/or type settlement. It is not a question of half a loaf of bread being better than a chance of getting no bread, but the chance of everyone getting a loaf of bread. The focus is on the difficult process of developing open communication, collaboration, and consensus. Often the parties work creatively to find a new solution that will maximize group goals and satisfy group interests. On the other hand, when the approach to conflict management involves denial, compromise, accommodation, or dominance, some residual frustration often develops within some members of the group and the conflict comes up again and again and seems to fester.

Peaceful settlement of disputes requires a mutual trust and confidence that all parties are operating cooperatively in the best interest of the organization. The common functions of the intern in a dispute are to help remove road blocks and distortions, bring to the surface people's interests and concerns, reduce tensions, find areas of agreement, determine possible solutions, redefine problems, develop acceptable agreements, help achieve consensus, and ensure group ownership.

Conflicts usually evolve in relation to the position or solution someone is suggesting and usually not over the core interests that have caused individuals to take a given position. Interests should be used as the primary focus of negotiating the merits of conflicting proposals. There are usually a number of positions that will satisfy everyone's interests. S. Roger Fisher and William Ury (1981) suggest,

> When you do look behind opposed positions for the motivating interests, you can often find an alternative position which meets not only our interests but theirs as

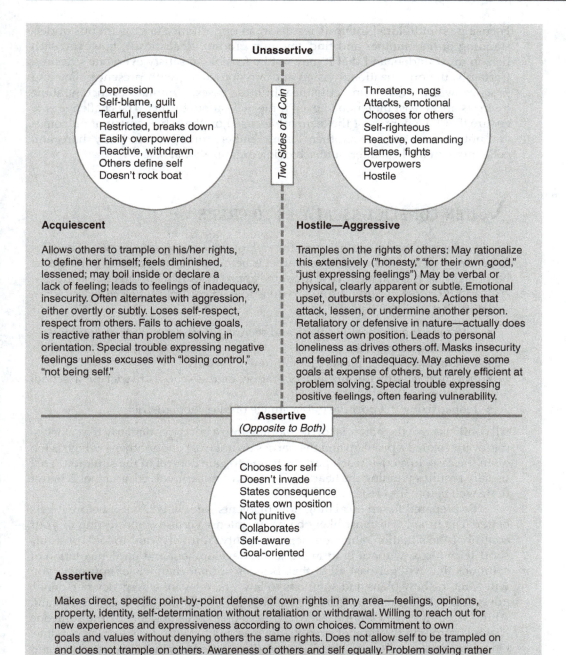

Unassertive

Two Sides of a Coin

Depression
Self-blame, guilt
Tearful, resentful
Restricted, breaks down
Easily overpowered
Reactive, withdrawn
Others define self
Doesn't rock boat

Threatens, nags
Attacks, emotional
Chooses for others
Self-righteous
Reactive, demanding
Blames, fights
Overpowers
Hostile

Acquiescent

Allows others to trample on his/her rights,
to define her himself; feels diminished,
lessened; may boil inside or declare a
lack of feeling; leads to feelings of inadequacy,
insecurity. Often alternates with aggression,
either overtly or subtly. Loses self-respect,
respect from others. Fails to achieve goals,
is reactive rather than problem solving in
orientation. Special trouble expressing negative
feelings unless excuses with "losing control,"
"not being self."

Hostile—Aggressive

Tramples on the rights of others: May rationalize
this extensively ("honesty," "for their own good,"
"just expressing feelings") May be verbal or
physical, clearly apparent or subtle. Emotional
upset, outbursts or explosions. Actions that
attack, lessen, or undermine another person.
Retaliatory or defensive in nature—actually does
not assert own position. Leads to personal
loneliness as drives others off. Masks insecurity
and feeling of inadequacy. May achieve some
goals at expense of others, but rarely efficient at
problem solving. Special trouble expressing
positive feelings, often fearing vulnerability.

Assertive
(Opposite to Both)

Chooses for self
Doesn't invade
States consequence
States own position
Not punitive
Collaborates
Self-aware
Goal-oriented

Assertive

Makes direct, specific point-by-point defense of own rights in any area—feelings, opinions,
property, identity, self-determination without retaliation or withdrawal. Willing to reach out for
new experiences and expressiveness according to own choices. Commitment to own
goals and values without denying others the same rights. Does not allow self to be trampled on
and does not trample on others. Awareness of others and self equally. Problem solving rather
than reactive. Self-enhancing and other-enhancing. Operates through attempts to understand
self and other's needs and to strike a legitimate balance. Includes expression of both "positive"
and "negative" feelings—joy, love, irritation, sadness, personal likes and dislikes, agreement,
disagreement, and so forth.

FIGURE 13.1 **Assertive versus Unassertive Modes of Behavior**

Source: Assertiveness, Acquiescence, and Aggression: An Alternative Model.
Contributed by Paula Rohrbaugh, Ph.D., Psychologist, PMB #244, 4742 Liberty Road. S.,
Salem, OR 97302.

well. . . . Reconciling interests rather than compromising between positions also
works because behind opposed positions lie many more shared and compatible
interests than conflicting ones.

Focusing on individual interests results in an opportunity to grow in our understanding of one another and find common ground. Realistically, however, each person must understand that it may not be feasible to satisfy everyone's desires. Certainly, the organizational vision and mission, along with present policy and practice, will provide some guidance. In these cases, a number of incompatible interests are at least understood even if they all cannot be met. The challenge is to ensure that the energies of the team are focused on the achievement of outcomes and not on defeating one another. Team members must learn to trust, share, and collaborate in the best interest of achieving organizational objectives.

WHEN CONFLICT ESCALATES TO CRISIS

Every once in a while, conflict runs the risk of developing into a crisis. The time to be prepared for such escalating conflict is before it ever happens. When conflict becomes crisis it is too late to use the same approaches that are effective with conflict, and the most important thing to do is to gain control of the crisis. Crisis is a situation that runs the risk of:

- Endangering the health, safety, and security of students and/or employees
- Escalating in intensity
- Falling under close media or community scrutiny
- Interfering with the normal operation of the school district or a school building
- Jeopardizing the positive public image of the school district

All conflicts have the potential of developing into a crisis, particularly if a cataclysmic event created a problem and the parties do not trust one another—which is too often the case. In a crisis, each party is trying to gain control of the situation. That usually requires winning the hearts and minds of those involved, and that is better done well before the crisis.

Be prepared for an escalating flow of events—it will get worse before it gets better! The mood will most likely be panic, intense scrutiny, and testing of your control of the situation, almost a siege mentality. You will want to look past this short-term focus, without ignoring it, to the development and implementation of solutions that will get past all of this. Besides normal channels of approval, you will want to show plans and solutions to lawyers, relevant emergency personnel, government leaders, and others whose support and know-how will be relevant. At the same time, you want to take charge as quickly as possible before someone else is controlling the flow of events. Move as quickly and decisively as possible. Once you have put the crisis behind you, allow time for rebuilding, recovery, and healing.

PLANNING IN ADVANCE FOR A CRISIS

An important element of planning is the crisis communication component. The crisis communication plan should identify spokespersons and establish a clear administrative chain of command. It is important to develop a communication policy and identify an official spokesperson who is prepared for the tension and confrontation that may occur. The plan should spell out who is responsible for calling who, along with a list of all needed telephone numbers. There should be a hot line for rumor control and dispensing accurate information. The plan should include a backup communication system in case the primary system fails. This will most likely be in place at your school and you should study this plan so you can be prepared in case it is needed. You should have certain canned statements ready and add a prepared statement at the time of the crisis. If there is an identified spokesperson, you should refer all inquiries to that person. Be especially careful of the media. They can be important allies, but they can also fan the flames of crisis if you misspeak or give them anything that would place the school or school system in an embarrassing position. Become very familiar with the school system's crisis plan before you get very far into your internship.

Crisis can be classified as to its magnitude, your ability to control and influence events, time available, and the number and quality of possible solutions. You will want to get the negative news out as quickly as possible and then focus on resolution. The school division will want to speak with one voice and thus avoid conflicting stories, so all inquiries should be referred to one person. Keep complete records of everything throughout the process.

In order to be able to take charge, the administrator(s) will need to understand the circumstances, define the problem, rank the options, and move decisively. This begins with an acknowledgement of the crisis and the establishment of strong leadership in its resolution. It is essential to an effective resolution that the crisis management team maintains credibility and is accessible to the community and media. This means that you are always honest, prepared, and brief. You will want to put the most positive face on the situation without whitewashing over the truth. Be very free with "thanks" and other recognition (see Chapter 12) for the help you are receiving.

It is very important that you keep cool, don't argue or loose your temper, and stay in control. Always be careful about what you say in public or in the presence of media. Bridge negative questions with positive answers. Do not answer "what if" questions that ask you to predict the future, and don't answer questions that are not asked. It is essential that you maintain your credibility even when others may be trying to destroy it. Most important, understand the facts and be prepared.

• **Form 13.1** •

Conflict Management Styles

Please circle the degree to which the statement is closely related to your beliefs and behavior as a leader. It is often best to give your first response or thought regarding each of the statements. Try to discern among those behaviors that are more like you and those that you would be very unlikely to do. Discern the subtle differences in your behavior. The scale is: very likely (VL), likely (L), unlikely (U), or very unlikely (VU) to behave like this.

1. I will talk to a staff member and ask the person to limit his or her personal conversations with other employees.   VL   L   U   VU

2. I decide who is right and insist that one person go along with the other person's decision.   VL   L   U   VU

3. I will not confront an individual because it might increase the problem or cause the person to hide the problem.   VL   L   U   VU

4. I will call a person in my department together with an employee from another department in which he or she was having a professional conflict, along with the other employee's supervisor, to discuss and resolve the problem.   VL   L   U   VU

5. I try to get everyone to accept a staff member's behavior with the understanding that we all must work together.   VL   L   U   VU

6. I get people together and try to examine values, interests, and shared visions in order to develop consensus and make decisions.   VL   L   U   VU

7. I let problems go because they often will go away on their own.   VL   L   U   VU

8. I tell employees that they must not allow problems outside of work to influence the work effort. Otherwise, employees can do pretty much as they wish.   VL   L   U   VU

9. I will tell a person that I would feel very comfortable firing him or her if inappropriate behaviors continued.   VL   L   U   VU

10. I ask employees for their input and listen before making my own decision, because that might help to keep harmony and stability in our organization.   VL   L   U   VU

11. I am willing to trade important information with others in order to get the problem solved through joint efforts.   VL   L   U   VU

12. I deliberately seek input from all involved employees even though it takes considerably more time to handle conflicts in this manner.   VL   L   U   VU

13. When I believe that I am right, I try to maximize my gains and minimize my losses within the organization.   VL   L   U   VU

14. I often do not tell other people what I really think about their behavior because it might damage our relations and interfere with our organization's plans.   VL   L   U   VU

15. I ignore the mistakes of my staff members, knowing that they will do better in the future.　　VL　L　U　VU

16. I make sure everyone gets something from the decision.　　VL　L　U　VU

17. I communicate to employees that they can safely challenge my ideas and practices if it helps lead to the targeted results.　　VL　L　U　VU

18. I emphasize the benefits of my approach over other individual's ideas to avoid misunderstanding and to make it clear that I am ultimately responsible.　　VL　L　U　VU

19. I do not bring important issues up for discussion if I perceive that potential disruption will outweigh the benefits of resolution.　　VL　L　U　VU

20. I maintain cooperation and satisfy my employees if the issue is more important to them than it is to me.　　VL　L　U　VU

21. I feel comfortable pointing out to an individual that their work behavior runs counter to the spirit and goals of our organization and that I expect changes in response.　　VL　L　U　VU

22. I try to find an integrative solution to the conflict so every person's concerns are recognized and viewed as important.　　VL　L　U　VU

23. I achieve quick, temporary settlements to complex problems when they are very controversial.　　VL　L　U　VU

24. I do not confront my staff members for their inappropriate behaviors if they do not hinder our organization's long-term goals.　　VL　L　U　VU

25. I do not require things to be done my way, but instead support the concerns and desires of my staff members.　　VL　L　U　VU

26. I am inclined to reprimand an employee if it eliminates the conflict or problem.　　VL　L　U　VU

27. I try to meet the expectations of other staff members and provide for their interests.　　VL　L　U　VU

28. I try to work with other employees in order to see the problem from all sides and find solutions that are mutually beneficial.　　VL　L　U　VU

29. I let my staff members take responsibility for solving the problem when there is little opportunity for my concerns to be met.　　VL　L　U　VU

30. I get employees to be flexible and change some of their beliefs, because it is the fastest way to achieve mutual understanding and arrive at a solution to the problem.　　VL　L　U　VU

Source: This instrument was developed by Dr. William G. Cunningham and Ms. Iryna M. Khrabrova based on research completed in the area of conflict management.

Conflict Management Styles Scoring Sheet

The Conflict Management Styles instrument scale has been converted to a numeric value according to degree as follows: 4 = very likely (VL), 3 = likely (L), 2 = unlikely (U), 1 = very unlikely (VU). Please circle the number that corresponds to the response you selected for each statement.

Statement	Compete/ Power	Accommodate/ Support	Avoid/ Do Nothing	Collaborate/ Participate	Compromise/ Negotiate
1					4 3 2 1
2	4 3 2 1				
3			4 3 2 1		
4				4 3 2 1	
5		4 3 2 1			
6				4 3 2 1	
7			4 3 2 1		
8					4 3 2 1
9	4 3 2 1				
10		4 3 2 1			
11					4 3 2 1
12				4 3 2 1	
13	4 3 2 1				
14			4 3 2 1		
15		4 3 2 1			
16					4 3 2 1
17				4 3 2 1	
18	4 3 2 1				
19			4 3 2 1		
20		4 3 2 1			
21	4 3 2 1				
22				4 3 2 1	
23					4 3 2 1
24			4 3 2 1		
25		4 3 2 1			
26	4 3 2 1				
27		4 3 2 1			
28				4 3 2 1	
29			4 3 2 1		
30					4 3 2 1
Total					

Scoring: The thirty statements are divided into the five conflict management styles. Each style contains the numbers corresponding to the degree of the behavior you are likely to exhibit. Total the circled scores in each column and write that score in the total line at the bottom of the scoring sheet. The highest score represents your preferred style of dealing with conflicts. The second highest score is the back-up style that you tend to display when problems arise. The lowest total score suggests the style that you are least likely to use.

section **III**

ASSESSMENT, LICENSURE, AND OBTAINING AN ADMINISTRATIVE POSITION

This last section will help you obtain an administrative position. The completion of the internship experience typically fuels desire to become an educational administrator. Thinking begins to shift from what is still needed in order to achieve specific career goals to how you can obtain a position in administration. These reflections require a hard look at both professional preparation and readiness.

An initial start is becoming active in a practitioner-oriented association. These have conferences and publish newsletters, journals, and books and help administrative candidates to meet practicing administrators, learn of position openings, and stay current in their field. They have local and state meetings that continue to expand on the visibility developed during the internship experience.

Another big part of final preparation is determining what is still required in order to obtain administrative licensure. Over forty states require a master's degree with some administrative courses and educational experience for an administrative and supervision license. States are also clearly working hard to establish performance-based standards and assessments. Many states are also setting up alternative certification plans (Kaye, 2003).

One way some states determine how well one is prepared for meeting the ISLLC standards is to require completion of the Educational Testing Services School Leadership Licensure Assessment (SLLA), discussed in Chapter 14. This is designed to give the intern an opportunity to see how well prepared he or she is to meet the expectations presented in the ISLLC standards. A number of states now require candidates to earn a minimum "cut score" on this assessment in order to be licensed for administration within the state. Other states have their own assessment, and although the "state competencies" are similar to those of the ISSLC standards, they are not exactly the same. For example, the Texas test, TExES, does not follow the exact format of the SLLA. The SLLA is applicable to these state-designed exams but, as in all cases, is only one possible suggestion for preparing to take the state assessment. Studying these assessments also provides a way to think about situations you may face as an intern and later as a practicing administrator.

Licensure is important because it ensures that the future leader possesses the needed knowledge, skill, and abilities to ensure the health, safety, and welfare of our citizens. Once you have completed all program requirements, you should begin the application for state endorsement as an educational leader. This typically requires formal application and all supporting materials to be filed with the state certifying office within the state department of education. Most universities and colleges have an office that can assist in this process.

The final step to obtaining the position is to locate and apply for anticipated vacancies in the school district (see Chapter 15). Remember, school systems want to hire the best candidates and it is your responsibility to convince them that you are that person. The screening and selection process is as varied as the school districts; however, there are many similarities.

The hiring decision is made through the use of a screening and selection process and criteria. This typically occurs through the use of application and supporting materials and an interview in order to determine if the candidate best meets the qualifications for the job.

Chapter 15, the final chapter, outlines the process of obtaining an administrative position. Your preparation program, internship experience, and, hopefully, this text/handbook will go a long way in helping you to achieve your career goals. Good luck, and "Go for it."

chapter 14

Preparing for an Administrative Assessment

In the age of high stakes testing and accountability, our business leaders, media representatives, and legislators have begun requesting that today's school leaders perform well on an assessment as well as in a leadership program and internship. State legislators and licensing boards have responded by establishing assessments to evaluate candidates for the principalship. The Educational Testing Services School Leaders Licensure Assessment (SLLA) is one such assessment effort. Thirteen states now require the ETS/SLLA for administrative and supervision licensure, and a number of other states have developed similar types of assessments that are required in their states. One of these alternative assessments includes the TExES, used in the state of Texas to assess specific competencies. Other states are now considering the ETS/SLLA or some other form of assessment as part of the endorsement process. (For more information on the SLLA visit www.ets.org.)

Although all assessments probably have some similar content and formats, there are important differences. You should obtain information on the specific assessment that is required in your state. Hopefully, the SLLA format will be applicable to all state assessments and will help you prepare for any assessment that might be required by your state. Because administrative assessments are receiving greater attention, it is important for administrative candidates to look into the types of assessments that exist in their states.

This chapter presents the most common assessment and the one that most other assessments are modeled after, the Educational Testing Service (ETS) School Leadership Licensure Assessment (SLLA). Certainly, your administrative preparation program and your internship will help you do well on such assessments; however, it is also quite helpful to become familiar with these types of assessments. Therefore, this chapter discusses the SLLA and provides a sample of possible questions and responses. You can use this chapter to help prepare yourself to complete the appropriate assessment required in your state. It is a valued experience to respond to these questions and then to discuss your response with others. These questions can also be discussed during the seminar classes or even with your mentor.

STRUCTURE OF THE SLLA

The SLLA was funded by six participating member states of ISLLC. The Educational Testing Service was hired as the test's development contractor. The SLLA was created in order to uniformly assess the abilities of potential school leaders by asking participants to respond to situations of leadership. Candidates are asked to identify problems and solutions and are to use the six ISLLC standards as their guidepost as they solve the most current situations facing today's school leaders.

In each section of the test, the six ISLLC standards are the driving force behind successful answers to each question. The six-hour test is separated into three two-hour modules. The first module is broken down further into two one-hour sections. The second module consists of two one-hour case studies, and the third module involves seven information-oriented documents typical of those encountered by school administrators. All questions require written responses. When answering each question or scenario, candidates should frame their responses within the confines of the six ISLLC standards.

Test Format

- Module I: Evaluation of Actions I and II
    Two Hours (Each section is timed separately)
    Section I—Evaluation of Actions I: Short Vignettes (1 hour)
    Section II—Evaluation of Actions II: Longer Vignettes (1 hour)
- Module II: Synthesis of Information and Problem-Solving Cases (2 hours)
- Module III: Analysis of Information and Decision Making—Document-Based Questions (2 hours) (ETS, 2000)

Scoring the SLLA

Each module is scored separately. Scores for each exercise are summed by section and then weighted into a total score ranging from 100 to 200. The four sections are weighted accordingly:

- Module I: Evaluation of Actions I: 20%
- Module I: Evaluation of Actions II: 20%
- Module II: Synthesis of Information and Problem-Solving Cases: 30%
  Both exercises in this section are scored on a 4-point scale, with 3 the highest possible score and 0 the lowest. The response to the questions within each case are treated as a single response for scoring purposes, so only one score is assigned to each case.
- Module III: Analysis of Information and Decision Making: 30%
  The seven exercises are scored on a 3-point scale, with 2 the highest possible score and 0 the lowest. The responses to the two questions on each exercise are treated as a single response, so only one score is assigned to each exercise.

TIPS FOR COMPLETING THE SLLA OR OTHER ADMINISTRATIVE ASSESSMENTS

What follows are some general suggestions for preparing to take an administrative assessment. Your internship experience should help you to become familiar with the situations presented in these assessments. Here are some other general suggestions.

1. Learn what material is on the test.
   - Have a thorough understanding of the material on the assessment. This comes through a review of your leadership preparation and internship experiences along with a review of assessment guidelines and sample questions. (See Principal/Administrator Orientation and Preparation Study

Guide: a Self-Paced Tutorial for the School Leadership Licensure Assessment, vtcreply@aol.com, and other resources mentioned at the end of this chapter.)

2. Get an understanding of the test.
   - Review the sample questions offered in this chapter and the resources at the end of this chapter. Understand how the test is scored. Pay close attention to what is asked of you within each question.
   - Practice answering all questions provided in this chapter and other references.
3. Have a plan.
   - Read all the questions before beginning. Decide which questions are easier for you and answer those questions first. Be mindful that the questions are not arranged in order of difficulty.
   - Work quickly without rushing.
   - Trust your ability and knowledge.
   - Gather needed information provided in the questions and involve stakeholders in your solutions. Make sure you examine underlying causes, making comments and providing interpretation. You must show an understanding of the significance of the information provided.
   - You will get no points for merely repeating, summarizing, or paraphrasing information provided in the case with no interpretation.
   - Your plan should demonstrate that you value student achievement.
4. Watch the time.
   - Keep track of the time allowed for each section. Allow enough time to respond to all of the questions asked in all three modules.
5. Follow helpful tips for test day.
   - Get plenty of rest the night before. You can relax because you have done your planning the weeks before.
   - Relax with the confidence you have referred to guides and are prepared to take the assessment.
   - Pace yourself and maintain stamina and focus in order to complete a challenging six-hour assessment.
   - Make sure you address all components of the prompts.
   - Answer all questions.
   - Bring your test confirmation ticket and photo identification.
   - Bring several pens and pencils (blue or black ink and #2 pencils).
   - Eat breakfast before the test and bring a snack. (It is a six-hour test.)

Important Administrative Values Tested in Assessments

Be aware of the following beliefs or points of reference as you are framing your responses to an assessment:

1. Participatory Leadership
   a. School leaders should be actively involved in the educational process.
   b. The effective school leader takes an active role in all areas of education both inside and outside of the school building.
   c. School leaders lead by example.
   d. Team process is valued.
2. Shared Decision Making
   a. School leaders should include all the stakeholders involved when deciding school matters (consult multiple stakeholders and use the collaborative process).

    b. School leaders seek the input of the teachers and staff within their building when making decisions.

    c. Effective leaders are sensitive to diversity, recognize the viewpoint of multiple stakeholders, and make equitable decisions.

3. Problem Identification

    a. School leaders should be able to effectively investigate, analyze, assess, and address problems as they arise within the educational context.

    b. School leaders offer research-based solutions to problems as they arise.

    c. School leaders understand the connections among causes, solutions, and school improvement.

    d. School leaders are effective problem solvers.

    e. School leaders know what information is needed and how to obtain it.

4. Interpretation of Data

    a. Effective school leaders are able to analyze data and assess what the data are telling them.

    b. Effective school leaders understand the complexity of problems and the interdependence of data.

    c. School leaders use data to drive the decision-making process.

    d. School leaders use data to identify areas of weakness within curriculum and/or instruction.

    e. School leaders use data to help solve problems and to monitor progress.

5. Curriculum and Instruction

    a. Effective school leaders are the instructional leaders within their building and are knowledgeable of instructional approaches.

    b. School leaders are always looking to improve and update the curriculum.

    c. School leaders look to implement research-based instructional methods into the classroom.

    d. Effective school leaders understand the connection between instruction and discipline.

6. All Students Can Learn

    a. Effective school leaders must believe that all students can learn but they may learn in different ways.

    b. School leaders believe that all students have a right to a quality education.

    c. School leaders consider the impact of decisions on students, maintain an instructional focus, and use instructional time wisely.

7. Other

    a. Effective leaders value teachers and treat them with respect as professionals.

    b. Effective leaders believe in comprehensive programs for professional development.

    c. School leaders understand the importance of political support for what they do.

    d. School leaders recognize the importance of both short- and long-term strategies.

    e. School leaders recognize the importance of keeping everyone informed.

These types of belief systems, along with the ISLLC standards, give a glimpse of the values that graders of the SLLA and other state assessments possess and follow when reading test takers' responses. You will improve your chances of receiving a high score if you are able to construct your responses based on such core beliefs. (See also Form 5.1 in Chapter 5.)

EDUCATIONAL LEADERSHIP ASSESSMENT

The sample questions in the appendix to this chapter (beginning on page 164) provide an opportunity to practice for an administrative assessment. They also provide an opportunity for you to practice responding to the types of matters that will occur during your internship and as a practicing administrator. These examples are similar to the ETS material listed at the end of this chapter, (the ETS materials provide extensive coverage of the SLLA), but provide a slightly different slant to the assessment. This appendix is provided to stimulate your thinking about assessments and administrative activity. You will want to look over other materials to properly prepare to take an administrative assessment. (See resources for the SLLA below, especially the *Principal Adminstrative Orientation and Preparation Study Guide.* For more information visit vtereply@aol.com.)

PRACTICE MAKES PERFECT

Each state that chooses to use the SLLA as part of the administrative and supervision licensure process will set their own cut score to determine a passing score. Educational Testing Service will automatically send the candidate's results to the candidate and to the state in which the individual is applying for license. The assessments in the appendix will be helpful for all internship students, in that these type of experiences might be expected to occur during their internship experience and might be part of any administrative assessment. These types of activities help to prepare interns to take on the responsibilities of educational leadership by complementing internship experiences. The exercises provided in the appendix will help you become familiar with realistic situations that might be a part of your internship experience and/or educational leadership assessment. Good luck on any assessment that you complete as part of your endorsement process.

RESOURCES FOR THE SLLA

Council of Chief State School Officers. Retrieved July 1, 2005, from www.ccsso. org/projects/Interstate_School_Leaders_Licensure_Consortium

Council of Chief State School Officers. Retrieved July 1, 2005, from www.ccsso.org/ content/pdfs/isllastd.pdf

Cunningham, W., Owings, W., and King, W. (2006). *Principal/administrator orientation and preparation study guide: A self-paced tutorial for the school leadership licensure assessment.* Richmond, VA: Virginia Tidewater Consortium for Higher Education. (vtcreply@aol.com)

Educational Testing Service. (2000). *School leaders licensure assessment study kit book 1 Introduction Module I: Evaluation of actions I.* Princeton, NJ: Author.

Educational Testing Service. (2000). *School leaders licensure assessment study kit book 2 module I: Evaluation of actions II.* Princeton, NJ: Author.

Educational Testing Service. (2000). *School leaders licensure assessment study kit book 3 module II: Synthesis of information and problem solving.* Princeton, NJ: Author.

Educational Testing Service. (2000). *School leaders licensure assessment study kit book 4 module III: Analysis of information and decision making.* Princeton, NJ: Author.

University of Virginia Curry School of Education. (n.d.). Retrieved July 1, 2005, from www.curry.edschool.virginia.edu/adminsuper/slla.html

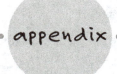

A SAMPLE EDUCATIONAL LEADERSHIP ASSESSMENT

appendix

MODULE I—EVALUATION OF ACTIONS I (ONE HOUR)

Test takers will be given one hour to complete this section of the SLLA. This particular module is referred to as "Short Vignettes" because it is made up of ten brief scenarios, each followed by questions to be answered regarding that scenario. Each describes a situation a principal might experience and be expected to deal with.

Points to consider when completing Module I:

- Focus your answer on the specific questions being asked within each scenario.
- Base your responses on the relevant ISLLC standards.
- Remember to read all ten scenarios first and choose the easiest one first. The vignettes are not arranged in order of difficulty.
- Provide lots of relevant information, show collaboration with staff and community, assess readiness, build support, provide resources, and celebrate success.
- Responses should be as brief as possible and may take on any format that answers the question asked.
- Remember your time. You have one hour to complete ten scenarios (this averages out to six minutes per vignette).

Ten sample test questions taking the format for Module I: Section I of the SLLA assessment are provided here.

1. The parent of a middle school student writes a letter to her daughter's principal asking that her daughter be moved to a different team. After a brief phone conversation with the parent the principal grants the request. Do you agree with the principal's decision? Evaluate the decision.

2. A first-year teacher approaches her principal because she is frustrated with the behavior of her second-block class. The principal schedules a meeting with the teacher for the next week to discuss the matter. How should the principal prepare for the meeting? (See sample response on the next page.)

3. A veteran teacher who is nearing retirement tells you, the principal, that he feels he should not attend the next staff development meeting because he is nearing retirement. He states that "by the time we see the benefits of these new practices in instruction, I will have already retired." How should this situation be handled? What should be the expected outcomes?

4. After reviewing the State Learning Objectives (SOL) testing schedule that was prepared by the guidance office for the coming week, a teacher approaches her middle school principal with complaints. She is upset that her planning time has been eliminated and she feels she is administering too many tests. After listening to her complaints the principal tells the teacher that the schedule is set and she will have to handle the situation as best she can. Do you agree with the principal's decision? Give a rationale for your opinion.

5. At 3 p.m. on a Friday afternoon a local news reporter calls to inquire about an accident that occurred at your elementary school that morning. He and his cameraman would like to stop by for an interview. What should be the principal's response and course of action?

6. The parents of a fourth-grade student call to express their desire for their daughter to refrain from appearing in the upcoming holiday pageant. They feel the material in the pageant conflicts with their family beliefs. The pag-

eant is a week away and the student is scheduled to play a leading role. How should this situation be handled? Give a rationale for your response.

7. The seventh-grade team leader approaches the principal frustrated over the failure of her teammates to cover their duty stations effectively between classes. The principal states that, as team leader, she should learn to handle those types of problems herself and if she cannot then she could expect to be removed from the position. Do you agree with how this principal handled the situation? Provide an analysis for your response.

8. The morning following a recent home basketball game, a local high school principal receives a phone call from a community leader who is concerned with the behavior of a faculty member at the game. According to the community leader, the "cheering" faculty member's actions were felt to be inappropriate. How should the principal respond to this influential member of the community? What action should be taken with the teacher?

9. The principal of a small elementary school receives a phone call from the superintendent requesting that the school budget be trimmed by 15%. The superintendent has requested a proposal be brought to the meeting scheduled for next week. How should the proposal be constructed? What points should be made at the meeting?

10. In October, a high school principal receives additional funding of $1,000 to be spent for staff development. The principal immediately decides to spend the money on a cooperative learning in-service for the faculty. The principal feels that cooperative learning is the key to improving classroom instruction. Do you approve of the principal's decision? Give an analysis of your response.

Sample Answer for Question 2

In order to prepare for the meeting the principal should:

1. Talk with the teacher about coming to visit for a couple of "informal" observations in order to understand the environment of the classroom. During observation, the principal would be looking specifically for classroom management issues along with student behavior. The principal would also watch instructional methods to see if boredom is causing students to misbehave. Other issues may be with directions provided, responses to student inquiries, questioning skills, or other instructional issues.
2. Talk with a few teachers that she closely works with, the department head, and her supervisor to obtain their feedback on how she might be able to motivate students to improve their behavior.
3. Find an experienced teacher who is good with discipline and who would be willing to accept the role as the teacher's mentor.
4. Arrange with the teacher for her to talk with the department chair and her supervisor to gain more assistance.

MODULE I—EVALUATION OF ACTIONS II (ONE HOUR)

This portion of the assessment is referred to as the "Longer Vignettes." It contains six scenarios that may be encountered by school administrators as they conduct the functions of their job. The six scenarios all focus on current teaching and learning issues that face today's administrators. Test takers are asked to articulate the problem and provide resolution as it applies to teaching and learning.

Points to consider when completing the second portion of Module I:

• Read all six vignettes before beginning; answer the easiest ones first.

- Identify what issues need to be addressed and how.
- Analyze the problem that exists and develop a strategy that resolves the problem.
- Focus your responses on the immediate items that need to be addressed and then move to future concerns.
- Base your responses on the ISLLC standards.
- Try to cover all aspects of the problem that you can.
- Make sure the responses fit the situation; be specific, comprehensive, and convincing.

Six sample test questions using the format from Section II of the SLLA assessment are provided here.

1. A parent writes a letter to the high school principal requesting that the science curriculum be revised due to the slant toward evolution. The letter goes on to state that the parent has also formed a committee of parents who share the same view. How should the principal address this matter?

2. An elementary principal walks down the third-grade hallway, where he hears and observes a first-year teacher's classroom that appears to be in total chaos. Later that day the principal receives a phone call from a parent of a child in that classroom who has concerns about the learning environment. The principal assures the parent that he will look into the matter and get back in touch. What should the principal do next?

3. The students of a very successful high school football coach are consistently turning out low-performing history scores on the state's standards of learning test. This problem has been occurring for the past three years while the football team has made it to the state playoffs each of those three years. What should be done by the principal in this situation?

4. A middle school team leader position becomes available. The position is at the seventh-grade level, where four teachers have five years or more experience and three teachers have three years or less. What steps should the principal take in order to fill this position?

5. The school division has just added a new technology position for your high school. Create a plan of action for filling this new position. The superintendent has given you the latitude to place this new position anywhere in the school, as well as to perform any job function you deem to be important.

6. A high school principal is approached by one of the AP History teachers at his school. The teacher is concerned that she is not adequately challenging a particularly advanced group of students in her third-block class. The teacher would like for the principal to observe the class and then provide feedback. How should the principal prepare for the observation? What should take place after the observation? Develop a plan for the observation and post-observation.

Sample Answers to Question 6

In order to prepare for the observation the principal should:

1. Schedule a pre-observation conference.
2. Before the pre-observation conference the principal should review the curriculum for AP History.
3. During the pre-observation conference the principal should:
   - Establish what the teacher would like to have observed (i.e., a particular group of students).
   - Establish goals for what the teacher would like to achieve from the observation.

- Select an observation tool that will match the objective.
4. Schedule at least three informal observations.

After the observations the principal should:

5. Schedule a post-observation conference where he would complete the following:
   - Review his informal observations with the teacher. Does his perception align with what the teacher feels occurred?
   - Review with the teacher the data he collected.
   - Receive teacher feedback on his data.
   - Along with the teacher, develop a plan of instruction for the advanced group of students.
6. Discuss the possibility of inviting the supervisor for gifted education to join them in looking into the teacher's concern.
7. Schedule a followup meeting to check on progress.

MODULE II—SYNTHESIS OF INFORMATION AND PROBLEM SOLVING (TWO HOURS)

These cases are unlike the previous vignettes because they focus on requiring test takers to use all of the ISLLC standards when formulating their responses. For each case study, students are asked a series of four to five questions regarding that particular case. Test takers are given a two-hour block of time to complete the two case studies.

Each case is purposefully complex, and successful completion will require test takers to demonstrate a standards-based approach when handling each case. Each case will also present a variety of documents that give additional information into the case. These should be used when you formulate each response. Typically one case is based on an elementary school and the second is based on a middle or high school setting.

Points to consider when taking Module II:

- Take time to study each case; you have two hours to answer two cases.
- Be sure to address what is asked within each case.
- Select from all documents relevant information to help you analyze and answer the questions.
- Make sure there is a consistent focus on students and their learning.
- Involve key stakeholders in the process.
- Responses should be detailed, specific, and convincing.
- You have approximately one hour per case study.
- Although each case study will have one ISLLC standard that dominates the response, all of the ISLLC standards should be used while framing your response.
- Consider the chronology of steps needed for successful achievements of desired goals (see Chapter 12).
- Be very specific with each suggestion you make.
- Each answer should demonstrate an understanding of the complexity of each issue, along with a solution to each issue that will be equitable to all stakeholders involved.
- Distinguish between primary issues and those of secondary importance, or mere symptoms.

Case: Bent Creek Middle School

Use the scenario and the data provided below as the basis for answering the questions.

Scenario 1: You are the newly appointed principal of Bent Creek Middle School, after serving eight years as an assistant principal of a neighboring middle school. The superintendent has requested a meeting with you for September 1. The purpose of the meeting is outlined in the memo provided below. Additional information is provided to establish a context for the meeting.

Documents

- School fact sheet
- Discipline data
- Memo from superintendent requesting September 1 meeting
- Bent Creek Middle School student survey

Questions

1. What additional information would you seek and from whom?
2. What are the major problems facing the school culture of the building?
3. What initial steps would you take prior to meeting with the superintendent?
4. What should be the goals of the recommended plan?

School Fact Sheet

- Bent Creek Middle School enrolls 750 students.
- Enrollment consists of grades 6–8.
- Students are grouped into teams with two teams comprising each grade level.
- Bent Creek is located in a rapidly growing suburban area of a city that is also rapidly growing.
- Student/teacher ratio is 23:1.
- Faculty attendance is 89%, the lowest in the district.
- The PTA is very active, with volunteers always eager to help.

Discipline Data

School Year: 2006–2007

Grade Level	Number of Students	Number of ISS	Number of OSS
6	103	80	9
7	112	94	10
8	149	120	21

Memorandum from the Superintendent

TO: Principal of Bent Creek Middle School

FROM: Superintendent of Clearwater School District

DATE: July 1, 2007

SUBJECT: School Discipline

Welcome to the Clearwater School District and to your appointment as principal of Bent Creek Middle School. I look forward to working with you to further the success of the Clearwater School District.

As you may recall from our discussion of the current discipline situation, changes need to be implemented and fairly quickly before this situation gets out of hand. As you are aware, discipline referrals are remarkably higher than any other middle school within the district. I would like to meet with you on September 1 at 10:30 a.m. to discuss your plan for reducing the number of referrals at Bent Creek Middle School.

I look forward to hearing your thoughts and vision for Bent Creek Middle School.

Bent Creek Middle School Student Survey

How do you feel about the following:	Strongly Agree	Sometimes Agree	Sometimes Disagree	Strongly Disagree	No Opinion
1. I like my school.	10	10	70	10	0
2. Teachers like their job.	10	5	10	70	5
3. Discipline is handled by teachers fairly.	5	5	75	10	5
4. The principal cares about the students.	5	40	50	5	0
5. I feel safe at school.	25	5	60	10	0
6. There are many opportunities to participate in activities outside of class.	30	20	20	20	10
7. Administrators are fair.	20	20	55	5	0

Sample Answer to Case: Bent Creek Middle School

1. **Additional information needed:**
   - While I have the previous school year's referral data, I would like to have the data going back at least five years in order to establish any trends. I would obtain this information from the school discipline database.
   - I would like to see the data from the feeder elementary schools and high school in order to look for patterns. I would obtain this information from the respective school's assistant principals and principals.
   - I would then take the data and disaggregate a step further (male, female, spec. ed., SES, etc.).
   - Meet with faculty members individually to get their perspectives on the discipline situation in order to find out more about their discipline policy and procedure.
   - Meet with members of PTA individually to get their perspective on student discipline.
   - Review outline of current discipline policy.
   - Visit classrooms where discipline referrals are high in order to get a better handle on what is going on.
   - Talk to team leaders and supervisors to get a variety of viewpoints.

2. **Problems facing the school culture:**
   - 80% of students suggest they do not like their school.
   - 80% of faculty negatively view their job (may play a large role in low faculty attendance).
   - 85% of students believe discipline is unfairly handled.
   - 70% of students do not feel safe at school.

   These four viewpoints will have a dramatic affect on school culture. According to this information, both the students and the teachers feel a disconnection between themselves and the school. Students feel discipline is unfair, and even more alarming is the fact that students feel unsafe at school. I would be interested to also see test scores for the school. I believe it is hard for students to learn when they do not feel safe. I also think that discipline could be perceived as unfair because of low teacher attendance. Substitute teachers may not always be aware of discipline policy or may not always be as consistent with their discipline.

3. **Initial steps:**
   - Meet with faculty individually to assess discipline policy and to address incentives for increased faculty attendance.
   - Discuss this issue with team leaders, supervisors, and feeder elementary schools and high school principals.
   - Ask for volunteers to serve on a discipline committee that will review needed information and develop a plan for school improvement. Encourage some teachers to volunteer for this committee.
   - Have the committee look over the information collected in the response to question 1 and visit schools that have similar socio-economic, racial mixes but that have excellent school spirit and behavior.
   - Finalize a plan for school improvement according to committee recommendations.
   - Meet with PTA representatives to gain their support for the proposed plan.
   - Document the status of the planning effort in writing and be ready to present to the superintendent at a future meeting.

4. **Goals of the plan:**
   - To develop a uniform discipline policy to be used across grade levels and subject areas
   - To improve the spirit within the school

- To develop a procedure that will address issues early before they escalate to referral status
- To increase faculty attendance and visibility in order to increase student safety
- To initiate staff development that addresses issues of discipline within the school
- To reduce referrals and increase student and teacher morale within the building

MODULE III: ANALYSIS OF INFORMATION AND DECISION MAKING (TWO HOURS)

This section is comprised of seven documents, each followed by two questions. Test takers are given two hours to assess the documents and answer the questions based on the six ISLLC standards. One or more of the standards may apply to each document.

Points to consider when completing Module III:

- Answer the easiest questions first; documents are not arranged in order of difficulty.
- Responses may be in any format (paragraph, bullets, numbers, etc.).
- Identify evidence that supports possible causes for problems as well as types of problems being experienced.
- Pace yourself; you have seven documents to cover in two hours.
- Be careful to focus on issues involving teaching and learning.
- Interpret information given in the document, including any patterns.
- Recognize additional information required, and specify how it will be obtained.
- Focus your answer on the specific questions being asked within each scenario.
- Try to assess what the data are telling you.
- Again, answer only what is being asked.

Document 1

The following is a letter mailed to a middle school principal.

Dear Principal:

I am writing to inform you of a situation with our daughter that has recently come to our attention. My daughter has come home complaining about the boys in her class making inappropriate remarks to her and her friends in the hallway between classes. She has told us that it has occurred three times over the past five days and usually takes place between her 1st and 2nd bell classes.

As an 8th grade student, our daughter has been very active in various activities, along with SCA. Up until now, her experiences at Shallow Water Middle have been very positive.

I would like to thank you in advance for any assistance you may be able to provide. We look forward to hearing from you in regards to this matter.

Sincerely,

Bob Smith

Questions

1. Before contacting the parents, who would you contact, and why?
2. What can be done in order to prevent this in the future?

Sample Answers for Document 1

Document 1 (Question 1): Who would you contact and why?

1. Question the girls to find out who is involved. What specific things are being said and/or done? Find out if this is happening to other girls as well.
2. Contact teachers who are located in this section of the building to establish if they have seen or heard the incidents as described.
3. Talk to the guidance counselors to see if they are aware of such problems.
4. Question the boys involved to hear their side of the events.
5. Get back to the parents and keep them informed of the status of what is being done.
6. If there has been physical contact, I may need to talk with the youth service officer.

Document 1 (Question 2): What can be done in order to prevent this in the future?

1. If this incident is indeed occurring, be sure the matter is addressed and consequences are applied.
2. Ask teachers to be visible in hallways between classes.
3. Have security monitors make sure they are walking through the hallways during class changes.
4. Have conversation with boys involved to explain sexual harassment and its consequences (possibly consider the need for a school-wide program).
5. Set up opportunities for students to discuss sexual harassment problems with counselors, teachers, and administrators. (Provide staff development for those involved in dealing with students who believe they have been sexually harassed or assaulted. Also, provide a central contact for referrals.)
6. Be certain to keep parents notified as much as possible while being mindful of privacy laws.

Document 2

The following is a memo from a teacher who is requesting a transfer.

TO: Sallie Stews, Principal

FROM: Mo Artega, Teacher

DATE: March 15

SUBJECT: Teaching Assignment

Since the beginning of the school year I have been very unhappy with my present teaching assignment. I am no longer comfortable teaching 5th grade math at Broad Road Elementary. I am writing you to inform you of my desire for a transfer.

As you are aware with the construction of the new elementary school across town, most of my teaching companions have left for the new building. I believe I would be much happier transferring to the new location.

I would like to request a meeting with you to discuss this matter in greater detail. Please let me know what time would be best for you.

Questions

1. What points would you like to address at the meeting?
2. What actions(s) would you take? Explain your answer.

Document 3

The following shows SLO test data for Western Mill High School.

SLO Test Data					

Subject: Science by sub groups
Percent Passing: 70%

Grade	Caucasian	Black	Hispanic	Special Education	IEP
9	85%	35%	97%	14%	3%
10	86.5%	55%	98%	19%	4%
11	89.45%	57.5%	99%	35%	10%
12	91.2%	64%	100%	38%	15%

Questions

1. What are the instructional issues shown in the data?
2. What additional information would you seek before meeting with the science department to assess the data?

Document 4

The following is a letter to the editor submitted to the local newspaper.

Not Fun and Games

My son is finishing his sophomore year at Forest Grove High School. With two weeks left to go on the school calendar, he has been playing bingo, watching movies, and sitting outside getting some sun. Why is this being done at school? I asked my son this same question and was told, "Dad, we finished our SLO tests. School is over!" If school is over, why are my tax dollars paying for high dollar baby-sitting? Why can't the test be pushed back two weeks and use the additional time for instruction? These are important questions for our local school officials.

Questions:

1. What are the curriculum and instruction issues contained in the letter?
2. As the principal, how would you respond?

Document 5

The following shows the results of a teacher survey conducted at the end of the year at Berkshire Elementary School.

Results of Teacher Survey

Scale:
SA   Strongly Agree
A   Agree
D   Disagree
SD   Strongly Disagree

Questions	Responses			
	SA	A	D	SD
1. I feel comfortable giving administration input and feedback.	5	50	40	5
2. I think we have relevant opportunities for staff development.	60	10	20	10
3. I feel we have an adequate amount of team planning time.	20	20	30	30
4. I think students are fairly and sufficiently disciplined by administration.	10	20	60	10
5. I feel safe at school.	5	20	50	25
6. There is good school spirit within our building.	5	5	55	35
7. I use the new school-wide lesson plan creator often.	80	5	5	10
8. Teachers are treated with respect by students.	10	20	40	30
9. Teachers are treated with respect by administration.	10	10	40	40
10. Teachers have the freedom to implement the curriculum as they see fit.	30	30	30	10

Questions:

1. Based on the information provided in the survey, what are the curriculum and instructional issues?
2. As the principal, what additional information would you seek?

Document 6

Read the following letter and respond to the questions regarding the request of a parent of a high school student.

Dear Principal:

I am writing to express my concerns regarding the issue that occurred with my son, Adrian Sanchez, on Monday, January 14. My son was instructed to go to the office during homeroom because of a dress code violation. He told the teacher that he was not going to the office. As a result, he was sent home that morning and was given a letter stating that he would have to serve a three-day out-of-school suspension for "noncompliance."

I disagree with the three-day suspension. I feel that three days is an unfair punishment for this incident. I support the school's dress code policy and

I also agree that his refusal to obey a teacher was wrong and he should be punished. However, I feel that three days is too severe in this incident.

I would like for you to reconsider this punishment. I look forward to hearing from you in regards to this matter.

Sincerely,

Luciliana Sanchez

Questions:

1. What are the school discipline issues associated with this letter?
2. What additional information should the principal obtain before responding to the letter?

Document 7

The following is a staff profile for Mount View Elementary School.

Staff Profile	
Teacher Experience	
1–5 years	10
6–10 years	15
11–20 years	5
Over 21 years	20
Total Teachers	**50**
Teachers with Master's Degree	38
Provisional Teachers	9

Questions:

1. What are the curriculum and instructional issues with this type of staff?
2. What predictions can you make in regards to staffing for the future at Mount View Elementary?

chapter 15

Obtaining an Administration Position

After completing the internship, the last educational matter in any preparation program is Job Hunting 101. Obviously, this process begins with an effort to identify whether you want a position in administration, and, if so, what exactly you want to do, where you want to live, and the type of school system in which you want to work. These types of questions probably began before you formally entered a preparation program and will continue after you leave.

Regardless of the position or location, the school district will be looking for administrative candidates who get involved in instruction, understand and can interpret and analyze assessment data, and who are active in committee work and in other areas of administrative responsibility. You will want to volunteer to chair school committees, volunteer for district-level committees, and be well informed and prepared. These administrative experiences, including the internship, provide opportunities for visibility, development, and confidence building by providing you with opportunities to engage in leadership and administrative tasks. The relationships that you establish with your mentor and others will be important to your obtaining a position. You will need advocates who can make you more visible in the district and state, recommend you to others, and help clarify your career goals.

The school system will be looking for candidates who they believe will have the most positive impact on student learning. Merzano, Waters, and McNulty (2005) completed a meta-analysis that indicated "principals can have a profound effect on the achievement of the students in their schools." Their meta-analysis defined twenty-one leadership responsibilities that are similar to some of the theoretical literature found in other chapters of this book and other sources. Some of these twenty-one characteristics that had the highest correlation are situational awareness; outreach; monitoring/evaluating; discipline; resources; order; knowledge of curriculum, instruction, and assessment; and change agent, to name a few. It is wise for the interviewee to be familiar with such work and to be prepared for questions related to important characteristics of effective school leaders.

The candidate with the more diverse experience is often given more favorable consideration. That means experience at different grade levels, in different jobs, and in different schools. It may be necessary to take on some less desirable or unwanted jobs in order to place yourself in a position for the job that you do want. Screening and selection committees look for experiences like involvement on school improvement committees, in-services attended, involvement in professional associations, presentations that were made, performance at your current assignment, your ability to be a team player, conferences attended, books and professional journals read, enthusiasm, perseverance, and so on.

Interviewers often stress enthusiasm along with other important administrative skills and dispositions. Enthusiasm and passion create commitment, and commitment is the power behind success. The "We won't let it fail" attitude goes a long way toward achievement. Certainly the desire for success is necessary, but no more so than enthusiasm, which provides the entrepreneurial drive. Creating passion and enthusiasm within your staff will be one of your greatest challenges and certainly will require you to model these behaviors.

You will want to be familiar with current issues, particularly those that the school system is presently facing. You will want to look at the most recent books and articles that provide an overview of the educational context, leadership, and appropriate behaviors to promote student achievement (for example, Cunningham & Cordeiro, 2006; Marzano, Waters, & McNulty, 2005). A good list of readings will help prepare you to answer questions that will occur during the interview. Selection and screening committees also look for personal qualities such as hard working, competent, professional, dedicated, courageous, ethical, positive, likes people, perseverance, and good manners. High among the qualities being looked for are follows through, does not give up, gets the job done, and does good work.

Your appearance will also be very important. You will want to dress the part, act the part, and walk and talk the part (see Chapters 5 and 6). Make sure that anything you write is well conceptualized, clearly stated, and grammatically correct. Most job consultants would suggest that you develop your own style, but to approach it in a conservative manner.

Do not limit yourself geographically, culturally/environmentally, or any other way in your search. You may not be able to get your first choice regarding a job; however, there are other opportunities for leadership and you may need to start in an administrative position that is not your ideal. Don't worry, this will get your foot in the door, give you experience, and it does not lock you into a lifetime choice.

THE SCREENING SELECTION PROCESS

Typically, the entry-level position in educational leadership is the supervisor or assistant principal position. In fact, the assistant principal is the major recruitment position for the principalship and most other administrative positions. Typically, those who are promoted are people who have demonstrated their capabilities, are highly visible, and have developed an active network of powerful colleagues. Typically a "sponsor" is very important for assisting the individual to achieve career goals. Another characteristic that seems high on the list of influences for promotion is loyalty. Disloyalty is considered to be failure to support the boss, defying district orders, or publicly questioning superiors. However, when such troubles do develop in your existing district, it does not seem to be a detriment to being promoted in another school district (Marshall et al., 1992).

It would be very difficult to come up with one standard set of criteria of what is looked for in hiring school administrators. Characteristics that are often mentioned include a commitment to excellence ("goes above and beyond"); a born leader (no, not the son or daughter of the superintendent, but taking an active role in leadership); admirable work habits (professional, accurate, hard working); dedicated to professional development (further educational plans, membership in professional associations, interest in in-service development, attendance at conferences, regularly reading professional books, and keeping up); and passion for excellence (strives for superior results). Other characteristics include diverse positions, settings, and achievements; appropriate preparation; ability to work well with people; experience in planning and managing; expertise in curriculum and instruction; a reputation for excellent work; good health and attendance; and being someone who loves and cares for children. Each district will have its own set of criteria regarding characteristics for promotion to administrative positions. Some of these will be written and others will be an unwritten part of the work culture. It is wise to try to get a good handle on what your school district is looking for in assessing candidates for administrative positions.

For some of the staff involved in the interview process, their first impression will be determined by the cover letter and vita. Your cover letter should introduce you, express your interest, highlight relevant academic and work experience, explain why you want the position, and highlight your career goals. It should be very well presented, so check grammar, spelling, style, and intent.

Your vita is a very important document providing a record of your important experiences and activities and will serve as a document or passport to help open the door to greater professional responsibilities and power, a promotion to leadership. The form of the vita is quite important but the substance is essential. Your vita should include the following:

Personal history
Educational history
Professional positions
Honors and awards
Professional associations
Professional activities
Editorial activities
Grants
Papers presented
Publications
Professional interests
Community services
Professional references

Neatness, organization, clarity, attention to detail, format, and writing quality all count in a vita. Gaps in dates on the vita and frequent moves are red flags—areas for concern. Your ethics begin with your vita, so always be honest, but at the same time, you want to impress the reader with your qualifications for the position. The Appendix at the end of this chapter provides a sample vita.

INTERVIEW

Remember, at this point teaching ability is not as important as leadership ability and personal characteristics. What can you do for the school in the future if you are placed in a leadership position? You will want to collect as much information as possible about the administrative position that you are applying for. A good place to begin is the job description for the position. Information can also be obtained from the evaluation form, the policy manual, the school improvement plan, data about the school (see Form 7.4), discussion with other staff, and so on.

The purpose of the interview is to assess whether you have the know-how and knowledge ("Can he or she do the job?") and to determine if you have the motivation and confidence ("*Will* he or she do the job?"). The burden is on you, the interviewee, to provide the information needed to convince the interviewers that the answers to those two questions are in the affirmative.

This process begins with the review of the vita. Does the individual have appropriate experiences and professional development? Are the vita and supporting materials clear, concise, well written, thoughtful, and rich in content? Do the references support the candidate as an outstanding future administrator? What is the appearance of the materials?

There is a delicate line between selling yourself and not coming across as egotistical. You will be safe if you focus on how your qualifications will benefit the school system. What are their interests? The style of your materials and resume should be readable without a lot of jargon and wordy expressions, and not in an overly aggressive, formal, academic, or needy tone. The tone should be sincere and avoid both exaggeration and restraint. Make yourself as strong a candidate as possible without lying. As mentioned, the paradox is establishing self-confidence without appearing conceited.

The interview is probably the most important part of the selection process. You will want to look very professional and yet be at ease and comfortable. Listen carefully to the questions being asked and make sure that you understand the questions. Avoid making assumptions. It is all right to paraphrase or restate a question to make sure you understood. You can also ask questions for clarification. Respond by providing the information that the interviewers are requesting. It is best not to use a lot of drama, humor, testimonials, and long stories during your interview. Keep answers brief and concise, but convincing that you are the person for the job. Politeness and common courtesy will go a long way in developing a positive relation with interviewers. Do not become distracted with thoughts like "I don't think I want this job." Control your desire to mentally argue. During the interview stay focused; you will have plenty of time after the interview to deliberate on such questions. Be prepared to discuss anything unusual in your background like gaps not accounted for, short durations in any one job, complete changes in your professional goals, and inconsistencies of any sort.

Your involvement and hard work will provide you with the answers to difficult interview questions. When you are asked "What will you do if . . . ?" you will know because you have already done it or observed it in "real life." It is necessary for you to roll up your sleeves and engage in authentic situations where you are the administrator in order to truly learn what is required to perform the job of a principal or other administrator. This will give you the needed background to feel confident during your interview and to be better prepared to respond to interview questions.

You will want to be thoroughly prepared for the interview. Most good interviewers use open-ended questions, which will require you to elaborate on the question or situation provided. You will have very limited amounts of time, so you need to focus your comments on what is important and what will convince the interviewer to hire you for the position. Know how to use your academic and professional experiences to convince others that you are perfect for the job. Downplay and whitewash any negative information in your background, but do not lie or deny information—such as not doing well in a course, having a weak recommendation, being fired, or other bad experiences. Convert such questions into the types of changes you have made, what you learned from the experience, and how you turned the negative into positive that would make you an excellent employee.

Be prepared for followup questions (see the "other" section on the next page) and recognize that when you are being encouraged to provide more information on a topic, it is an important topic that needs more careful focus. Interviewers are trying to determine if your pattern of thought matches the needs of the district and/or school. They are wondering what you can do for the school in the future. What you have done in the past got you the interview. Now what you can do for the school will get you the job. Finally, be careful of your body language—eye contact, gestures, posture, and hand movements.

Here are examples of some questions you might be asked during an interview:

Work experience: How do you spend a typical day on your present job?

Education: If you had your education to do over again, what would you do differently? Why?

Motivation: What kinds of situations or circumstances cause you stress? What do you want in your next job that you feel you are not getting in your present position?

Self-assessment: Can you describe a difficult obstacle you had to overcome? How did you handle it? What would you consider to be your greatest achievement to date? Why?

Goals: What are some things you will want to avoid in future jobs? What do you feel you need to develop in yourself to be ready for this job?

Human relations: Is it important to you whether or not staff like you? If you could change your personality to help you get along better with people, how would you change? If you had to name the one thing that helps teachers or parents or administrators to respect you, what would it be?

Educational methods: How effective do you think the Reading Recovery Program is for slow readers? What kind of curricular changes or innovations did you suggest in your last job assignment? Why? What data would you want to monitor to determine the effectiveness of an instructional program within a school?

Stability: How would you react when a teacher questions your authority in front of another teacher? If a parent said you were unfair, what would you do?

Other: How would you describe the basic responsibilities of a principal? Please describe your last boss. How did that person deal with teachers? As a principal you will be evaluated; what criteria should we use? What do you believe about being a principal that will bring you the greatest satisfaction? What strategies does the principal have for raising state standard test scores? Making/maintaining AYP? Closing the achievement gap? How does the principal work with the teacher whose state standard test scores are not up to par? Please describe a good faculty meeting. What is the objective of a good faculty meeting? You find a student down in the hall after a class change. What would you do? On what basis do you assess the performance of a teacher? Also, in today's world you can be expected to be asked quite a few data-driven questions during the interview (see Chapter 14).

In answering questions, it is often good to summarize or restate your main points, but avoid being too repetitive. Interview questions that are particularly good at revealing a person's character place candidates in situations and ask them how they would handle the dilemmas being faced. Interviewers get at the candidates' values by developing oppositional situations. For example, loyalty to a supervisor versus a staff member, truth to a parent versus silence for a child's welfare. It is very helpful to participate in mock interviews that can be set up with your mentor or other practitioners, fellow students, or your university instructors. It is very beneficial to practice interviewing prior to being called in for a real interview.

Have some questions in mind to ask when your interview is complete. You will want to develop your questions around the information/reports that you have collected to learn more about the position, school, and school system. You might notice an educational program that is being used within the school district or school and ask some questions for clarification. The job description or other information will spell out the responsibilities or expectations for the job, and you might want to ask clarifying questions about the specific role that you might have if placed in this position—for example, immediate challenges, school system philosophy of educational leadership, school community relations.

Some other questions for the prospective employer might include:

- What types of professional development support exist for educational administrators?
- Why did the person who was last in this position leave?
- What is the benefit package that goes along with this position?
- What would be the scope of my responsibilities?
- What do you consider the major challenges of this position to be?
- What opportunities exist for me to really make a contribution to this school/ school division?
- To whom will I report? What is his or her management style?
- What major objectives or initiatives are you planning for the near future in which I would be involved?
- A year from now, what do you want to see accomplished by the person you select to fill this position?
- What kinds of projects or assignments do you plan for me to work on first, if I am the successful candidate?
- When would I be expected to start?

It is important not to overdo this. Those completing the interview have limited time, so you should select only a few questions that are very important to you and that will help you build a positive impression with the interviewees. Do not pull out a list of questions. Remember, your questions will reveal what is important to you. Poor, inadequate, or inappropriate questions can undo what otherwise was a fine interview, so they are quite important. Determine how and when you will find out the results of the screening/hiring process. Express appreciation and follow up with a letter of appreciation.

Perceiver System

There are also a number of structured formats for conducting interviews. In these systems, all candidates are asked the same set of questions and the interviewers have specific response concepts in mind. If the interviewers hear that concept in the candidate's response, one point is awarded for that question; if the concept is not mentioned, the candidate gets no points for the question. Thus, the responses given by the person being interviewed are scored and the individual's total score is used to determine if they will be hired/promoted. Usually questions are organized around themes. This system can be created by the school division or the interviewers, or can be a standard system like the Perceiver System that was developed by Gallup. Gallup has completed extensive research on the Perceiver System and this is the most prevalent system used in the United States today.

Here are a few hypothetical questions and "look fors" so you can get a feel for these systems:

Question	Listen for
Are good teachers born?	Teachers must like children and want to help them.
How can you help your teachers?	Provide resources and support; stress continuous development for everyone.
What idea have you implemented in your school?	Describes a specific idea in detail and discusses its success and/or failure.
How do you typically treat people?	I treat them fairly and value them, but I can discriminate between appropriate and inappropriate behavior.

Assessment Center

Some school systems use an assessment center approach, whereby they observe candidates for administrative positions in an environment, with simulated situations that an individual will face as an administrator. Trained assessors observe and rate the candidates as they participate in various activities. These are the same types of activities that occur during the internship process. The candidates are rated on a set of relevant skills or dimensions based on the evidence presented from all the experiences. The National Association of Secondary School Principals Assessment Center is the best known assessment center in education. The NASSP assessment/development process is shown in Figure 15.1.

The score on the assessment center is provided to the school district and the candidate, and is used to help make promotion decisions and/or for setting up a personal professional developmental plan for the candidate.

You would be wise to determine how the recruitment, screening, and selection process is being completed in your district. You can then better prepare so that

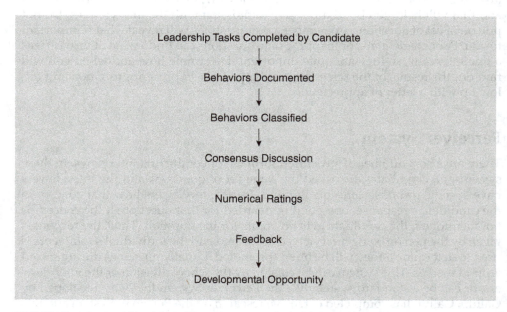

FIGURE 15.1 **The NASSP Assessment/Development Process**

you can do your best during this process. Of course, this process begins with the internship itself, and if you do not do a good job in the internship, it will significantly lower the chances that you will be able to be promoted in that district. The chances may also be reduced in other districts if the poor performance is mentioned by one of your references—or even through more informal channels. Therefore, being promoted may require an effective internship experience.

NEGATIVE FACTORS EVALUATED DURING THE EMPLOYMENT INTERVIEW

What follows is a list of negative factors that were determined by interviewers during the interview process. These are factors that were influential in not hiring individuals. The factors include:

1. Poor personal appearance
2. Overbearing, overaggressive, conceited, "superiority complex," know-it-all attitude
3. Inability to express self clearly—poor voice, diction, grammar
4. Lack of planning for career, no purpose or goals
5. Lack of interest and enthusiasm—passive, indifferent
6. Lack of confidence and poise, excessive nervousness and ill-at-ease
7. Poor scholastic record—just got by
8. Makes excuses, evasive, hedges on unfavorable factors in record
9. Lack of tact
10. Lack of courtesy, ill mannered
11. Lack of maturity
12. Condemnation of past employers
13. Lack of social understanding, poor social skills
14. Marked dislike for academic work
15. Lack of vitality
16. Failure to look interviewer in the eye
17. Limp, fishy handshake
18. Indecisive
19. Sloppy application form
20. "Merely shopping around" attitude
21. Wants job only for a short time
22. Little sense of humor
23. Lack of knowledge in field
24. Emphasis on who is known
25. Cynical
26. Low moral standards
27. Intolerant, strong prejudices
28. Narrow interests
29. No interest in community activities
30. Inability to take criticism
31. Lack of appreciation for the value of experience
32. Radical ideas
33. Asks no questions about the job
34. Attempts to put pressure on interviewer
35. Lazy
36. Unwilling to go where he is sent
37. Indefinite responses to questions

Your "rite of passage" has been completed when you accept your first administrative position. This is an integral part of your preparation and internship and should not be left to chance. The best way to prepare is to ensure you have the type of real-world activities in your internship experience that you will be expected to know for your job interview and when you begin your administrative position. Having completed your preparation program, shadowing, practicum, and internship will help to ensure that you are well prepared, knowledgeable, and ready to move forward to the next stage in your career. This is the process of transformation. Have courage and good luck on your noble journey as you complete a new passage in your professional life.

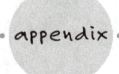
appendix

SAMPLE VITA

Roberta A. Sinclair
320 Oceanview Drive
Virginia Beach, Virginia 23458
Work: 757-942-1686
Fax: 757-432-8705
Home: 757-911-3228
Email: rsinclair@aol.com

Personal History

I am Roberta A. Sinclair. I was born and raised in Winston-Salem, North Carolina, and graduated from Parkland High School. I received a Bachelor of Arts in Education from the University of North Carolina at Chapel Hill. I wanted to teach science to high school seniors but later decided that upper elementary would give me more opportunities for employment. I had a wonderful student teaching experience in a school not far from my home. I taught several of my best friends' brothers and sisters.

While attending a conference for language art teachers in the summer of 1998, I met Sandra Kinbaum, Virginia Beach Public School's Assistant Superintendent of Instruction. We talked about our school experiences and she convinced me to teach in an open classroom in Virginia Beach beginning in the fall.

Sandra told me there were lots of eligible bachelors in Virginia Beach. So off I went to Virginia Beach. I taught at College Park Elementary for three years. I met my husband there. We dated for a year and were married in June 2001. I have been teaching at Great Neck Middle School since 2001. I love science, especially environmental science. My students and I have been oyster gardening in the Lynnhaven River for the past four years. I have won awards for my work with the environment and hope to have an article published in the *Scholastic Magazine* next year about oyster gardening and its importance to our environment.

Most of my students thought that if you were born in poverty you would always live in poverty. They are a difficult group to teach but I see the gleam in their eyes when they can read novels, write letters to governmental officials, and perform complicated math problems on the board in front of their peers. I knew I could make a difference in the lives of these children.

However, I am hoping to make a career change to administration upon completion of my leadership program at Old Dominion University. Using my experience and love for learning, it is my plan to take a school to new heights. I see every day as a new adventure and fondly look back on my life with much happiness.

Educational History

Old Dominion University   Summer 2006–Present
Norfolk, VA 23529
Master of Science in Education—Educational Leadership; GPA 3.92

University of North Carolina at Chapel Hill   August 1993–May 1998
Chapel Hill, NC 27708
Bachelor of Science—Elementary Education, Grades 4–7; GPA 3.73

Professional Positions

Great Neck Middle School   2001–Present
Virginia Beach City Public Schools
Middle School Teacher (Life Science, Grade 6, Testing Specialist)

College Park Elementary   1998–2001
Virginia Beach City Public Schools
Elementary School Teacher (Grades 4 and 5)

Adjunct Instructor for Old Dominion University (PT)   2004–Present
Career Switchers Program in Science Methods

Honors and Awards

Virginia Beach Environmental Award, 2006
Elizabeth River Start School Teacher Award, 2006
Channel 3 Educator Recognition Award, 2005
VBCPS Teacher of the Year, 2001 and 2004
Wal-Mart Teacher of the Year, 2003
Old Dominion University Honors Institute for the Advanced Study
    of Teaching, 2003–2005
Who's Who Among America's Teachers, 2005
Who's Who in Education, 2004 and 2006
Who's Who in American Education, 2002 and 2003
Who's Who in Southern Women, 2001, 2003, and 2004
PTA Teacher of the Month, October 2002, February 2003, and May 2005

Professional Associations

Association for Supervision and Curriculum Development	2003–Present
National Staff Development Council	2004–Present
National Science Teacher Association	2001–Present
National Council of Teachers of Math	1998–2001
Parent Teacher Association	1998–Present
Virginia Education Association	1998–2002

Professional Activities

Co-Chairperson, GNMS—Math/Science Academy Steering Committee	2002–Present
VBCPS Mentor Advisory Board Member	2002–Present
Partners in Education Coordinator	2003–Present
Co-Chairperson, Academic Achievement Committee	2002–2004
Chairperson, VBCPS Science Textbook Adoption Committee	2002–2004
GNMS PTA Corresponding Secretary	2002–2003
Chairperson, Grade Level 5	2000–2001
Chairperson, CPES Science Curriculum Committee	1999–2001
Co-Chairperson, School Safety Committee	1998–2000

Community Services

Lynnhaven River Water Quality Investigator	2004–Present
Chesapeake Bay Foundation Curriculum Writer	2003–Present
Nauticus Teacher Advisor and Curriculum Writer	2002–2005
Volunteer, Norfolk General Hospital	2001–2004
Bible Sunday School Teacher	1998–2002

Professional References

Peter Penn, Principal, Great Neck Middle School
Bill Katzenmeyer, Professor, Old Dominion University
Sammy Hernandez, Mayor, City of Virginia Beach

BIBLIOGRAPHY

Ashburn, E., Mann, M., and Purdue, P. (1987). Teacher mentoring: ERIC clearinghouse on teacher education. Paper presented at the Annual Meeting of the American Education Research Association, Washington, DC.

Bass, G. (1990). The practitioner's role in preparing successful school administrators. *NASSP Bulletin, 74,* 529:27–30.

Beck, J. (1994). The new paradigm of management education: How knowledge merges with experience. *Management Learning, 25,* 2:95–100.

Beyer, B. (2004, Summer). Ethical standards in leadership practice. *NCPEA Educational Leadership Review, 5,* 2:53–58.

Billet, S. (1996). Situated learning: Bridging socio-cultural and cognitive theorizing. *Learning and Instruction, 6,* 3:263–280.

Blake, R. E., and McCanse, A. (1991). *Leadership dilemmas–Grid solutions.* Houston, TX: Gulf Publishing.

Blake, R. R., and Mouton, J. (1978). *The new managerial grid.* Houston, TX: Gulf Publishing.

Bolman, L., & Deal, T. (1993). *The path to school leadership: A portable mentor.* Newbury Park, CA: Corwin Press.

Bolman, L., and Deal, T. (2003). *Reframing organization: Artistry, choice, leadership.* San Francisco: Jossey-Bass.

Bond, S. S. (2004, April). Taking the high roads. *Principal Leadership, 86,* 3:204–209.

Brandt, R. (1992, February). On rethinking leadership: A conversation with Tom Sergiovanni. *Educational Leadership, 49,* 5:46–49.

Brause, R. (2002, April). Doctoral dissertation: *Dilemmas for doctoral students, doctoral courses and doctoral faculty.* Paper presented at the Annual Meeting of the American Education Research Association, New Orleans, LA.

Brown, G., and Irby, B. (2001). *The principal portfolio.* Thousand Oaks, CA: Corwin Press.

Brown G., Irby, B. J., and Chance, J. W. (1996). Reflective performance scale. In *Administrative portfolio evaluation system institute manual.* Huntsville, TX: Sam Houston State University Press.

Browne-Ferrigno, T. (2003, October). Becoming a principal: Role conception, initial socialization, role-identity transformation, purposeful engagement. *Educational Administrative Quarterly, 39,* 4:468–503.

Browne-Ferrigno, T. (2004, Summer). Principal excellence program: Developing effective school leaders through unique university–district partnerships. *NCPEA Educational Leadership Review, 5,* 2:24–36.

Browne-Ferrigno, T., and Muth, R. (2001, November). *Becoming a principal: Role transformation through clinical practice.* Paper presented at the annual meeting of the University Council of Educational Administration, Cincinnati, OH.

Browne-Ferrigno, T., and Muth, R. (2004, October). Leadership mentoring in clinical practice: Role socialization, professional development, and capacity building. *Educational Administration Quarterly, 40,* 4:468–494.

Bull, B., and McCarthy, M. (1995, November). Reflections on the knowledge base in law and ethics for educational leaders. *Educational Administration Quarterly, 31,* 4:613–631.

Camburn, E., Rowan, B., and Taylor, J. (2003, Winter). Distributed leadership in schools: The case of elementary schools adopting comprehensive school reform models. *Educational Evaluation and Policy Analysis, 25,* 4:347–373.

Capasso, C., and Daresh, J. (2001). *The school administrator internship handbook.* Thousand Oaks, CA: Corwin Press.

Center for Research on the Context of Teaching. (2000). *Year four: Assessing results.* Evaluation Report. Stanford, VA: Author.

Chance, E. (1990, August). *The administrative internship: Effective program characteristics.* Paper presented at the Annual Meeting of the National Council of Professors of Educational Administration, Los Angeles, CA.

Chao, G. T., Walz, P. M., and Gardner, P. D. (1992). Formal and informal mentorships: A comparison on mentoring functions and contrast with non-mentoring counterparts. *Personal Psychology, 45,* 619–636.

Chen, M. (1991, April). *Between teaching and administration: The dual loyalty of aspiring teachers.* Paper presented at the Annual Meeting of the American Educational Research Association, Chicago, IL.

Clutterbuck, R. (1987). *Everybody needs a mentor.* London: Institute Press.

Collins, A. (1997, December). *Cognitive apprenticeship and the changing workplace.* Keynote address to the 4th Annual International Conference and Post-Compulsory Educational and Training Centre for Learning and Work Research, Griffith University, Queensland, Australia.

Collins, J. (2001). *Good to great.* New York: HarperCollins.

Copeland, M. (2003, Winter). Leadership of inquiry: Building and sustaining capacity for school improvement. *Educational Evaluation and Policy Analysis, 25,* 4:375–395.

Cordeiro, P., Krueger, J., Parks, D., Restine, N., and Wilson, P. (1993). Taking stock: Learnings gleaned from universities participating in the Danforth Program. In M. Milstein and Associates (Eds.), *Changing the way we prepare educational leaders* (pp. 17–38). Newbury Park, CA: Corwin Press.

Cordeiro, P. A., and Smith-Sloan, E. (1995, April). *Apprenticeships for administrative interns: Learning to talk like a principal.* Paper presented at the Annual Meeting of the American Educational Research Association, San Francisco, CA.

Council of Chief State School Offices. (1996). Interstate School Leadership Licensing Consortium (ISLLC) standards for school leaders. Washington, DC: Author.

Covey, S. (1989). *The 7 habits of highly effective people.* New York: Simon and Schuster.

Crews, A. C., and Weakley, S. (1996). *Making leadership happen: The SREB model for school leadership development.* Atlanta, GA: Southern Regional Education Board.

Crosby, F. (1999). The developing literature on developmental relations. In A. J. Nurrell, F. Crosby, and R. Ely (Eds.), *Mentoring dilemmas: Developmental relations within multicultural organizations.* Hillsdale, NJ: Lawrence Erlbaum.

Cunningham, J. (1998, February). *The workplace: A learning environment.* Paper presented at the First Annual Conference of the Australian Vocational Education and Training Research Association, Sydney, Australia.

Cunningham, W. (1982). *Systematic planning for educational change.* Palo Alto, CA: Mayfield Publishing Company.

Cunningham, W. (1991). *Empowerment: Vitalizing personal energy.* Atlanta, GA: Humanics New Age.

Cunningham, W., and Cordeiro, P. (2006). *Educational leadership: A problem based approach.* Boston: Allyn & Bacon.

Cunningham, W., and Gresso, D. (1993). *Cultural leadership: The culture of excellence in education.* Boston: Allyn & Bacon.

Daresh, G. (2004, October). Mentoring school leaders: Professional promise or predictable problems? *Educational Administration Quarterly, 40,* 4:495–517.

Daresh, G., and Playko, M. (1992). Perceived benefits of a preservice administrative mentoring program. *Journal of Personnel Evaluation in Education,* 1:15–22.

Daresh, J. (1988). Learning at Nellie's elbow: Will it truly improve the preparation of educational administrators? *Planning and Change, 19,* 3:178–187.

Daresh, J. C. (1987, April). *The beginning principalship: Preservice and inservice implications.* Paper presented at the Annual Meeting of the American Educational Research Association, Washington, DC.

Daresh, J. C. (1993, April). *The arrival of the new principal: Reactions of staff.* Presented at the 1993 AERA annual meeting, Atlanta, GA.

Daresh, J. C. (2002). *What it means to be a principal: Your guide to leadership.* Thousand Oaks, CA: Corwin Press.

Daresh, J. C., and Playko, M. A. (1997). *Beginning the principalship: A practical guide for new school leaders.* Thousand Oaks, CA: Corwin Press.

DeSpain, B.C., and Livingston, M. (1997). The importance of school administrative experience for the educational leadership professor: A view of student perceptions. *The AASA Professor, 29,* 4:7–14.

Deutsch, M. (1973). *The resolution of conflict: Constructive and destructive process*. New Haven, NJ: Yale University Press.

Duke, D. (1998, April). The normative context of educational leadership. *Educational Administrative Quarterly, 34*, 2:165–195.

Ehrich, L., Hansford, B., and Tennent, L. (2004, October). Formal mentoring programs in education and other professions: A review of the literature. *Educational Administration Quarterly, 40*, 4:518–450.

Elmore, J. (2002). The administrator as teacher: Reflections of a retired dean. In Michael L. Birkel (Ed.), *The inward teacher: Essays to honor Paul A. Lacey*. Richmond, IN: Earlham College Press.

Farkas, S., Johnson, J., and Duffett, A. (2003). *Rolling up their sleeves: Superintendents and principals talk about what's needed to fix public schools*. New York: Public Agenda.

Fisher, R., and Ury, W. (1981). *Getting to yes: Negotiating agreements without giving in*. New York: Penguin Books.

Forrest, M., Turban, D. E., and Dougherty, T. (1996). Issues facing organizations when implementing formal mentoring programs. *Leadership and Organizational Development Journal, 17*, 3:27–30.

Foster, L., and Ward, K. (1998). The internship experience in the preparation of higher education administrators: A programmatic perspective. *The AASA Professor, 222*, 2:14–18.

Foster, W. (1986). *Paradigms and promises: New approaches to educational administration*. Buffalo, NY: Promethus Books.

Gardner, J. (1990). *On leadership*. New York: Free Press.

Geisman, T., Morris, J., and Lieberman, M. (2000). Selecting mentors for principal interns. *Journal of School Leadership, 10*, 3:233–247.

Gentz, B., and Murphy, J. (2005, January). Embracing confusion: What leaders do when they don't know what to do. *Phi Delta Kappan, 86*, 5:367–373.

Golary, R. (1992). School-based management pitfalls: How to avoid some and deal with others. *The School Community Journal, 2*, 1:38–52.

Golary, R., and Golary, M. (1995). *The power of participation: Improving schools in a democratic society*. Champaign, IL: Research Press.

Griffiths, D., Stout, R., and Forsyth, P. (1988). *Leaders for America's schools: The report and paper of the National Commission on Excellence in Educational Administration*. Berkeley, CA: McCutchan.

Grogan, M., and Andrews, R. (2002, April). Defining preparation and professional development for the future. *Educational Administration Quarterly, 38*, 2:233–256.

Hackmann, D., Schmitt-Oliver, D., and Tracy, J. (2002). *The standard-based administrative internship*. Lanham, MD: Scarecrow Education.

Halpin, A. (1966). *Theory and research in administration*. New York: Macmillian.

Hansford, B., Tennent, L., and Ehrich, L. (2003). Educational mentoring: Is it worth the effort? *Educational Research and Perspective, 39*:42–75.

Henderson, R. L. (1989, October). *The educational administration internship: A revised curriculum*. Paper presented at the Annual Meeting of the University Council for Educational Administration, Scottsdale, AZ.

Heslep, R. (1997, February). The practical value of philosophical thought for ethical dimensions of educational leadership. *Education Administration Quarterly, 33*, 1:67–85.

Hessel, K., and Holloway, J. (2002). *A framework for school leaders: Linking the ISLLC standards to practice*. Princeton, NJ: Educational Testing Service.

/I/D/E/A/. (1991). *AASA Instructional Leadership Team Program*. Dayton, OH: Institute for the Development of Educational Activities.

Irvin, L., and White, D. (2004, February). Keys to effective leadership. *Principal Leadership, 62*, 6:20–25.

Johnson, S. (1990). *Teachers at work: Achieving success in our schools*. New York: Basic Books.

Jentz, B., and Murphy, J. (2005, January). Embracing confusion: What leaders do when they don't know what to do. *Phi Delta Kappan, 86*, 5:367–373.

Jones, J. (1993). *High-speed management*. San Francisco: Jossey-Bass.

Kaye, E. (2003). *Requirements for certification*. Chicago: University of Chicago Press.

Kindler, H. (1996). *Managing disagreement constructively*. Menlo Park, CA: Crisp Publications.

Kram, K. (1985). Improving the mentoring process. *Training and Development Journal, 39*, 4:40–43.

Laken, A. (1973). *How to get control of your time and your life*. New York: Peter H. Wyden.

Lashway, L. (2003). *Inducting school leaders.* Eugene, OR: Clearinghouse on Educational Policy & Management. (ERIC Digest No. 170)

Leadership Quest. *How to succeed in your internship or your first year as an educational administrator.* Eugene, OR: Author. (ERIC Digest ED479074)

Leithwood, K. (1992). *Transformational leadership and school restructuring.* Eugene, OR: ERIC-RIEO.

Leithwood, K., and Duke, D. (1997). A century's quest to understand school leadership. In J. Murphy and K. Seashore Lewis (Eds.), *Handbook for research on educational administration.* San Francisco: Jossey-Bass.

Leithwood, K., Jantzi, E., and Coffin, G. (1994). Preparing school leaders: What works? *Connections, 3,* 3:1–7.

Leithwood, K. A. (1987). Using the principal profile to assess performance. *Educational Leadership, 45,* 1:63–66.

Leithwood, K. A., and Stager, M. (1986, April). *Differences in problem-solving processes used by moderately and highly effective principals.* Paper presented at the annual meeting of the American Educational Research Association, San Francisco, CA.

Lemley, R., Howe, M., and Beers, D. (1997). *Quality school leaders series—The new principal: Formulas for success.* Leadership training associated with the National Association of Secondary School Principals. Reston, VA: NASSP.

Lester, P., and Pascal, I. (2004). *Field-based learning for school administrators: Creating and monitoring on-site opportunities using national standards.* Lancaster, PA: Proactive-Publications.

Likert, R. (1967). *The human organization: Its management and value.* New York: McGraw-Hill.

Lindley, F. (2003). *The portable mentor.* Thousand Oaks, CA: Corwin Press.

Lovely, S. (2003). *Staffing the principalship,* Alexandria, VA: Association for Supervision and Curriculum Development.

Lovely, S. (2004, March/April). Surviving the first year and beyond. *Principal, 84,* 4:22–36.

Lumsden, L. S. (1992). *Prospects in principal preparation.* Eugene, OR: ERIC Clearinghouse. (ERIC Digest No. 77-EDO-EA-92-10)

MacKenzie, A. (1990). *The time trap.* New York: AMACON.

Marshall, C., Mitchell, B., Gross, R., and Scott, D. (1992, January). The assistant principalship: A career position or a stepping-stone to the principalship? *NASSP Bulletin, 76,* 540:80–88.

Martin, G., Wright, W., and Danzig, A. (2003). *School leader internship.* Larchmont, NY: Eye on Education.

Martin G., Wright, W., Danzig, A., Flanary, R., and Brown, F. (2005). *School leader internship: Developing, monitoring, and evaluating your leadership experience.* Larchmont, NY: Eye On Education.

Marzano, R., Waters, T., and McNulty, B. (2005). *School leadership that works.* Alexandria, VA: Association for Curriculum Development.

McAvoy, J., and Rhodes, D. (2003, September/October). Top 10 mistakes that principals make. *Principal, 83,* 1:20–22.

McCreight, C. (2004). *Handbook for practicum students and interns in educational administration.* Mequon, WI: Stylex Publishing.

McEwan, E. (1997). *Leading your team to excellence: How to make quality decisions.* Thousand Oaks, CA: Corwin Press.

Merriam, S. (1983). Mentors and protégés: A critical review of the literature. *Adult Quarterly, 33,* 3:161–173.

Mertz, N. T. (2004, October). What's a mentor, anyway? *Educational Administration Quarterly, 40,* 4:541–560.

Meuller, K. K., Shea, S., and Andrews, R. L. (1989, October). *Deliberative inquiry: A process to organize the knowledge base of educational administration.* Paper presented at the Annual Meeting of the University Council for Educational Administration, Scottsdale, AZ.

Mezirow, J. (1990). *Fostering critical reflection in adulthood: A guide to transformative and emancipatory learning.* San Francisco: Jossey-Bass.

Milstein, M. (1993). *Changing the way we prepare educational leaders.* Mubury Park, CA: Corwin Press.

Milstein, M., and Krueger, J. (1997). Improving educational administration preparation programs: What we have learned over the past decade. *Peabody Journal of Education, 72,* 2:100–116.

Milstein, M., Bobroff, B., and Restine, L. (1991). *Internship programs in educational administrations: A guide to preparing educational leaders.* New York: Teachers College Press.

Milstein, M. M. (1990). Rethinking the clinical aspects of preparation programs: From theory to practice. In S. L. Jacobson and J. A. Conway (Eds.), *Educational leadership in an age of reform.* New York: Longman.

Milstein, M. M. (1992, October/November). *The Danforth Program for the Preparation of School Principals (DPPSP) six years later: What we have learned.* Paper presented at the Annual meeting of the University Council for Educational Administration, Minneapolis, MN.

Moller, J. (1996, April). *Education reflective principals in a context of restructuring.* Paper presented at the annual meeting of the American Educational Research Association, New York.

Morgan, P., Gibbs, A., Hertzog, C., and Wylie, V. (1997). *The educational leader's internship: Meeting new standards.* Lancaster, PA: Technomic Publishing.

Morgan, P., Hertzog, C., & Gibbs, A. (2002). *Educational leadership: Performance standards, portfolio assessment, and the internship.* Lanham, MD: Scarecrow Press.

Murphy, J. (2002, April). Educational leadership. *Educational Administration Quarterly, 38,* 2:172–189.

Mueller, K., Shea, S., and Andrew, R. (1989, October). *Deliberative inquiry: A process to organize the knowledge base of educational administration.* Paper presented at the Annual Meeting of the University Council for Educational Administration. Scottsdale, AZ.

Murray, M., and Owens, M. (1999). *Beyond the myths and magic of mentoring: How to facilitate an effective mentoring program.* San Fancisco: Jossey-Bass.

Muse, I., and Thomas. G. (1988). *Mentoring: A handbook for school principals.* Provo, UT: Brigham Young University Press.

National Commission for the Principalship. (1990). *Principals for our changing schools: Preparation and certification.* Fairfax, VA: Author.

National Policy Board for Educational Administration. (1989). *Improving the preparation of school administrators: An agenda for reform.* Charlottesville, VA: Author.

National Policy Board for Educational Administration. (2001). *Standard for Advanced Programs in Educational Leadership.* Arlington, VA: Author.

National Staff Development Council. (2000, December). *Learning to lead, leading to learn: Improving school quality through principal professional development.* Oxford, OH: Author.

Nelson, R. (2000). *The rewards of recognition.* Motivation, Inc. (800-575-5521)

Peoples, K. (1998, March). *Flexible learning and staff development: An educational perspective.* Address to Open Training Service Seminar, Flexible Learning Center Action Research Staff Development Project, Melbourne, Australia.

Peters, T. (1998). *Lessons in leadership presents articles and columns.* Presented at a workshop in the Tom Peters Distinguished Speaker Series, WYNCOM.

Peters, T., and Waterman, R. (1982). *In search of excellence.* New York: Harper & Row.

Peterson-delMar, D. (1994). *School-site councils: The hard work of achieving grassroots democracy.* Eugene, OH: OSSC Bulletin 37(6). (ERIC Document No. ED 368 058)

Polite, V. C., McClure, R., and Rollie, D. L. (1997, January). The emerging reflective urban principal: The role of shadowing encounters. *Urban Education,* 31:466–489.

Portin, B. (2004, April). The roles that principals play. *Educational Leadership, 62,* 8:14–18.

Pounder, D., and Crow, G. (2005, May). Sustaining the pipeline of school administrators. *Educational Leadership, 62,* 8:56–60.

Raelin, J., and Schermerhorn, J. (1994). A new paradigm for advanced management education: How knowledge merges with experience. *Management Learning, 25,* 2:95–100.

Rebore, R. (2001). *The ethics of educational leadership.* Upper Saddle River, NJ: Prentice-Hall.

Restine, L., Krueger, J., and Milstein, M. (1990, October). *PRAXIS: A response to effective leading and learning.* Paper presented at the Annual Meeting of the University Council of Educational Administration, Minneapolis, MN.

Restine, L. N., Milstein, M. M., and Broboff, B. M. (1989, October). *Selection of the knowledge base for administrative internship programs.* Paper presented at the annual meeting of the University Council for Educational Administration, Scottsdale, AZ.

Roche, A. (1979). Secular trends in human growth, maturation, and development. *Monographs of the Society for Research in Child Development, 44,* 3:1–120.

Schon, D. (1983). *The reflective practitioners: How professionals think in action.* New York: Basic Books.

Schon, D. (1987). *Educating the reflective practitioner.* San Francisco: Jossey-Bass.

Senge, P. (1990). *The fifth discipline.* New York: Doubleday Currency.

Sergiovanni, T. (2005). *The principalship: A reflective practice perspective.* Boston: Allyn & Bacon.

Sergiovanni, T., and Starratt, R. (2001). *Supervision: Human perspectives.* New York: McGraw-Hill.

Shapiro, J. P., and Stefkovich, J. A. (2001). *Ethical leadership and decision making in education: Applying theoretical perspectives to complex dilemmas.* Mahwah, NJ: Lawrence Erlbaum.

Short, P., and Greer, J. (2002). *Leadership in empowered schools.* Upper Saddle River, NJ: Pearson Education.

Short, P. M. (1997). Reflection in administrator preparation. *Peabody Journal of Education, 72,* 2:86–99.

Silver, P. (1986). The Center for Advancing Principalship Excellence. Champaign: University of Illinois.

Smith, P. (2003, Spring). Workplace learning and flexible delivery. *Review of Educational Research, 73,* 1:53–88.

Southern Regional Education Board. (2004). *Preparing a new breed: It's time for action.* Atlanta, GA: Author.

Southern Regional Education Board. (2005). *The principal internship: How can we get it right?* Atlanta, GA: Author.

Southworth, G. (1995). Reflections on mentoring for new school leaders. *Journal of Educational Administration, 33,* 5:17–28.

Stogdill, R. (1981). Traits of leadership: A follow-up to 1970. In B. Bass (Ed.), *Handbook of leadership.* New York: Free Press.

Sweeney, J. (1982). Research synthesis on effective school leadership. *Educational Leadership,* 39:346–352.

Sweitzer, H., & King, M. (2004). *The successful internship: Transformation and empowerment in experiential learning.* Belmont, CA: Brooks/Cole-Thompson Learning.

Thomas, K. (1976). Conflict and conflict management. In M. Dunnette (Ed.), *Handbook of industrial and organizational psychology.* Chicago: Rand McNally.

Thomas, K., and Bennis, W. (1972). *Management of change and conflict.* Baltimore, MD: Penguin Books.

Thomas, K., and Kilman, R. (1979). Thomas-Kilman conflict assessment. Mountain View, CA: CPP and Davis Black Publishing.

Tschannen-Moran, T. (2005, Spring). Innovative university programs: College of William and Mary. *UCEA Review, XLVI,* 2:13–14.

UCEA. (2001). *Policy governing membership in UCEA: UCEA Membership Policy and Procedures.* Columbia, MO: Author.

Wanous, J. (1983). *Organizational entry: Recruitment, selection, and socialization of employees.* Reading, MA: Addison-Wesley.

Wasden, D. (1988). *The mentoring handbook.* Provo, UT: Brigham Young University Press.

Wheatley, M. (1992). *Leadership and the new science.* San Francisco: Berrett-Koehler.

Whipp, R., Adams, B., and Sabelis, I. (2002). *Making time.* Oxford, England: Oxford University Press.

Williamson, R., and Hudson, M. (2001, August). *The good, the bad, and the ugly: Internships in principal preparation.* Paper presented at the Annual meeting of the National Council of professors of Educational Administration, Houston, TX.

Zellner, L., Jinkins, D., Gideon, B., Doughty, S., & McNamara, P. (2002). *Saving the principal: The evaluation of initiatives that made a difference in the recruitment and retention of school leaders.* ERIC:EDRS/MFO1/PCO1.

INDEX